The Author
Paul Einzig was born in Transylvania
in 1897 and educated at the
Oriental Academy of Budapest and
the University of Paris, where he
earned his doctorate degree in
political and economic sciences. He
held various posts on leading
London financial newspapers
between 1921 and 1956, including
long periods as foreign editor and
political correspondent. He is at
present London Correspondent
of the **Commercial and Financial
Chronicle** in New York. He is the
author of over fifty books, mainly on
foreign exchange and related
subjects.

THE EURO-DOLLAR SYSTEM

THE
EURO-DOLLAR SYSTEM

Practice and Theory
of International Interest Rates

BY

PAUL EINZIG

Fourth Edition

MACMILLAN
ST MARTIN'S PRESS

© Paul Einzig 1964, 1967, 1970

First edition January 1964
Reprinted with alterations March 1964
Second edition 1965
Third edition 1967
Fourth edition 1970

Published by
MACMILLAN AND CO LTD
Little Essex Street London W C 2
and also at Bombay Calcutta and Madras
Macmillan South Africa (Publishers) Pty Ltd Johannesburg
The Macmillan Company of Australia Pty Ltd Melbourne
The Macmillan Company of Canada Ltd Toronto
St Martin's Press Inc New York
Gill and Macmillan Ltd Dublin

Library of Congress catalog card no. 67–20894

Printed in Great Britain by
R. & R. CLARK LTD
Edinburgh

CONTENTS

v

PREFACE TO THE FOURTH EDITION

Since I revised this book for its third edition some three years ago the Euro-dollar market has undergone a number of changes, calling for a very extensive revision and amendment of its material. The importance of that market increased during 1968–69 far beyond expectations. Although ever since its inception I consistently predicted its growth, I must confess I was taken by surprise by the sudden acceleration of the pace of its growth. In 1968, and even more during the current year, the volume of Euro-dollar deposits showed a really spectacular expansion. At the same time Euro-dollar rates showed an unexpectedly steep rise. The combined effect of these two tendencies in the sphere of international finance, on world economy and on the economy of the United States, was very considerable, and has opened up perturbing possibilities.

Euro-dollars, and to a much lesser extent other Euro-currencies, have come to play a very important part as a means for speculation in foreign exchanges and in gold. Ever since their origins they have always provided an alternative device to that of forward exchanges as a means for going short in devaluation-prone currencies or for going long in revaluation-prone currencies. But it was not until the last year or two that the extent of the use of such facilities in connection with speculation has become sufficiently large to bear at times comparison with the volume of speculation by means of forward exchanges. Euro-dollars have become the principal device for speculating in gold and for financing gold-hoarding. They now also play a prominent part in speculating in commodities as an alternative to speculation in their futures market.

Euro-currencies have also come to play a decisive role in the financing of new issues in the Euro-bond market and in the development of the secondary market in them. Since the volume of such operations increased very considerably during 1968, they created a considerable additional demand for Euro-currency facilities. A sharp decline in activities in Euro-bonds during 1969 was almost entirely the result of the rise in Euro-dollar rates to a level at which the cost of financing new issues became excessive and prices in the secondary market declined.

But in addition to the increased importance of Euro-dollars in the international financial sphere, they have come to play a very important role also in the domestic economic spheres in many countries — not least in the domestic economy of the United States. Rising interest rates in the Euro-dollar market led to an all-round increase of interest rates everywhere, an increase which began or threatened to begin to affect unfavourably economic conditions within the countries concerned.

At the time when I was preparing the third edition of this book, the influence of Euro-dollar rates on domestic interest rates and on domestic economies was confined more or less to countries which had been in the habit of borrowing Euro-currencies on a large scale. In the meantime it has become a major factor affecting also lending countries such as Germany and intermediary countries such as Britain. The sharp rise in Euro-dollar rates during 1969 has been primarily responsible for the repeated rounds of Bank rate increases and for the general rise in every kind of short-term interest rates all over the world. Anyone who was inclined in the past to underrate the importance of the Euro-dollar system was forced by the rise in 1969 to reconsider this opinion.

At the time of writing, it is as yet impossible to assess the full significance of the rise in the volume of Euro-dollars and in their interest rates on the world economy. It all depends on whether the trend will become reversed in good time to avoid the grave consequences of the maintenance of world interest rates at crisis level. There must surely be a limit beyond which the high cost of raising new capital and of current financing of business activities would entail disastrous consequences.

The fact that the Euro-dollar system is capable of producing highly destructive effects and of creating dangerous situations is liable to increase the number of its critics and opponents. But the system is here to stay for better or worse, whether its critics like it or not. In any case its critics ought to be reminded that the system as such should not be condemned merely because it lends itself to abuses. Any institution is liable to be used for the wrong purpose or in the wrong way. The monetary system itself has been criticised since time immemorial, because it has been grossly misused on innumerable occasions from its early origins to our days. Yet nobody would think of suggesting that it was a mistake for mankind to adopt the use of money and that it would have been wiser to stick to barter. The Euro-dollar system, like the monetary system as a whole and like many other institutions, has immense potentialities for good as well as immense potentialities for evil.

Critics ought to be reminded that the upward trend of Euro-dollar rates, which has caused so much harm and which threatens to cause a great deal more, is not due to influences inherent in the system. It is almost entirely due in the present instance to the ill-advised monetary policy pursued by the authorities of the United States, criticised in detail in Chapter 17, by which they are doing immense harm to world economy through permitting American banks to attract billions of dollars from the Euro-dollar market.

This experience alone calls for an extensive revision of the material in this book. I deemed it advisable, owing to the importance of the change, to deal with it in greater detail in an additional chapter, even if the conditions it deals with are purely temporary. Apart from this major amendment, I also found it necessary to bring the book up to date by covering the wide range of less important changes in the technical operation of the system and its economic implications. But after due consideration I decided to abstain from basing the revised edition of this book on the assumption that the present abnormal extent of American borrowing is permanent. I assume that a return of the conditions that prevailed before American borrowing came to assume spectacular dimensions is only a question of time.

Although the Euro-dollar system has now been in existence as an important institution of the international financial system for something like twelve years, it is still far from having settled down to a more or less definitive form. It remains subject to frequent alterations, not only of a kind that force their attention on the general public, but also of the kind that are liable to remain unnoticed by anyone who is not actively engaged in the Euro-dollar market. Many of these changes are of a purely technical character. Nevertheless economists and others concerned only with the broader aspects of the system are earnestly advised not to underrate such technical changes. The contemptuous reference by a well-known monetary economist to technical details of foreign exchange which, according to him, are of interest to banking accountants only, discloses a tendency which is bound to widen the existing gap between foreign exchange theory and foreign exchange practice and which threatens to complete the divorce of the former from the latter.

P. E.

120 CLIFFORD'S INN,
LONDON, E.C.4

January 1970

PREFACE TO THE THIRD EDITION

THE most important change that took place in the Euro-dollar system since this book was revised for the second edition two years ago was the emergence of a market in London dollar certificates of deposits in 1966. It is described and analysed in some detail in Appendix I.

The statistical tables have been brought up to date. In the main text, too, additions and alterations were made to cover developments during the last two years.

Experience during those two years has fully confirmed the main conclusion of this book — that the Euro-dollar market has become a permanent integral part of the international financial system. While even two years ago the question whether Euro-dollars have come to stay was subject to heated controversy, today there is hardly anybody who would dissent from my affirmative answer.

The new material on London dollar certificates of deposits is based on my article on the subject that appeared in the December 1966 issue of the *Banca Nazionale del Lavoro Quarterly Review*.

P. E.

120 CLIFFORD'S INN,
  LONDON, E.C.4

January 1967

PREFACE TO THE SECOND EDITION

A DRASTIC revision of the material published in the first edition of this book has become imperative because of the far-reaching changes that occurred in the Euro-dollar market within a few months after its publication. Losses suffered by banks as a result of defaults by borrowers of Euro-dollar deposits confirmed my warnings against too indiscriminate lending and induced many lenders of Euro-dollars to be more prudent in their operations. To some extent the trend towards the expansion of the volume of transactions has slowed down, and holders of dollars have now become less keen on lending for periods of years. Wider profit-margins are now expected and obtained, and there is more discrimination. Many Americans have repatriated their deposits from the Euro-Dollar market.

For these reasons alone I felt justified in deciding in favour of a revision of my material. In any case, various new aspects of the subject had to be considered. The development of activity in the market of foreign dollar bonds in Europe made it necessary to examine the impact of that market on Euro-dollars. The change in the attitude of Central Banks towards the Euro-currency markets calls for comments. Above all, additional experience has been gained in the operation of the system since I originally collected my material during the first half of 1963. Many aspects of the subject have been examined more closely in the meantime, and a great deal of official material has been produced.

I felt, therefore, that the time had come for a re-examination of the operation of the system with all its manifold implications. The fact that this re-examination is made so soon after the publication of the original edition calls for no apology, having regard to the fact that when I wrote that book the Euro-dollar system was in the middle of its institutional evolution.

Preface to the Second Edition

It has changed a great deal during the last year or two and, even though it is still subject to further changes in detail, it seems to me that in its broad outlines it has now reached its more or less definitive form.

Recent experience has amply confirmed my view that the system has come to stay. Although several major influences responsible for its creation have more or less ceased to operate, the Euro-dollar market has survived their eclipse. It had its ups and downs, but it can now be definitely claimed to have become an integral part of the international financial machinery.

P. E.

120 Clifford's Inn,
London, E.C.4

April 1965

PREFACE TO THE FIRST EDITION

WHEN during 1957 the London foreign exchange market drifted gradually into transacting regular business in dollar deposits, it is doubtful if any of those engaged in this new activity, or those who had sanctioned it and supervised it, were aware that they were engaged in initiating a revolutionary reform of the monetary system. I am sure they all looked upon it as a convenient and profitable device, without even thinking about its broader implications. Likewise, when I set out to prepare this book I intended it simply as a practical description of a technical device of limited importance and of limited interest.

It took me some time, in the course of my inquiries into the Euro-dollar market, to realise that it has brought about an institutional change of outstanding importance in the international monetary system. I can hardly blame, therefore, practical specialists if they too failed to discover that the new system, by creating a truly international money market with an independent international interest structure of its own, has brought about a fundamental change with very far-reaching effects. The full significance of these effects is yet to be ascertained. But we already know enough about this new system to realise that we ought to know a great deal more about its practical and theoretical aspects.

Until about 1960 the market in foreign currency deposits was virtually unknown outside foreign exchange departments. The new system was hardly ever described in detail, let alone analysed. It was not as much as mentioned in the Radcliffe Report on the Working of the Monetary System or in the four volumes of its evidence. Although witnesses were heard by the Committee right up to April 1959, for nearly two years after the distinct emergence of the Euro-dollar market, none of the practical bankers, officials, or theoretical economists who gave written or verbal evidence had deemed it worth while to refer to it. If any member of the Committee was aware at all of its existence he could not have thought it important enough to deem it worth while to question expert witnesses on it.

Yet it should have been obvious by then that the new device had introduced an entirely new element into the international credit structure, which was bound to have a strong impact on money markets, discount markets, foreign exchanges, foreign trade financing, domestic interest structures, speculation, arbitrage, and the banking system.

For the first two or three years of its existence the Euro-dollar market — as it came to be known later — commanded very little attention. From about 1961 much has been done to repair the omission. Foreign currency deposits are now dealt with much more frequently in the financial columns and their rates are now quoted regularly. Changes in the trend and other interesting developments are now frequently commented upon. A fair amount of descriptive material, with explanations, appears in various official publications and bank reviews. The financial Press, too, often publishes detailed articles showing familiarity with the broader implications of the subject.

Beyond doubt, the requirements of the small but select public interested in the subject are now better served than they were a few years ago. Nevertheless, Keynes's famous remark on forward exchange, made in 1922 : 'There are few financial topics of equal importance which have received so little discussion or publicity', which is no longer valid about forward exchange, may be said to apply even now, to a diminishing extent, to the market in foreign currency deposits. In particular the progress of its theoretical examination leaves much to be desired.

One of the reasons why most of those qualified to deal with the broader implications of the new system have failed so far to show an active interest in it is that it is still in a state of flux and is subject to frequent changes. Anyone who has no opportunity to follow such changes quite closely is liable to be out of date in his comments. The rules of some of the Euro-dollar practices are still rather vague. Nevertheless, enough has emerged in a sufficiently definite form to warrant attempts to produce a comprehensive survey of its various aspects. Much of the material published recently is undoubtedly highly valuable, and it implies no criticism to their authors to suggest that there is room for a great deal more.

It was with much misgiving that I embarked upon the difficult task of dealing with the theoretical as well as practical aspects of this difficult subject. Even though I was greatly assisted by the published material quoted in the text or in the bibliography, and derived much information about more recent developments from the financial Press, I had to collect most of my material through direct inquiries among bankers engaged in this operation. I take this opportunity for expressing my gratitude to the managers and staffs of the various foreign exchange departments for their generous help. Only after having paid them many scores of visits did I begin to feel justified in attempting to describe the working of this fascinating system. In the course of my work I had to re-visit them again and again in order to check some additional point, and I am greatly indebted to them for their patience in answering my questions.

I cannot help feeling that someone actually engaged in Euro-dollar operations might have been better qualified to give a detailed account of all their various aspects. The reasons why, in spite of entertaining such doubts, I felt justified in undertaking the task are fourfold.

None of the foreign exchange dealers seems to be eager to undertake it. Even an ex-dealer, H. E. Evitt, avoided treating the subject in recent revised editions of his practical textbook on foreign exchange. Yet, I was told by the Institute of Bankers Library and also by others that there is a strong and urgent demand for a book on the subject.

Although I had no experience in foreign exchange dealing, let alone in Euro-dollar dealing, I had spent much time before the war, and again in more recent years, in talking to foreign exchange dealers. I feel I am justified in claiming to have picked up in the course of my inquiries as much practical detail as anyone who is not himself a dealer could reasonably be expected to pick up.

Anyone actually in the market is liable to present a somewhat one-sided picture, based as it would be on his own necessarily one-sided experience. Even the most active and experienced foreign exchange dealer is only likely to see part of the market, and he is less favourably placed than a 'neutral' observer for securing information from rival dealers who see the market from a different angle.

Finally, while most practical dealers must have forgotten more about the practical aspects of the subject than I am ever likely to know, very few of them would feel qualified to attempt also its theoretical analysis.

This last point brings me to the second half of my self-imposed task. Even though several writers on Euro-dollars have dealt with its broader theoretical aspects and with its policy aspects, I am sure they would readily admit that no single individual could reasonably be expected to exhaust such a difficult new subject. In my *History of Foreign Exchange* I gave an account of the very gradual way in which foreign exchange theory had struggled into existence. It will take the cumulative efforts of many of us to produce a really satisfactory Euro-dollar theory. I am aware that this book has not said the last word on the subject — apart from other reasons, because, as I remarked above, the system is in the course of evolution and is liable to undergo extensive changes. New practices are likely to supplement or replace existing ones and new situations are likely to arise.

Owing to its highly technical character and its broad implications, a satisfactory study of the Euro-dollar system calls for a combined effort of practical specialists and theoretical economists. I hope that my present attempt will assist students in guiding them in the maze of that intricate system, and that it will encourage foreign exchange dealers to try to master its theoretical aspects.

Although this book aims at examining the entire system of foreign currency deposits in general, I purposely focused my attention on Euro-dollars. Had I tried to deal in detail with all Euro-currencies it would have greatly added to the complications of my description and analysis. In the interest of clarity

I have made only casual references to other Euro-currencies. But to repair this omission, I have added a separate chapter dealing briefly with them.

Finally, a word about the view, expressed to me from more than one quarter while I was working on this book — that it was a sheer waste of effort, because the Euro-dollar market was a passing phenomenon and would disappear before the book was published. Even if it were so, it is a sufficiently interesting phenomenon to deserve a description as a phase in financial history which might reappear. But I am not worried about the prospects of its disappearance.

I am satisfied that the advent of the Euro-dollar system constitutes a long-overdue institutional change. It has brought a great improvement in the sphere of international banking facilities, and it has removed an anomaly by separating wholesale banking from retail banking. If the present book will achieve nothing beyond making its readers realise that the Euro-dollar system has come to stay, it will have achieved something worth while. For it is to the interest of practical bankers and of economists to accept the new institution as an integral part of our international economic system, instead of under-rating the importance of the change by looking upon it as purely temporary.

Towards the close of the seventeenth century Madame de Sévigné remarked about her great contemporary Racine: '*Il passera comme le café*', meaning that his reputation, like the habit of coffee-drinking — which was a novelty in the West in her days — would prove to be a mere passing fashion. Both coffee and Racine have survived, however. And so will, I am confident, the Euro-dollar system.

P. E.

120 CLIFFORD'S INN,
    LONDON, E.C.4

June 1963

CHAPTER 1

INTRODUCTORY

FOREIGN currency deposits are, as the term implies, deposits in the denomination of some currency other than that of the country in which they are deposited. Alternatively they may be defined as deposits held with banks outside the countries whose currencies are deposited. Accordingly, Euro-dollars are dollars deposited with banks outside the United States. Although their name suggests that they are deposited in Europe, this need not necessarily be the case. Technically the term is not strictly correct, because a large proportion of Euro-dollar deposits is usually re-deposited outside Europe — for instance, in Japan. It would not be correct to try to tighten the definition by saying that Euro-dollars were originally re-deposited in Europe, even though subsequently they may have been re-deposited outside Europe. For a large proportion of Euro-dollars was originally deposited in Canada before they came to find their way to Europe. But they only became Euro-dollars from the moment they were re-deposited in Europe.

The use of the term is acceptable, if only because of the distinction it implies between U.S. dollars deposited in Canada — which would be included under the term 'foreign currency deposits' — and those deposited in Europe. Such distinction is indeed essential, because of the totally different ways in which, and the totally different purposes for which, the two categories of dollars deposited outside the United States are used. U.S. dollars held by Canadian banks — the total of which was for a long time larger than that of dollar deposits re-deposited in European countries — are used, or were used for a long time, entirely for the purpose of re-lending the dollars in New York. The resulting movements of funds between the United States and Canada were of relatively small significance

1

from the point of view of their effect on the international monetary system. Financial and monetary links between the United States and Canada have always been very close, and the development of that practice has not introduced an institutional change.⌐

The development of an active market in dollar deposits redeposited in Europe has created a new situation and has constituted a very important institutional change. For this reason, even if purists are entitled to object to the term on the ground that it does not always indicate accurately the geographical location of the deposits, the use of a term that indicates the distinctive character of the dollars concerned, is substantially justified.

There is, admittedly, less justification for use of the term Euro-sterling and other Euro-currencies which are deposited with banks outside their respective countries. After all, since London is decidedly in Europe (*pace* de Gaulle), all sterling deposits there could be called Euro-sterling if it were worth while to state something so obvious. Likewise, D. marks deposited in Western Germany, Swiss francs deposited in Switzerland, etc., are obviously deposited in Europe. On the face of it there seems to be no point in using a term implying that, when these currencies are deposited in a European country other than the respective countries of their own, they are deposited in Europe. Since, however, these currencies, when deposited outside their countries, perform a function very similar to that of Euro-dollars, it seems justified to indicate this important fact by employing a term similar to that employed for describing dollar deposits re-deposited in Europe.

Through constant usage in the small but expanding literature on the new system, the term 'Euro-dollars' has come to convey much more than mere indication of geographical location. It has come to convey something even more than just deposits in terms of a foreign currency. Such deposits had existed since time immemorial, but Euro-dollars are something different. A Euro-dollar market in the sense in which the term is understood has only been in existence since 1957, but there have been innumerable precedents for accepting deposits in

2

terms of some foreign currency. Those who seek to minimise the significance of the new development are of course in a position to point out that already in the early 'fifties Italian banks were borrowing systematically dollar deposits from French banks, and that about the same time, or possibly even earlier, Communist-controlled banks adopted the habit of camouflaging their ownership of some dollar deposits by re-depositing them with European banks. Bankers whose memories go back to the inter-war period may remember that during the 'twenties there was active business in sterling and dollar deposits in Berlin and Vienna.

Some students of banking history succeeded even in tracing back transactions in sterling deposits in foreign countries to before 1914, producing concrete evidence about their existence in the late nineteenth century. In my own *History of Foreign Exchange* I recorded the medieval practice of drawing bills payable at the quarterly fairs in terms of foreign currencies other than those of the countries of payment. It seems reasonable to assume that, since business was actively transacted in foreign currencies at such fairs, such bills were often paid out of or into foreign currency deposits. A thorough historical research would probably disclose many more definite early precedents. Even so, the conclusion inferred from such precedents, that the market in Euro-dollars of which we became familiar in the late 'fifties was not an innovation, seems to be entirely unjustified.

After all, the fact that in Ancient Rome Crassus sold real property against payment in instalments does not in any way affect the fundamental character of the change represented by the spectacular development of hire-purchase during the post-war period. Nor is there any justification for minimising the significance of the accelerated progress in automation that has been taking place in recent years, on the ground of some isolated instances of primitive automatic mechanical devices in the seventeenth century or before.

The argument that in these two instances the difference between various stages of evolution is merely one of degree, overlooks the fact that, when a difference in degree is so striking

3

as it is in the instances quoted above as well as in the instance of Euro-dollars, it becomes a difference in kind. Moreover, in the case of Euro-dollars there is, in addition to the striking difference in degree, quite a good deal of difference in the basic nature of the functions performed by them and those performed by foreign currency deposits in previous instances. Never before has there been a broad international market in them. The emergence of a structure of international interest rates that are distinct from, and largely independent of, national interest rates is something entirely new. It is without parallel in modern economic history.

The nearest thing to systematic dealings in foreign currency deposits was the market in sterling and dollar 'swap and deposit' transactions in Berlin and Vienna during the 'twenties. It was not, however, a truly international market comparable with the Euro-dollar market that has come into being in recent years. Transactions in sterling and dollar deposits in Central Europe after the first World War may have affected the reichsmark and the Austrian schilling, and they had certainly influenced credit conditions in Germany and Austria. But they produced no noteworthy effect outside these countries. They certainly had not assumed sufficiently large dimensions to become a factor of consequence in the London or New York money markets, nor could they have affected sterling or the dollar to any perceptible degree. They were limited and one-sided markets of essentially local significance. The deposits acquired in connection with swap transactions did not change hands but were held by the borrower until maturity. The rates that were quoted in those markets did not constitute international interest rates in the sense that Euro-dollar rates do.

By contrast, the volume and nature of transactions in Euro-dollars, their large and active turnover, and the wide range of their employment, has constituted an institutional change of the utmost importance. It has created a truly international money market, and has developed a structure of international interest rates that is entirely without precedent. Until its advent, money markets were essentially national, even if a high degree of solidarity existed between them — largely through the mechanism of forward exchanges which tended to compensate differences between levels of interest rates. Although national interest rates had always been subject to international influences, they could be controlled to a large degree by the monetary authorities of the countries concerned. While the structure of international interest rates in the Euro-dollar market is naturally influenced by interest rates in New York that are charged or allowed by American banks and are controlled by the American monetary authorities, it is to a large degree independent of them. Indeed, the market owes its very existence to the fact that interest rates on Euro-dollar deposits are outside the control of the United States authorities and of American banks. The same is true about the much narrower markets that exist in Euro-sterling and in other Euro-currencies. Interest rates quoted in them are largely independent of the respective policies pursued by the banks and the authorities of the countries whose currencies are the subject of the transactions. Therein lies the main theoretical significance of the new device.

The Euro-dollar market owes its practical significance largely to the wide variety of sources from which it is supplied, the equally wide variety of the destination of the dollar deposits, and the immense variety of uses to which these dollars are put, whether in international finance and commerce, arbitrage of every kind, or speculation. It is no exaggeration to say that the development of this market has given rise to a new branch of banking activity. Nothing comparable could be claimed to have occurred in connection with any of the precedents concerning transactions in foreign currency deposits.

The domestic economies and financial markets of even the most important countries cannot remain immune from trends generated by Euro-dollar transactions. For this reason those in charge of foreign exchange policies and monetary policies have to follow the market closely. They may find themselves impelled to initiate new policies and techniques to cope with it. The Euro-dollar system deserves the attention of everybody concerned with problems of foreign exchange or credit policy, whether in a capacity of Treasury official, Central bank official, banker, businessman, financial editor, or academic student of the monetary system. Its operation gives rise to a very wide variety of such problems. It has introduced new influences affecting the situation from the point of view of the merchant, the arbitrageur, the bullion dealer, and other practical operators.

The theoretical economist's duty is to analyse the operation of the new system in order to ascertain the set of rules that the new international money market and the new structure of international interest rates obey. This calls for the study of influences affecting Euro-dollar rates and the volume of Euro-dollar transactions. It calls for the investigation of the impact of the new device on interest rates, exchange rates, the volume of domestic credit resources, and international liquidity. It is necessary to give careful thought to the extent of the credit risk, economic risk, and even political risk involved in building up this additional international credit structure.

There is also the broad question to be considered whether the system as a whole tends to make for stability or instability, whether and to what extent it tends to equalise interest structures in various countries and to eliminate discrepancies between interest rates for various maturities. In conclusion it is necessary to answer the question whether the appearance of the system is likely to prove to be on balance a change for better or for worse.

A question of the utmost theoretical as well as practical significance that had to be examined is whether this important new device has come to stay or not. Opinion among bankers and financial commentators as well as official opinion in various countries is sharply divided on this question. It may help to find the right answer if the origin and evolution of the system is studied. Those who believe that it is purely temporary attribute its appearance and expansion to the coincidence of some fortuitous circumstance such as the high Bank rate and exchange restrictions adopted in Britain in 1957, or the artificially low interest rates allowed on time deposits in the United States. No doubt these factors and many others contributed towards the development of the system. A study of its brief but instructive history shows, however, that whenever one or other of the special influences ceased to operate something else turned up to prevent the disappearance of the new device. Admittedly the volume of Euro-dollar transactions and the level of Euro-dollar rates had their ups and downs. The underlying trend in the turnover has, however, been distinctly upward, and it became considerably accentuated in the late 'sixties.

It is probably correct to assume that the immediate impetus to the expansion of transactions in Euro-dollars, to an extent that they became a factor of importance, was given by the 7 per cent Bank rate and the restrictions imposed on certain types of foreign trade financing by the British authorities in 1957. Once the previous insignificant trickles of isolated transactions developed into a stream of active turnover in a regular market, it came to be fed by additional streams joining it. During the late 'fifties its development was greatly assisted first by German borrowing and then by Italian borrowing, and later by Japanese borrowing. The liberalisation of exchange controls in a number of countries at the end of 1958 resulted in the development of markets in other foreign currency deposits, even though Euro-dollars continued to dominate the scene.

The ups and downs of the British Bank rate, the dollar scares and gold rushes, the flights to the D. mark or the Swiss franc, appeared to have made no difference to the underlying expanding trend of the market. Influences affecting it at one time or other included the appearance of London branches of American banks as borrowers of Euro-dollars, the employment of part of U.S. dollars held by Canadian banks in the London market, the discovery by the larger American corporations of the new facilities for earning high yields on deposits, the changes in the attitude of various Central Banks which sometimes encouraged the development of the market and at other times discouraged it. The revision of Regulation Q in 1962, to enable American banks to compete with the Euro-dollar market in attracting official dollar deposits, which was widely expected to be the end of the new device, has hardly affected it. On the basis of this experience it is not unreasonable to suppose that, notwithstanding the many views expressed to the contrary, Euro-dollars have come to stay. This question will be examined in great detail in the concluding chapter. Here let it be sufficient to say that the permanent character of the new system is now entirely beyond question, because evidence of its viability seems to be overwhelmingly strong and, to all appearances, conclusive. Its advantages have outweighed its disadvantages to such an extent that there appears to be an unanswerable case in favour of assuming its permanent existence.

Although by the late 'fifties Euro-dollars and other Euro-currencies came to be dealt in systematically not only in London but also in Paris and some other European financial centres, London is entitled to claim credit for the initiation and development of the new system. The City has proved once more its immense vitality and the adaptability of its organisation and techniques to changing circumstances and requirements. By creating a new important device for use in the foreign exchange market, in the money market, in international trade, and in domestic credit expansion in countries with inadequate liquid financial resources, the London banking community has earned the gratitude of all the countries which have directly or indirectly benefited by the new device.

To prove that the above remarks are not inspired by any bias in favour of London I propose to quote the following passage from an article by a leading French financial commentator, Paul Turot, on the Euro-dollar market, appearing in the April 1961 issue of *Banque* : 'London was in the best position to benefit by the higher degree of monetary freedom [as a result of the return to convertibility in 1958], thanks to its excellent technical organisation and to the abundance of specialised personnel which were lacking in other markets. It was consequently in London that the market which has come to be called the Euro-dollar market had first developed.'

The efforts of the London community to develop the new facilities received much encouragement from the British official attitude in favour of the system. The British authorities could have prevented its development — as they have prevented the development of active dealings in Euro-sterling in London — through a rigid use of their powers of exchange control. They refrained, however, from doing so, no doubt because they realised the advantages of developing London into the leading market in Euro-dollars. They were presumably aware that its expansion must reduce the use of sterling as an international currency. Nevertheless, they must have felt it to be to the advantage of London's position as an international banking centre that it should attract business in terms of foreign currencies. Even before the Radcliffe Report pronounced itself in that sense, they came to realise that what mattered was not so much whether international trade was financed in sterling as whether it was financed through London.

Foreign dollar bonds issued in Europe are often referred to as 'Euro-dollar loans'. There is no justification for such a use of the term. Although such loans may be paid for with the aid of Euro-dollars, they can also be paid for by other means — with dollars held by non-residents or bought for that purpose in Switzerland, Germany, etc., or with special dollars that can be bought for foreign investment by residents in Holland, Belgium and other countries. The employment of the term to indicate foreign dollar loans would imply that all dollar assets belonging to Europeans constitute Euro-dollars, which is clearly incorrect. The term should be confined to foreign dollar deposits re-lent by a bank resident outside the United States.

In the following chapters an attempt will be made to examine the various practical aspects of the new system, to analyse its various theoretical aspects, and to consider its various policy aspects. It is my contention that, so far from being a mere technical device the study of which could and should be left to the specialist, it is a major factor which is liable to influence many aspects of the domestic economies as well as the international economy, and which calls for a thorough re-thinking of monetary theory and policy and even of economic theory and policy.

CHAPTER 2

ORGANISATION OF THE MARKET

EURO-DOLLARS were until recently not a special type of dollars, and there was nothing to distinguish them from ordinary dollars beyond the fact that they may have been re-deposited with a European bank. This may sound like stating the obvious. Yet it was very frequently overlooked. A great many people imagined that Euro-dollars were a special category of dollars, somewhat similar to the various types of reichsmarks before the war or the various types of sterling after the war. All such special types of currencies had separate exchange rates, because there were differences between the ways in which their holders were entitled to use them. On the other hand, dollars re-deposited in Europe were just ordinary dollars in the United States, interchangeable with other dollars. There was, and is, no exchange rate (as distinct from interest rate) for Euro-dollars.

In this latter respect the position is the same concerning Euro-sterling and other European currencies. In their case there has always been some difference between their use and that of the respective basic currencies. In the case of Euro-sterling, holders of non-resident sterling — which alone is qualified for becoming Euro-sterling — are entitled to transfer their holdings freely, as distinct from sterling held on resident accounts which is subject to exchange restrictions. In the case of D. marks, Swiss francs, and, since more recently, French francs, there are restrictions on the payment of interest on deposits held by non-residents. As far as the Euro-dollar is concerned, there was until recently no discrimination whatsoever. There were no official restrictions in the United States, and the same restrictions which applied to dollar deposits under Regulation Q applied to the payment of interest to non-residents. A holder was entitled to lend his dollars abroad without any restrictions. Any holder of dollars in the United States, whether resident or non-resident in the United States, was entitled to convert his holding into Euro-dollars by re-depositing them with a European bank. Following on the application of various unofficial 'guidelines', since January 1968 American residents are no longer entitled to lend their dollars freely in the Euro-dollar market.

During the late 'fifties, and even more during the 'sixties, dealing in Euro-dollars and other foreign currency deposits has been a very important source of activity and income of banks in Western Europe, the Middle East, the Far East, and other parts of the world. This activity has been pursued all along by the foreign exchange departments of banks in spite of the fact that a transaction in a Euro-currency does not necessarily involve a foreign exchange transaction. It simply consists in the lending and borrowing of a deposit which is in terms of a currency other than that of the country or countries in which the transaction takes place.

The term 'deposit' is to some extent a misnomer. For, properly speaking, the 'placing' and 'taking' of Euro-dollar deposits is a loan transaction. On the basis of this fact it is argued sometimes that logically the Euro-dollar market should form part of the money market instead of the foreign exchange market. It is true, in a great many instances, the transfer of a Euro-dollar deposit from the lender to the borrower is followed immediately by a foreign exchange transaction. Indeed, in many instances it is actually linked with a foreign exchange transaction. Basically, however, the transaction involves not the exchange of one currency against another but a loan in terms of a foreign currency, repayable in the same currency.

In a sense the Euro-dollar market has created a money market which is parallel with the local money market, providing rival facilities. In fact, during the early period of its existence, when transactions in Euro-dollar deposits in London were handled almost entirely by merchant banks, it was often referred to as the 'merchant banks' money market'. The standard dates for which most transactions in Euro-dollars are concluded are substantially identical with those of the money market and the discount market. Nevertheless, for practical considerations the market in Euro-dollars and in other foreign currency deposits has been from the very outset an integral part of the foreign exchange market. The following are the main reasons why it is more convenient that Euro-dollar business should be transacted by foreign exchange departments rather than by the money market departments of the banks :

(1) By definition the market for foreign currency deposits deals in foreign currencies and is therefore essentially international, while the money market is organised for transacting business in terms of the local currency and is overwhelmingly local. It is true, bank bills dealt with in Lombard Street originate largely from foreign trade. But even in this respect the trend since the war has been towards an increase of the proportion of domestic bills. As for Treasury bills, dealings in which now constitute the bulk of transactions in Lombard Street, they are essentially local, even if a by no means negligible proportion is usually acquired on foreign account.

(2) As pointed out above, foreign deposit transactions are very often linked with foreign exchange transactions, without which many of them could not come about, since they are undertaken solely for the sake of swapping the proceeds into the local currency or into a third currency. They often form part of some space arbitrage or time arbitrage which can only be carried out in the foreign exchange market. They lead to a considerable amount of foreign exchange business, both spot, swap and outright forward, and foreign exchange departments would in any case have to handle these. It would slow down the dealing if two departments were involved instead of one.

(3) Transactions in foreign deposits often serve as an alternative to foreign exchange transactions. Banks, when in temporary need of dollars, may prefer to borrow them in the form of Euro-dollar deposits rather than buying them or obtaining them through swap transactions. Conversely, discrepancies between maturity dates of Euro-dollar deposits may in given circumstances

be more conveniently met with the aid of swap transactions or uncovered spot transactions instead of Euro-
dollar transactions. It is, therefore, only reasonable
that foreign exchange departments should handle transactions arising from using an alternative device to
foreign exchange transactions. The need for making
arrangements between two departments would cause
delay which would be disadvantageous at times when
rates are liable to move at any moment.

(4) Very often either lenders or borrowers of foreign currency deposits are foreign banks. Foreign exchange
dealers are acquainted with them. They are in daily
contact with these banks in connection with their
foreign exchange operations, and their well-established
personal relationships are therefore helpful also in
foreign currency deposit transactions.

(5) Foreign exchange dealers are in a better position than
anybody outside the foreign exchange market to judge
the correct limit for the amount of foreign currency
deposits that can be loaned safely to any one bank.
They are also more familiar with conditions abroad and
are therefore in a better position to judge the safety
limit for commitments in any one country.

(6) Since foreign exchange departments are already organised for transacting business in foreign currencies, the
extension of their activities to cover the placing and
taking of foreign currency deposits involves very little
additional expense, such as the cost of separate private
lines to brokers for dealing in Euro-dollars. Although
telephone bills for long-distance calls and telewriter
expenses are bound to increase as a result of this additional activity, as a general rule not many additional
dealers are required. On the other hand, money
market departments would have to employ additional
specialist staffs.

Under British exchange restrictions only banks authorised
to deal in foreign exchanges ('authorised dealers') may transact
business in foreign currency deposits in the London market or

13

between London and foreign centres. Most authorised dealers are in fact more or less actively engaged in such transactions. We saw earlier that originally it was mostly in the hands of the merchant banks who had practically created the market. Subsequently, British overseas banks, London branches or affiliates of foreign or Commonwealth banks, and finally some affiliates of clearing banks, came to operate in Euro-dollars through their fully-owned subsidiaries. Only a relatively small minority of the authorised dealers has a large turnover. In the foreign exchange departments of banks which actively deal in foreign currency deposits some dealers specialise in foreign currency deposits.

No attempt has been made in London to organise a market in the sense of creating a meeting-place such as had existed for foreign exchange during more than three centuries at the Royal Exchange and still exists in several continental financial centres. Even in those centres no Euro-currency business is transacted at the section of the Bourses set aside for foreign exchange dealing. As in London, all Euro-currency deals within the same market are transacted by means of telephone between banks and brokers. Business with banks in other centres is arranged either by long-distance telephone or by teleprinter.

A certain amount of Euro-currency business with foreign centres is now transacted through brokers.

Like the foreign exchange market, the Euro-dollar market is confined to inter-bank dealings. Even the largest non-banking firms have to deal with banks. They have no access to foreign exchange brokers. Dealings of banks with their non-banking customers are discussed in the next chapter.

London is by far the most important market in Euro-dollars. It is practically the only market where it is possible to deal in large amounts at any time in both ways. In fact, many London banks usually quote rates in both ways. Continental Euro-dollar markets, with the exception of Frankfurt and Zürich, are inclined to be borrowers' markets during much of the time. London has also the advantage of having a unique foreign exchange market in dollars and an excellent money market and discount market, which helps towards ensuring the

14

efficiency of the Euro-dollar market. Moreover, none of the continental centres has such close connections with countries on other continents, even though they may have closer connections with each other.

Next in importance to London is Paris. Its turnover in Euro-dollars is quite large, though much smaller than that of London. There are Euro-dollar markets also in Frankfurt, Amsterdam, the three Swiss banking centres (Zürich, Basle, and Geneva), and in Milan and Vienna. In the Middle East there is some activity in Euro-dollars in Beirut, Tel-Aviv, and Cairo. A market has also been created in Singapore.

There is a very large turnover in U.S. dollar deposits in Montreal and Toronto, though it can hardly be called a market, because usually all the U.S. dollar deposits received by the Canadian banks are promptly re-lent in some financial centre outside Canada. For a long time they were employed almost entirely in loans to Wall Street. In 1963 one of the money brokers in New York began to deal in Euro-dollars, as a sideline to dealing in Federal Funds. It confines its role to that of an intermediary.

Paris is by far the largest market in Euro-sterling. There is also much dealing in it in Switzerland. While in London there is a limited market in Euro-sterling held by non-residents, there is no market in New York either in Euro-dollars or in Euro-sterling, because Regulation Q limits interest on deposits in foreign currencies as well as in dollars, irrespective of whether they are held by residents or non-residents. Subject to exchange control, American banks may lend on the Euro-dollar market up to twelve months. In 1969 the rates rose above those they charged to prime borrowers.

Foreign exchange brokers play an important part in the markets in foreign currency deposits. In London all the ten brokers act as intermediaries in Euro-dollar transactions. They usually specialise in certain Euro-currencies or in particular types of maturities such as very long or very short Euro-dollars. Some of their dealers specialise in Euro-currencies. Although the use of brokers is not so universal as in the case of foreign exchange transactions, most banks prefer to make use of them.

The Foreign Exchange Brokers' Association owned from 1964 to 1968 a firm which dealt in Euro-currencies direct with foreign banks.

Many banks specialise in certain types of transactions. Some of them aim at snatching a quick turn by simply acting as intermediaries between borrowers and lenders for the sake of a narrow profit margin between the dealing rates they quote. Others swap into sterling the Euro-dollars they borrow, and employ the proceeds in Lombard Street or in special credits, while others again use it for financing foreign trade. Some banks specialise in particular currencies or in using the Euro-dollars for financing trade in particular countries or groups of countries. There is also some specialisation in respect of maturities. Some banks are very active in using foreign currency deposits in covered interest arbitrage, while others are prepared to use them in time arbitrage involving calculated risks or even in operations in which to create open exchange positions.

Although, as we shall see in the next chapter, it is possible to transact forward business in Euro-dollars, and to a very much less extent in other Euro-currencies, there is no forward market proper. Nor are there market transactions in options. Practically all transactions are for delivery in two days.

Many attempts have been made to estimate the total outstanding amount of Euro-dollars and other foreign currency deposits. As the same deposits are liable to be re-deposited a number of times and might appear repeatedly in statistical returns of various countries, a correct calculation must be confined to the amount of original deposits re-deposited outside the United States or other countries concerned. The only authentic figures are those published by the Bank for International Settlements. In its annual report for 1968–69, the total of short-term liabilities and assets in foreign currencies of the principal non-American commercial banks were $33·5 billion and $37·4 billion respectively at the end of 1968. Only part of such deposits comes within the definition of Euro-currencies. The figures are reproduced in Appendix II.

The London Euro-dollar market is very efficient, in that it

is capable of absorbing large and sudden changes in the supply
or in the demand without unduly affecting the rates — except
those of very short deposits. Margins which were rather wide
during the early stage of the development of the market have
narrowed considerably. With the rise in rates they broadened
again in 1969. Very often London acts as intermediary between
borrowers and lenders of Euro-dollars in the same foreign
country. For instance, Italians often borrow in London Euro-
dollars belonging to other Italians.

While the Bank of England is the very centre of the money
market and the discount market, and it has also come to play
a very active part in the foreign exchange market, it plays
no active part in the market for foreign currency deposits.
Its attitude towards that institution may be described as one
of benevolent neutrality. The organisation of this market has
been left to private initiative in the sense that it has no direct
access to the central institution. But ever since 1967 there has
been much evidence of official intervention in the form of
lending by the Bank for International Settlements.

Although the organisation of the Euro-dollar market is still
in a state of flux, the extent to which this new institution has
developed in a very brief space of time is indeed remarkable.
It has greatly added to the value of the facilities offered by
the London banking centre, not only in the sphere of international finance but also in that of domestic finance. One of
its contributions to London's international banking facilities
is the market in London dollar certificates of deposits that
developed in 1966. It is described and analysed in Appendix I.

CHAPTER 3

PRACTICES AND TECHNIQUES

THE development of the practices and techniques of the Euro-dollar market has made remarkable progress within a short space of time, but, like the organisation of the market, they are still far from having settled down to their final form. The purposes for which Euro-dollars are used and the ways in which they are sought to be achieved are open to changes, and such changes, as well as lessons learnt through trial and error, are apt to cause changes in practices. Nevertheless, some rules may be considered to have attained their definite form. In many ways these rules are very similar to those operating in respect of foreign exchange transactions.

Banks which are large dealers in Euro-dollars find it possible at times to 'marry' transactions, placing with a customer a deposit placed with them by another customer. Much more often, however, they have to find the counterpart in the market. This can be done either by contacting a bank in a foreign centre (or by being contacted by them), or locally, mostly through the intermediary of a foreign exchange broker. Some banks prefer to deal direct with each other, not only to save brokerage but also because it is felt that direct contact gives their dealers some idea how keen the other party is on transacting business at the rate suggested. For the same reason dealers prefer negotiating deals through long-distance telephone calls rather than through the impersonal teleprinter.

On the other hand, by dealing through brokers, banks find it less awkward to refuse names or to quote higher rates than those quoted to borrowers of first-rate standing, even though a bank approached directly by a would-be taker of Euro-dollars to whom it does not want to lend can avoid causing offence by saying that it has no Euro-dollar deposits to offer.

In foreign exchange dealings brokers confine themselves to indicating the type of bank that is offered as a counterpart, and do not disclose names until after the deal is concluded. In Euro-currency dealings they have to disclose the borrower's identity to the lender before the deal is concluded, once they are satisfied that the latter really intends to proceed with the transaction and does not merely want to sound the market. Brokers usually fight a subtle rearguard action against actually giving away names. To the inevitable question about the identity of the would-be borrower they usually reply : 'Merchant Bank ' or ' Clearing Bank affiliate ', or ' American bank ' etc. The would-be lender may not be content with this, and the broker's next step is to indicate how the bank ranks within its category, or he names a bank belonging to the same class. He may say : 'first-class', 'you have often accepted their name', etc. It is only if the would-be lender is not satisfied even with this indication that the broker discloses, with some reluctance, the actual name. All this takes time and it is largely because of such delays that business in foreign currency deposits is much slower than in foreign exchanges.

The reason why banks usually insist on knowing the actual potential borrower's name even if the broker assures them that they had been dealing with the bank in question regularly in the past is that conceivably their limit for that name may have been exhausted in the meanwhile. The limits placed on each name by every bank are a closely-guarded secret and are subject to change in either direction. All Euro-dollar transactions are unsecured credits, hence the importance attached to names by would-be lenders.

Situations are liable to arise in which the lending bank does not wish to renew a maturing deposit which the borrowing bank would like to have renewed. On such occasions the lender cannot shield behind the broker. The excuse that is frequently used on such occasions is : 'One of our large depositors did not renew his deposit so we must call in some of our deposits '. The debtor then borrows a deposit for a short period — which is usually much easier — and hopes to arrange for a longer deposit before the short deposit matures.

19

Banks deal directly with each other in foreign exchange transactions between two foreign centres, but a certain amount of Euro-currency deposit business between foreign centres is transacted through a new type of intermediaries called 'international brokers' that has arisen as a result of the development of the Euro-dollar market. There are several such brokers in Germany (in Hamburg and Munich), in Switzerland (in Lausanne and Geneva), and in Paris. German international brokers act as intermediaries between continental — mostly German — business firms and London or other non-German banks. International brokers in France and Switzerland act mainly as intermediaries for non-banking clients, but some foreign banks also avail themselves of their services occasionally and approach the London market through them instead of directly. International brokers sometimes arrange a deposit to be given to a London bank and then to be re-lent by the latter to a foreign borrower, possibly to one resident in the original depositor's own country. The advantage of this arrangement from the point of view of the foreign depositor is that he lends to a first-class London bank, so that the transaction involves practically no risk. Against this, he has to be content with a much lower interest.

In London both parties pay the broker a commission of $\frac{1}{32}$ per cent each, subject to several exceptions. In Paris the brokerage is $\frac{1}{16}$ per cent for both parties, which may partly account for the fact that margins on Euro-dollar transactions are wider there than in London.

There is often hard bargaining over rates, and such bargaining is harder for larger amounts and for longer maturity dates. For this reason, borrowers prefer to approach ten lenders for, say, $1 million each, rather than one lender for the whole of $10 million, though much larger single deals are not infrequent.

The standard maturities are similar to those of the forward exchange market and of Lombard Street — deposits at call, for seven days, for one month, three months, and six months. It is possible, however, to obtain quotations for almost any date up to twelve months. There is a trend towards a lengthening of maturities in which it is possible to deal. While in 1961 deposits for more than three months were a matter of negotiation, by 1963 deposits up to six months came to be transacted as a matter of routine and even for twelve months it was easy to deal. In special instances it became possible later to negotiate transactions for periods up to five years. In 1965 there was a setback, but the limit is now again five years.

There had been a certain amount of disagreement between London and continental markets whether the year should be reckoned, for the purposes of the Euro-currency deals, as 360 days and the month as thirty days, in accordance with continental practice, but eventually the British practice of reckoning the year as 365 days and each month according to the actual number of days it contains came to prevail.

As soon as a transaction is concluded, whether through a broker or directly, both parties confirm it in writing directly to each other. The lender sends the borrower a confirmatory note on the following lines :

FOR PAYMENT TO : City Bank of New York

Messrs. Merchant Bank, Ltd.
   250 Old Broad Street, E.C.2

Date: May 15th, 1963

DEAR SIRS,

   We confirm arranging to place on deposit with you the following currency :

$1,000,000

TO BE PAID BY	VALUE	AMOUNT	PERIOD	FROM	TO	RATE
National Bank of New York	May 17, 1963	$1,000,000	3 months	May 17, 1963	August 17, 1963	3%

We have instructed our correspondents as above to pay this sum to your account, value as stated.

per pro. London Overseas Bank Ltd.

(Signed) A. SMITH

21

The Euro-Dollar System

The borrower sends the lender the following confirmatory note :

FOR PAYMENT TO : City Bank of New York

Messrs. London Overseas Bank, Ltd.
120 Lombard Street, E.C.2

Date: May 15th, 1963

DEAR SIRS,

We confirm agreeing to take on deposit from you the following currency :

$1,000,000

TO BE PAID BY	VALUE	AMOUNT	PERIOD	FROM	TO	RATE
National Bank of New York	May 17, 1963	$1,000,000	3 months	May 17, 1963	August 17, 1963	3%

Please pay this sum for our account to our correspondent as above, value as stated.

per pro. Merchant Bank Ltd.
(signed) B. JONES

The lender cables instructions to his correspondent in the United States to pay into the borrower's account (or to some other account prescribed by the borrower) the amount of the contract. The borrower notifies his correspondent that such and such payment is to be expected on such and such date.

The broker also confirms the verbal arrangement concluded through him by sending copies of the contract to both parties. His commission is payable at the end of each month. He is entitled to his commission not only on the original deal but on each renewal.

Unless otherwise stipulated, all dealings in foreign currency deposits are treated as spot transactions, which means that lenders have to deliver the amount of the deposit on the third clear business day. As in the case of spot foreign exchange transactions, it is possible, however, to transact business in Euro-dollars for delivery on the same day ('value today'), or on the following day ('value tomorrow'). It is also possible to stipulate delivery in more than the customary two days, but this can only be done as a matter of routine for very short periods, usually up to seven days. Beyond that the arrangement is a matter for negotiation.

There is no regular forward market in foreign currency deposits, not even in Euro-dollars. Forward deals can usually be arranged, however, on terms, even though such transactions are not yet very frequent. They amount to a deferred loan of Euro-dollars. The lender of Euro-dollars for forward delivery covers himself by a long-short transaction. For instance, if somebody wants in a month's time a loan of Euro-dollars for three months, the lender borrows a Euro-dollar deposit for four months and re-lends it for one month. As a result, he gains possession of the dollars in a month's time for a period of three months and is therefore in a position to lend it. If he lends Euro-dollars for three months to be delivered in three months, he borrows for six months and re-lends it for three months.

As rates are usually higher for six months than for three months, such operations are likely to be costly for the borrower. The lender gets a low interest rate for the first three months and has to pay a higher interest rate for the whole six months. He has to charge, therefore, to the borrower a sufficiently high rate for the second three months to compensate him for his loss of interest during the first three months, plus a reasonable profit. The borrower is not likely to accept such costly terms unless he anticipates a rise in Euro-dollar rates during the coming three months. If the lender does not anticipate a rise he may be prepared to risk having an open commitment for three months and he may be willing to quote a rate that is not as high as the difference between the rate for three months and the rate for six months.

An alternative device is to give the customer an option, either in respect of the date on which he takes up the Euro-dollars he borrowed, or even in respect of the decision whether or not to avail himself of the loan at all. Such transactions are not practiced by many banks, and the rates they quote depend on the view they take about the borrower's genuine intention of taking up the Euro-dollars. While willing to accommodate a good customer, they wish to discourage gambling on the lines of 'heads I win, tails I don't lose'. Some banks are prepared to deal in Euro-dollars with a 'penalty clause', enabling their clients to back out of the contract. Conversely, the lenders may reserve the right to call in the deposit before it matures, against payment of a penalty. Such deposits carry a lower interest.

Business in the Euro-dollar market is transacted in large round amounts. The usual unit for Euro-dollar transactions is $1 million, although items of $500,000 and $250,000 also frequently change hands. Even items of $100,000 appear in the market at times. Amounts up to $10 million are not infrequent, and occasionally there are transactions of $100 million and even more. The rates for such large amounts are always a matter for negotiation, if only because it takes time for the lender to undo his commitment in the market without causing a rise in the rate that would wipe out his profit. London branches of American banks often deal in large amounts.

Transactions between bankers and their customers may be in smaller amounts but are also usually in round figures and not in broken amounts. There is nothing to prevent owners of smaller dollar deposits from re-depositing their dollars in London and most banks would be willing to open dollar deposit accounts for them. The interest paid on such deposits would be, however, distinctly lower than that paid on larger deposits changing hands in the Euro-dollar market. The rate would of course largely depend on the client.

An exception to the rule that in the market transactions are in round amounts is provided by Euro-dollar deposits lent to West German banks, which are often in broken amounts. The reason is that in Germany banks have to provide a 30 per cent reserve on non-commercial commitments in foreign currencies and only 20 per cent on commercial commitments. Because of this they often pass on to the London market the actual amount of their commercial transactions, rather than round it up, so as to avoid having to provide a 10 per cent reserve for the margin between the actual amount and the nearest round figure.

Many banks run books of graded maturities of their deposits, even though they take care not to have any overall commitments other than discrepancies between maturity dates. Some banks do not want to have even such discrepancies. They job in and out of the market, quoting borrowing and lending rates at the same time, for the sake of the margins between those two rates, which can be earned by re-lending immediately the amount borrowed or by re-borrowing immediately the amount lent. This profit at the rate of, say, $\frac{1}{4}$ per cent p.a. is supposed to compensate them for the risk of a default. Other banks prefer to take a bigger risk for the sake of wider profit margins, by taking a view on the future of Euro-dollar rates, lending long and borrowing short. They may also re-lend the amounts borrowed to industrial or commercial firms for periods well in excess of that of their Euro-dollar deposits, on the assumption that they will always be in a position to renew or replace the maturing deposits at rates at which the transactions remain profitable even if the rates have changed against them in the meantime. Some banks never swap into other currency than that of the deposit, while others often use their Euro-dollar deposits in the form of other currencies. Some banks are very active in employing such deposits for covered interest arbitrage, others are prepared to use them in operations which create open positions.

A practice which has developed in recent times is the lending of Euro-dollar deposits with an escape clause. Against payment of a penalty the lender of the deposit is able to regain possession of the amount before maturity. American corporations in particular, but also European Central Banks, often insist on the insertion of such a clause. An alternative solution has been found in 1966 in the application of the American system of transferable and marketable deposit certificates.

CHAPTER 4

INVESTMENT FACILITIES

EURO-DOLLAR deposits came into being largely because they were able to offer the foreign holder of dollars advantages he was unable to obtain through holding his funds in the form of time deposits in the United States or in other forms of short-term dollar investments possessing a comparable degree of security and liquidity. Foremost among the advantages that attracted and still attracts a large supply of dollar deposits into the Euro-dollar market is the higher yield compared with the artificially low deposit rates in the United States and with the low yield of otherwise suitable American short-term investments, kept down by the policy of cheap money.

Many foreign holders of dollars had grown tired of being content with a much lower yield on their American short-term investments than that obtainable on corresponding investments in their own countries. They did not wish to get out of dollars, but they were looking for opportunities to improve the yield on their holding. To some extent they sought to achieve that end by holding commercial paper, or some other forms of short-term investments which either did not exist before the war or were not considered suitable investment for foreign holders of dollars. Even the yield on such investments was inadequate, however. In the circumstances it was only natural that foreign holders of dollars should seize eagerly upon the opportunity provided by the emergence of the Euro-dollar system for securing a materially improved yield.

Although expert opinion is divided about the way in which the Euro-dollar system had actually originated, everybody agrees that from the very outset official dollar deposits re-deposited in Europe played a prominent part in providing the required resources. According to Mr. Robert D. Roosa, giving evidence before a Congressional Committee, the Euro-dollar deposits of Central Banks, Treasuries, and official international institutions amounted to some $2 billion towards the middle of 1962, and in the same year Altman estimated these official funds to constitute some two-thirds of the total of Euro-dollar deposits. The Bank for International Settlements stated in its report in June 1968 that at the end of 1967 the total was $3·1 billion.

During the early years considerations of yield must have been foremost in their minds. In more recent times Central Banks of some advanced countries came to be guided in their attitude towards lending Euro-dollars by broader considerations of monetary policy, to be discussed in Chapter 13. But the majority of the monetary authorities, especially those behind the Iron Curtain and outside Europe, continued to be influenced by the possibility of being able to earn a high yield without having to lower the liquidity or security of their short-term investment. On the other hand, considerations of monetary policy induced some Central Banks in more recent years to curtail their lending in the Euro-dollar market. Moreover, the relaxation of Regulation Q in favour of official dollar deposits reduced for a while yield differentials for official holders. Even so, although some Central Banks are believed to have withdrawn or reduced their Euro-dollar deposits, the proportion of Euro-dollars lent by official holders is believed to be still rather high. These holders include governments receiving large oil royalties in the Middle East and elsewhere; also the Bank for International Settlements which is known to employ large funds in Euro-dollars both for its own account and for the accounts of its various member Central Banks.

Next in importance to official holders of dollars among suppliers to the Euro-dollar market are commercial banks. They employ in Euro-dollars dollar deposits they hold on behalf of clients, and also their own deposits acquired and held in connection with interest arbitrage. Both commercial banks and Central Banks find time deposits eminently suitable for short-term investment, because, to use Roosa's words, 'their maturity and other terms can be flexibly adjusted to their needs'. Regulation Q made it unattractive, however, to hold dollar time deposits with banks in the United States.

Under Regulation Q the maximum interest rates American banks were permitted to allow on time deposits from 1957 to 1961 were 1 per cent from thirty to ninety days, $2\frac{1}{2}$ per cent from ninety days to six months, and 3 per cent over six months. From April 1968, they were permitted to pay $5\frac{1}{2}$ per cent from three months to six months, and $6\frac{1}{4}$ per cent over six months. Although Euro-dollar rates had their ups and downs, they were all the time — except for brief periods in 1958 for three months' deposits — appreciably higher than any of these rates. Above all, American banks are not permitted to pay interest on deposits for less than thirty days.

Before the development of the Euro-dollar market arbitrage funds were usually employed in U.S. Treasury bills or bank acceptances, while some other types of short-term investments also came to attract such funds to a limited degree. As and when the Euro-dollar market developed, arbitrageurs came to neglect other American short-term facilities. There was a real exodus of foreign funds out of the market for U.S. Treasury bills. Investments in Euro-dollar deposits at call became particularly popular as an alternative to investment in Wall Street loans. For technical reasons the employment of dollars in 'Federal Funds' over week-ends is from time to time a highly profitable line for London arbitrageurs.

It is understandable that foreign banks should seize upon the opportunity of being able to earn interest at a reasonably high rate on deposits at sight. Even though such deposits can be withdrawn without notice, in actual practice they are left very often with the borrower for quite a while. Such facilities combined the near-maximum of liquidity with a relatively high yield.

While banks came to employ most of their clients' deposits and their own arbitrage funds in Euro-dollars, it would not be correct to suggest that, as a result of the advent of the new device, banks reduced drastically their balances on current accounts in favour of Euro-dollars at call. Admittedly, such a practice would be technically feasible, for Euro-dollar deposits at call are only very slightly less liquid than dollar balances on current account with American banks. It is, however, a generally accepted practice among banks to keep reasonable working balances on their current accounts with each other, even though such employment of their funds is quite unprofitable. Had the European banks reduced their current account balances with their American correspondents, the latter in turn would have insisted on fixing a minimum balance as a condition of continuing to maintain the accounts.

Such balances are not maintained above the figure that is absolutely indispensable on a basis of reciprocity. Generally speaking, even before the advent of the Euro-dollar system, few banks ever held on current account more funds than was considered to be the minimum from the point of view of maintaining friendly relations with their correspondents. In any case, there is some slight difference between having the money actually in readiness on current account and having to give notice for the withdrawal of Euro-dollars at call before noon on the day when the money is required. Most banks would hesitate to cut down their working balances with their foreign correspondents to an extent that might expose them to the frequent necessity of overdrawing their accounts, even for a few hours.

Among non-banking investors in the Euro-dollar market those insurance companies which have large business in the United States are of outstanding importance. Although some of their premium reserves that are kept in dollars have to be held actually with an American bank in the United States, they are at liberty to keep much of their dollar funds in Euro-dollars. The sum total of Euro-dollars held by insurance companies is believed to be considerable. Other non-banking investors in Euro-dollars include the big oil companies and tobacco companies and some other firms of international standing. In Britain such companies have a general licence from the Bank of England permitting them to operate in Euro-dollars and in foreign exchanges in the same way as if they were authorised dealers. Both these types of firms are as often borrowers as they are lenders, while insurance companies are invariably lenders.

Many of the larger and more alert holders of refugee funds,

too, discovered the advantages of the new facilities. In most countries the rank and file of firms and private investors can only invest in the Euro-dollar market if they obtain special licence in each instance from the authorities. There are only a few countries, such as Canada, Switzerland, and West Germany, where corporations and individuals are free to lend their dollars in that market.

Prominent among early lenders in the market were Communist-controlled banks — the Moscow Narodny Bank in London, the Banque Commerciale de l'Europe du Nord in Paris, the State Bank of the U.S.S.R., and the banks of other Communist governments. At the beginning the rates they were prepared to accept on the Euro-dollar deposits were slightly below the standard rates, for the sake of establishing relationship with those Western European banks which until then were not prepared to have any dealings with them. Before very long they were able to obtain standard rates. The view was widely held that their main object was to conceal from the American authorities the size of their dollar holdings by disguising them as the holdings of London or Paris banks. In re-depositing their dollars, Communist banks wished to safeguard themselves against the risk of a seizure of their funds by the United States authorities in case of an aggravation of the Cold War. The possibility of legal action taken by creditors of Imperial Russia to attach Soviet deposits might also have been in the minds of the Soviet authorities. We saw above that considerations of yield could not have been altogether ignored by them.

But in all probability their main motive was a desire to prepare the ground for borrowing Euro-dollars at a later stage and to create a goodwill with London and Paris banks for that purpose. Many Treasuries, Central Banks, commercial banks, and large corporations of international standing had been in the habit of holding large dollar deposits with banks in the United States, in spite of the unsatisfactory yield, in the hope of being able to borrow later from the same American banks in case of need. Since, however, there is a ban in the United States on lending to Communist countries, there was no advantage from that point of view for Communist holders of dollars in accepting low deposit rates. On the other hand, they assumed that by lending to European banks there appeared to be a possibility that in due course they would be able to turn borrowers — which is precisely what has actually happened. About this more will be said in Chapter 8.

Conversely, while West Germany appeared in the Euro-dollar market in the first instance as a borrower, subsequently she reversed her role and became a large lender, as a result of a series of large balance of payments surpluses and the influx of hot money in West Germany. From the very outset France appeared simultaneously as borrower and lender since many Frenchmen held large dollar funds while others were in need of dollar credits. In the 'sixties balance of payments surpluses of Western European countries resulted in an accumulation of large official dollar balances, much of which assumed the form of Euro-dollars lent by the French, Italian, and other authorities. Even some under-developed countries outside Europe often operated in both directions in the Euro-dollar market, for, while the countries as a whole were in bad need of borrowing dollars, there were a great many wealthy corporations or individuals possessing large dollar balances which they came to employ in the market. The London and Paris banks, with which they deposited such dollars in preference to lending them to their fellow-countrymen, assumed thus in practice the role of guarantors of such funds when they were returned to the very countries whence they had come.

Keeping dollar deposits with Western European banks presents some obvious advantages to continental holders of dollars also because of the closer geographic proximity of the banks with which they hold their deposits. It is easier and less costly for them to keep in touch with their London banker to instruct him to change the form in which their funds are invested. This is particularly advantageous for those who want to conceal their dollar holding from the authorities of their own country of residence, from the point of view of existing or possible future exchange restrictions. It is more convenient for them to be able to pay visits to their London banker instead of having to send him instructions by cable or mail, and it is preferable to having to pay costly visits to New York. In any case the virtual identity of business hours in London and Western European centres makes it simpler for European holders of dollars to re-deposit them in London.

Moreover, the memory of the war-time blocking of Swiss assets in the United States still lingers on. It has made it appear expedient for continental holders of dollars to convert their dollar holdings into British dollar assets. This was deemed advisable in view of the possibility of a Communist invasion of their countries, the assumption being that in that case the history of the Swiss assets in the second World War might easily repeat itself. It is widely assumed that, as in 1940, the English Channel would effectively stop a Communist invasion, so that if continental dollar holdings appear as British assets, not being under enemy control, they would not be blocked in the United States.

Finally, foreign banks — including Central Banks — holding dollars find advantage in the new facilities from the point of view of being able to diversify their short-term investments. Even in advanced countries such as Germany, France, and Italy no adequate money market facilities are available for meeting present-day requirements for diversification that have arisen from the new conception according to which liquidity depends, not so much on the ratio of cash or of liquid assets to liabilities, as on the average maturity of assets compared with the average maturity of liabilities. This conception — which is still far from having emerged clearly — entails the adoption of systems of graded maturities of investments. The Euro-dollar market provides excellent facilities to meet this new requirement.

European banks are able to improve their liquidity structure thanks to the Euro-dollar market by buying dollars and lending them in the form of Euro-dollar deposits at call, and in doing so they feel justified in employing a larger proportion of their resources in a less liquid form. Alternatively, they are able to increase the proportion of liquid assets to short-term liabilities by borrowing Euro-dollars for, say, three months and re-lending them in the form of deposits at call or for seven days.

Yields obtainable in the New York and London money markets were not attractive during periods of pressure on the dollar or sterling, when the cost of covering the exchange risk on short-term investment tended to be distinctly higher than would have been justifiable on the basis of interest differentials. On the other hand, the employment of liquid resources in the Euro-dollar market had distinct advantages so long as forward rates were inclined to adapt themselves to interest parities based largely on Treasury bill rates. These advantages disappeared, however, as and when forward rates came to adapt themselves increasingly to parities based on Euro-dollar and other Euro-currency rates.

Hitherto we have only been dealing with investment in Euro-dollars by non-residents in the United States. Actually an increasing number of large American investors had also discovered these facilities and had taken advantage of them. Although most of those who had done so had been influenced by considerations of yield, fears of adoption of exchange control measures and considerations of fiscal evasion may also have played a part in inducing some Americans to re-deposit funds with banks outside the United States. For geographical reasons the bulk of such 'funk money' was deposited with Canadian banks, even though much of it found its way to European banks, either directly or through the intermediary of Canadian banks. Relatively few Americans cared to switch out of dollars into some other currency, and the difficulty and expenses of hoarding gold — which in any case was made illegal in 1961 — deterred them from resorting to that form of hedge. Subsidiaries of U.S. firms in Europe, Latin America and the Middle East came to employ their reserves in Euro-dollars until they were compelled to repatriate them in 1965.

The reason why this solution was not adopted on a much larger scale was partly that the overwhelming majority of Americans — apart from those residing in New York — were not internationally minded. The majority of those who were aware of the existence of the new investment facilities were reluctant to avail themselves of them. Apart from other reasons, there was a very widespread fear of exchange control being adopted in the country in which they would re-deposit their dollars. About this more will be said in Chapter 8. American banks have been doing their best to draw the attention of their clients to the existence of such a risk. To that end they require their American clients who instruct them to invest their funds in the Euro-dollar market to sign a declaration acknowledging that their attention was drawn to the fact that their funds would be subject to exchange restrictions, present or future, in the country where the funds are to be re-deposited.

The flow of American corporation funds to the Euro-dollar market became reversed in March 1965 as a result of President Johnson's appeal to Americans to repatriate their funds. In 1968 the four hundred largest corporations which had been in the habit of investing their funds in Euro-dollars came to be prevented from doing so through a tightening of the exchange control.

A new type of American short-term investment which is expected to compete to some extent with Euro-dollar facilities is the Certificate of Deposit. There is an increasingly active market in such certificates which enable holders of time deposits with American banks to mobilise their deposits before maturity. But rates of interest for periods up to twelve months are not high enough to provide an effective counter-attraction to the Euro-dollar market.

Having regard to the manifold advantages of the Euro-dollar system from the point of view of depositors, the surprising thing is not that the market has expanded to the extent it has but that it has not expanded earlier. Even now the estimated total of Euro-dollars falls short of total foreign-owned assets. One of the reasons for this, apart from fears of exchange restrictions, political risk in Europe, or commercial risk, lies in the fact that the market deals exclusively in very large units. Even though many banks in Europe would of course accept dollar deposits of much smaller amounts than the minimum units transacted in the market, the interest allowed on such amounts would be distinctly below the standard market rate. In any case, only large depositors are familiar with the system.

CHAPTER 5

BORROWING FACILITIES

DURING the late 'fifties the cost of borrowing by importers and exporters in London was relatively high, owing to the measures called for by the defence of sterling by means of a dear money policy. But this was offset, and more than offset during part of the time, by the benefit derived by borrowers from the wide discount on forward sterling. In the crisis year of 1957, however, the policy of high interest rates and the general credit squeeze was supplemented by specific bans on credits for financing trade between foreign countries and for re-financing trade beyond the original periods for which credits are usually granted. This made the discovery of an alternative device a matter of considerable importance. Refusal to meet such very genuine and legitimate requirements was in itself sufficient to create a demand for new facilities when they made their appearance in the form of Euro-dollar deposits.

The natural solution would have been for New York banks to seize upon the opportunity to take London's place in the financing of such trade. But, generally speaking, American banks were kept too fully occupied with expanding domestic credit requirements to be too keen on increasing their foreign commitments suddenly and substantially. Nor were any of the continental financial centres ready or able to step into the breach to anything like the full extent required. There was a distinct gap in the international financial machinery. In the circumstances the appearance of the Euro-dollar system was well-timed and providential.

Central banks and Treasuries were among those that stood to benefit by the new borrowing facilities, even though on balance they were, from the outset, overwhelmingly lenders in the Euro-dollar market. During the early years of the

35

Euro-dollar system some of them may have found it convenient at times to meet temporary pressure on their reserves, or to improve their reserve position on special occasions by means of obtaining Euro-dollar deposits. Since the increase of the International Monetary Fund's drawing rights and its increased willingness to render assistance, and since the establishment of close co-operation between Central Banks, they have been in a better position to cover such temporary requirements without having to borrow Euro-dollars, and now there is every reason to believe that most of the Central Banks outside the Iron Curtain appear exclusively as lenders.

Among Treasuries which have availed themselves of Euro-dollar borrowing facilities the Belgian Treasury has figured prominently as a systematic borrower of Euro-dollars on a fairly large scale over a period of years. Owing to the inadequacy of the facilities of the Brussels money market, whenever the Treasury's advances from the National Bank of Belgium approached the authorised ceiling, the Treasury raised funds by borrowing deposits in Euro-dollars or other Euro-currencies, whichever was cheaper, allowing for the cost of swapping the proceeds into Belgian francs. The purpose of the $20,000,000 loan placed by the Belgian Treasury in London in 1963 was to consolidate some of its Euro-dollar debts, but it resumed borrowing Euro-dollars once more almost immediately after the conclusion of that loan. The explanation lies in the Belgian National Bank's firm resistance to pressure to raise the ceiling for its advances to the government, in accordance with its tradition for sound finance.

The Soviet Government, too, and various other governments behind the Iron Curtain, have made in recent years increasingly strenuous efforts, through the intermediary of their State Banks and Communist-controlled banks, to attract Euro-dollar deposits. About this more will be said below.

Banks of various types in many countries welcomed the appearance of substantial additional credit resources represented by the growing supplies of Euro-dollar deposits. Even though the interest rates on such deposits were usually above the deposit rates these banks allowed on deposits in terms of their domestic currencies, until recently they were lower than the charges on sterling credits in London. Indeed, they were even lower than lending rates to prime borrowers in New York. Moreover, apart altogether from the difference in the cost of borrowing, the availability of the funds was in itself a great advantage and so was the relative ease with which such credits could be negotiated. To obtain a conventional bank credit in a foreign centre is, even for banking borrowers of good standing, seldom a routine operation. Although before the war there were reciprocal standing arrangements for drawing on *nostro* accounts or for acceptance credits, such arrangements had to be negotiated and from time to time re-negotiated. In view of the ever-changing situation this was not always easy, and at times it was rather delicate, and could even be extremely difficult. On the other hand, borrowing Euro-dollar deposits, at any rate for standard dates and for banks of first-class standing, is a routine matter and can be arranged in a matter of minutes.

The amount available to borrowers is flexible and if the would-be borrower is prepared to bid up the rates he can obtain the funds he needs — up to a point. Every bank puts a limit on the amount of Euro-dollars it is prepared to lend to every other bank. And if the market finds that a bank is prepared to pay unduly high rates the reaction is liable to be unfavourable. But since the borrowing bank is in a position to borrow simultaneously from a number of lenders in different centres, the grand total of Euro-dollars it is able to borrow is indeed considerable.

Borrowing of Euro-dollars by banks may serve the following purposes :

(1) To earn a quick return through undoing the transaction in the market, or in some other market, at the earliest possible moment at a somewhat more favourable rate. Many banks are only interested in such types of operations and are only prepared to deal with first-rate names. They are content with a profit margin of $\frac{1}{4}$ per cent, or even less if they deal directly with each other without the intermediary of a broker.

(2) To borrow and re-lend even without a profit, for considerations of prestige — to keep the bank's name

prominently before the market or to increase the figure of its deposits — or for the sake of establishing or strengthening some useful connection.

(3) To engage in various types of interest arbitrage, time arbitrage or space arbitrage with the aid of borrowed Euro-dollars or other Euro-currencies.

(4) To finance foreign trade operations with the aid of Euro-dollar credits, granted out of the pool of the bank's resources whose total is increased by the Euro-dollar deposits, in the place of sterling credits or of dollar credits granted by American banks in the United States.

(5) To swap into local currency in order to improve the liquidity position or to be able to lend to domestic customers in spite of a credit squeeze such as the United States experienced in 1968–69.

(6) To employ the proceeds of the swaps for special purposes, such as, in the case of British banks, granting short-term credits to local authorities or making deposits with hire purchase finance houses without having to curtail credit to regular customers in order to make funds available.

(7) To be able to finance a general domestic business expansion, as was the case of Japan until 1969.

Banks borrowing Euro-dollars often pass on the deposits in the same form in which they had received them — the same amount in the same currency for the same maturity. This is usually done when the object is to earn a quick turn in the market or to keep the bank's name before the market. It is also often done in operations of space arbitrage or interest arbitrage, but time arbitrage implies the lending of long deposits against borrowing short deposits or vice versa.

When Euro-dollars are borrowed for most other purposes the deposits usually lose their identity and their proceeds are absorbed in the pool of the bank's general resources. In respect of such use of Euro-dollars there is no direct relationship between the borrowing and lending transactions. Large round amounts of Euro-dollars may be re-lent in the market in large but different amounts, or they may be re-lent outside the market either in large amounts or in much smaller broken amounts. They are often re-lent for several different maturity dates. They can be re-lent either in dollars or in local currency or in a third currency. Often the Euro-dollars borrowed by banks are swapped into some other currency, then swapped again into yet another currency, or they are sold against some other currency with the exchange risk left uncovered.

One of the advantages derived by banks from being able to borrow Euro-dollars is that they can often adjust their foreign exchange commitments much more easily in that way than by means of conventional borrowing. Thanks to the new facilities they are no longer at the mercy of the foreign exchange market to the same extent as before. They are in a better position to avoid having to buy in the amounts of dollars they are due to deliver at a moment when the trend of the market is against them. They can also avoid having to renew maturing commitments by means of swap transactions on costly terms.

The same is true about merchants who have to pay dollars at a certain date and who may find it difficult to obtain a dollar credit in New York and too expensive to buy forward dollars for that particular date. Borrowing Euro-dollars enables them to defer the covering of their requirements until the spot rate or the forward rate has moved more in their favour. All these advantages diminish, however, as a result of the tendency of Euro-currency rates and forward rates to move in sympathy with each other.

Although merchants are not in a position to obtain Euro-dollar deposits at market rates — they have to pay, in normal conditions, between $\frac{1}{2}$ per cent and 2 per cent more — they can normally borrow at much lower interest rates than those charged for conventional credits. The banks' profit margins on Euro-dollar transactions with their customers are normally narrower than the difference between their standard lending rates and deposit rates, and even narrower than the difference between lending rates and deposit rates quoted to favoured big clients. This is so even in countries such as Britain or the United States. The discrepancy is apt to be wider in countries such as Germany or Italy, not to speak of Japan.

Originally Euro-dollar facilities lent for commercial purposes served almost exclusively the requirements of foreign trade, but gradually they came to be used extensively also to meet domestic requirements. This was found advantageous not only in countries with chronically inadequate credit resources but also in the United States, especially in the late '60s.

In 1957 and 1958 British and foreign banks lent Euro-dollars mainly for financing foreign trade formerly financed by sterling acceptance credits. But by 1959, and even more in 1960, Euro-dollars came to be employed on a large scale also for expanding domestic credits. Transactions for that purpose assumed considerable importance in 1961, especially in Japan, whose leading commercial banks gradually increased their Euro-dollar debts till the total reached something like $1 billion by the end of 1961. Italian banks first used Euro-dollars for financing foreign trade, even though the increased reserves of the Bank of Italy, resulting from Euro-dollar transactions, came to form the basis of domestic credit expansion. It was not until November 1962, however, that the Italian authorities gave the Italian banks a free hand to borrow Euro-dollars for the purpose of financing domestic trade. Euro-dollars were borrowed by a number of Asian countries in addition to Japan, partly through the intermediary of Israel and the Lebanon. Levantine financiers came to specialise in the market in foreign currency deposits and set up agencies in Switzerland and France to act as intermediaries for Euro-dollar credits. In Germany, too, several intermediaries are functioning for the purpose of arranging such credits for German firms, circumventing German banks.

Over and above all, London and Paris branches of the leading American banks have appeared as borrowers of Euro-dollars to an increasing degree. By the middle of 1969 Euro-dollar deposits borrowed by these branches were said to have exceeded $14 billion. They used the funds partly for financing American subsidiaries in Europe and for granting credits to finance foreign trade which would have been financed in New York. But by far the larger part of these deposits was lent to their own head offices in the United States, so that the dollars owned by foreign holders and re-deposited in the first instance in London or Paris, came to finance American domestic trade. This in spite of the fact that the profit margin on such transactions is much narrower than the one between domestic deposit rates and lending rates. One of the objects of these efforts to re-attract dollars from the Euro-dollar market in spite of the narrow profit margin is the competition between the leading American banks to acquire each others' deposits *via* London.

Some U.S. security dealers and brokers have acquired the habit of borrowing Euro-dollars in London instead of borrowing from New York banks. The latter became themselves in 1968–69 the largest borrowers of Euro-dollars.

Branches of Canadian banks, too, appeared from time to time as borrowers of Euro-dollars, mainly for the purpose of re-lending them in New York in the form of brokers' loans. Canadian banks with agencies in New York were particularly well placed for handling such transactions. But, as we remarked in the last chapter, after the setback of Wall Street in 1962, Canadian-held U.S. dollars began to find their way to the Euro-dollar market. This flow was reversed with the improvement of Wall Street in 1963 and has had its ups and downs since then.

British borrowing of Euro-dollars, mainly for Local Authorities and for hire-purchase finance houses, has been considerable from time to time. The authorities have become more liberal in permitting U.K. firms to borrow Euro-dollars.

Apart altogether from credit squeezes, which must recur from time to time in most countries, in some countries credit facilities are chronically inadequate to meet the abnormal requirements of their rapidly expanding economies. Especially in Germany, Italy, and Japan conventional credit was for many years both inadequate and very costly since the second World War. High interest rates to industrial and commercial borrowers are maintained in some countries not only by supply–demand relationship but also by cartel arrangements between banks. Thanks to the appearance of Euro-dollars, industrial and commercial borrowers were able to obtain credit facilities on terms much more favourable to them.

41

CHAPTER 6

NEW POSSIBILITIES FOR ARBITRAGE

THE market for foreign currency deposits provides ample additional scope for arbitrage by further increasing the intricacies of the international monetary system, and by adding new interest parities to the existing wide variety. Already before the advent of Euro-dollars there was a wider range of interest parities for arbitrageurs to choose between than in pre-war days. The choice between various short-term investment facilities in New York eligible for use in interest arbitrage widened during the 'fifties. For instance, commercial paper which was not used regularly by arbitrageurs before the war became for some time one of the favourite investment facilities in the post-war period. The American market in 'Federal Funds' came to attract much arbitrage funds from London in the 'sixties.

The appearance of Euro-dollar and other foreign currency deposit rates created new interest parities between those international interest rates, and also between them and national interest rates. This has greatly increased the likelihood of lasting and relatively substantial deviations of forward rates from some of their interest parities. After all, a forward rate can only conform to one interest parity at a time, so that if there are several different interest parities for each maturity the rate is bound to be over-valued in relation to some of them and under-valued in relation to others. When discrepancies between the various interest parities are not too wide forward rates may be able to settle somewhere between them in such a way that there is not sufficient intrinsic premium or discount against any of the interest parities to make transfers of funds for arbitrage worth while. But if the spread between various parities is very wide forward rates are bound to depart from some of them quite considerably, causing movements of funds

42

in one direction or another, and at times in both directions simultaneously.

The reason why the appearance of foreign currency deposit rates on the scene has widened discrepancies between various interest parities is that, while prior to their advent all interest parities were based on national interest rates, now the parities between various Euro-currencies and also those between them and national interest rates are based wholly or partly on international interest rates. These are affected by influences that do not affect national interest rates to anything like the same extent, if at all. Conversely, they are liable to remain partly immune to influences affecting national interest rates. The extent to which interest parities based wholly or partly on Euro-currency rates tend to move in sympathy with those based entirely on national interest rates is much less pronounced than the tendency for various interest parities based entirely on national interest rates to move more or less in sympathy with each other. Hence the more frequent, wider, and more lasting discrepancies between forward rates and some of their interest parities, providing opportunities for arbitrage transactions.

In theory forward dollar rates should tend to settle somewhere between interest parities based on Euro-dollar rates and those based on national interest rates. In practice they always tend to adjust themselves to that particular set of interest parities which happens to be favoured at a given moment by the majority of arbitrageurs. The fashion in this respect is apt to change from time to time. During the inter-war period the forward sterling-dollar rate usually tended to adjust itself to its interest parities based on London fine bank bill rates and either New York prime bill rates or rates on loans to Wall Street. During the early and middle 'fifties it was the parities between U.K. and U.S. Treasury bill rates that were of decisive importance. With the development of the markets in Euro-currencies the parities between Euro-dollar and Euro-sterling came to play an important part in determining the forward sterling-dollar rate, even though more often than not the Euro-sterling rate plays a passive part, being determined by the Euro-dollar rate and the sterling-dollar forward rate.

For some time in the early 'sixties the forward sterling-dollar rate tended to be somewhere between the parities of Euro-dollar rates with interest rates on credits to British local authorities and deposit rates paid by hire-purchase finance houses associated with leading British banks. It was these two rates that largely determined Euro-sterling rates, though the relationship was reciprocal.

Even though the relative importance of parities between Euro-dollar and other Euro-currencies compared with other interest parities is liable to change, they remain important most of the time, owing to the large volume of arbitrage transacted between Euro-currencies. Anyone needing Euro-dollars can choose between borrowing them in one of the European markets or buying or borrowing sterling and swapping it into dollars which can then be lent in the Euro-dollar market. Such transactions are not viewed with much favour in official circles which are anxious to keep arbitrage dollars and Euro-dollars strictly apart. Their segregation would run, however, contrary to the laws of human nature when there is a profit margin in favour of switching from the one to the other. A ban could only be enforced effectively by drastic exchange control measures that would paralyse the operation of the free market. In the absence of such restrictions forward rates always tend to adjust themselves to a level at which there is little financial advantage in preferring one alternative of securing Euro-dollars to the other alternatives.

We shall see in Chapter 14 that more often than not Euro-sterling rates are determined by the interplay of forward rates and Euro-dollar rates. They are the effect rather than the cause of changes in forward rates and never the cause of changes in Euro-dollar rates. There has always been a certain degree of reciprocity in the relationship between interest parities and forward rates, the latter influencing the former in some measure, as well as being influenced by them. But the extent to which changes in Euro-sterling rates are the effect of changes in forward rates is much more pronounced than the extent to which forward rates normally affect national interest rates. What matters from the point of view of arbitrage, with which we are concerned in this chapter, is that there is a strong tendency towards equilibrium between Euro-dollar–Euro-sterling parities and sterling-dollar forward rates. Owing to the spectacular increase in the volume of Euro-dollars during the second half of 1969, such equilibrium often came to be achieved through the influence of Euro-dollar rates on forward rates.

Situations in which it is profitable to transfer short-term funds between two centres simultaneously in both directions have become much more frequent as a result of the operation of interest parities based on Euro-currency rates on both sides or on one side. For instance in July 1969, when an increase of American demand for Euro-dollars caused a rise in their rates, it was profitable for a time to transfer Euro-sterling into Euro-dollars, until the adjustment of forward rates to Euro-sterling–Euro-dollar interest parities became complete, while during the transition period it was also profitable to transfer funds in a reverse direction, from New York into British local authority loans.

The development and expansion of the Euro-dollar market has greatly increased the volume of funds available for arbitrage. In the old days the frequently recurrent inadequacy of the resources available for that purpose was largely responsible for the development of lasting and substantial discrepancies between forward rates and their interest parities. Foreign exchange departments were usually allotted a fixed working capital and any additional funds required by them for use in some profitable interest arbitrage operations had to be obtained from the Treasurer of their bank, who often refused to meet their request or charged a very high book-keeping interest on the amount loaned to the foreign exchange department. The availability of larger funds for arbitrage in the form of Euro-currency deposits tends to reduce deviations of forward rates from the interest parities which are favoured by arbitrageurs. Even so, the inevitable discrepancies due to the increasing number of interest parities and their wider interest differentials make the achievement and maintenance of more or less complete equilibrium more difficult than before.

The new funds provided to foreign exchange departments

gave rise to additional short-term investment possibilities, enabling banks to depart from the conventional types of investments associated with interest arbitrage in the past. So it is not only the supply of arbitrage funds that has increased but also the demand for them. Nevertheless, the existence of larger funds for arbitrage purposes means that, while on the one hand discrepancies inviting arbitrage transactions are likely to be wider, more frequent, and more lasting, on the other hand movements of funds making for adjustment at least to some interest parities are apt to be on a larger scale.

The term 'arbitrage' is interpreted in this chapter in its broadest sense covering not only arbitrage in the conventional sense but also 'lender-arbitrage' or 'borrower-arbitrage' — the decision of lenders or borrowers other than arbitrageurs to borrow or lend on the most advantageous terms obtainable, allowing for forward rates — 'hedger-arbitrage', 'trader-arbitrage' and 'speculator-arbitrage'. The development of the Euro-dollar system affected the following types of arbitrage in that sense of the term :

(1) Space arbitrage to take advantage of the discrepancies between Euro-dollar rates quoted at any given moment in various markets.

(2) Interest arbitrage between Euro-dollars and other Euro-currencies.

(3) Interest arbitrage between Euro-dollars and conventional short-term investments.

(4) Time arbitrage between long and short Euro-dollars.

(5) Time arbitrage between long and short Euro-dollars on the one hand and other long and short Euro-currencies on the other.

(6) Time arbitrage between long and short Euro-dollars on the one hand and long and short dollar swaps on the other.

(7) Arbitrage between Euro-dollars and forward gold.

(8) Lender or borrower arbitrage, covered or uncovered, between Euro-dollars and other Euro-currencies.

(9) Hedger-arbitrage between Euro-dollars and other facilities.

(10) Trader-arbitrage between Euro-dollars and other facilities.

(11) Speculator-arbitrage between Euro-dollars and other facilities.

Arbitrage in space may assume the form of bilateral, triangular or multilateral operations. It is, for instance, more profitable at times to acquire in Switzerland Euro-dollars and swap them into sterling in London while at other times it is better to borrow Euro-sterling or swap into Euro-sterling in Switzerland. The discrepancy may be wide enough to make it worth while to operate in one market and undo the operation in the other market. Sometimes the transaction goes through one or more intermediate market before it reaches its final destination.

Arbitrage in space is at times profitable, because Euro-dollar rates are liable to be influenced by purely local factors in particular markets. This is true especially of very short Euro-dollar rates which are very sensitive and are apt to get out of equilibrium as a result of unexpected withdrawals of funds from the Euro-dollar market. In view of the near-perfect organisation of the market, and thanks to the operation of long-distance telephone and teleprinter, such discrepancies are not likely to be wide or of a lasting nature. There was for a time a tendency for Euro-dollar rates to be higher in Paris than in London, without leading to offsetting arbitrage on a sufficient scale.

There is a great deal of arbitrage between Euro-dollars and other Euro-currencies. Since the market in Euro-dollars is much larger, arbitrage transactions tend to adjust other Euro-currency rates to Euro-dollar rates, allowing for the forward exchange. It is only when operators trust the stability of the currencies concerned to a sufficient extent to engage in uncovered arbitrage that discrepancies between Euro-dollar rates and other Euro-currency rates tend to be unrelated to forward rates. Thus, when the dollar rate is in the vicinity of its lower support point and the support point is trusted, holders of other Euro-currencies may be prepared to acquire Euro-dollars without feeling the need for securing themselves against its depreciation. Very often, however, it is profitable to cover the exchange regardless of questions of confidence. For instance, when the forward dollar rate is at a premium against sterling, arbitrageurs switching from Euro-sterling into Euro-dollars stand to benefit by the premium. In such situations they might sell the forward dollars even if the spot sterling-dollar rate were at 2.42, so that there could be no reason to expect a further depreciation of the dollar.

Strictly speaking, all transfers of dollars into Euro-dollars constitute interest arbitrage between conventional short-term investments in New York and the Euro-dollar market. Interest arbitrage occurs when holders of dollar deposits or investments transfer their funds into Euro-dollars or when the increase of national interest rates in New York or the discovery of some high-yielding investment facilities there results in the return of funds from the Euro-dollar market.

Time arbitrage between long and short Euro-dollar deposits has developed into a very important branch of arbitrage. There is a fairly strong speculative element in such operations, because banks borrowing short Euro-dollars against lending long Euro-dollars have no means of knowing for certain how Euro-dollar rates are likely to change by the time the short deposit matures. If they anticipate a fall in interest rates, or even if they expect interest rates to remain unchanged, it appears profitable to borrow short and lend long. Since most of the time short rates are lower than long rates they may be able to make a profit even if they have to renew their short loans at a slightly higher rate than the original rate. On the other hand, short rates would have to be abnormally high to enable them to earn a profit on lending short against borrowing long.

The relative strength of the conflicting anticipations by the market as a whole influences the relative levels of long and short deposit rates, in addition to the incidence of commercial, etc., transactions. Active dealers in Euro-dollars, while en-deavouring to balance their total deposits placed with their total deposits taken, allow discrepancies to develop between the amounts placed and taken for any particular maturity. They go long for certain dates and go short for other dates, according to the view they take of Euro-dollar rate trends for various maturities.

Time arbitrage transactions are carried out also between Euro-dollars and other Euro-currencies. A bank may switch three months' Euro-sterling deposit into one month's Euro-dollar deposit if it expects that in a month's time their relative interest rates will change in its favour. Or it may do so if it expects that within a month renewal of the transaction could be effected more favourably in view of a change in the forward rate.

In my *Dynamic Theory of Forward Exchange* I dealt at some length with the so-called equilibrium line of forward rates for various maturity dates. That equilibrium line is not a straight line, because interest parities based on interest rates on the same investments but for various maturity dates hardly ever represent the same percentage per annum. The rates of long and short Euro-dollar rates are also apt to differ fairly widely. This provides ample scope for divergencies between long and short Euro-dollar rates and those between long and short forward rates, providing opportunities for profitable arbitrage.

Reference was already made in previous chapters to the use made of Euro-dollars in conjunction with gold-hoarding operations. There could be until 1968 arbitrage on discrepancies between the forward price of gold and the cost of financing gold-hoarding with the aid of Euro-dollars. Even though the forward price was usually based on the cost of such operations, at times one of the methods of speculation was marginally cheaper. The same is true about operations in silver.

Decisions to finance foreign trade transactions in one currency in preference to another are influenced to a large degree by the cost of borrowing in the form of Euro-dollars or other Euro-currencies. Such decisions constitute arbitrage in the broader sense — trader-arbitrage is the term adopted by Spraos — because they are determined by considerations very similar to those determining the movements of funds for arbitrage. In Britain Euro-currency credits are subject to license.

Decisions of arbitrageurs are influenced to a large extent by the view they take about the need for covering the exchange risk. Those engaged in hedging operations, foreign trade, or speculation may also be confronted with a similar choice. All such decisions are in reality a combination of an operation of covering, hedging, or speculation with an arbitrage operation.

For instance, in 1961 Western European exporters borrowed Euro-dollars and Euro-sterling and sold the proceeds because this was a cheaper way of covering their exchange risk than by selling forward dollars or forward sterling at a big discount or by borrowing in New York or London respectively. This was the result of the speculative pressure on the dollar and on sterling which caused the forward rates to depreciate to an intrinsic discount. Had the forward rates been at their interest parities in relation to the Euro-dollar or the Euro-sterling rate there would have been no advantage in borrowing Euro-currencies and selling the spot exchange in preference to selling forward dollars or sterling outright.

If trader-arbitrage and hedger-arbitrage were always covered it would go a long way towards readjusting discrepancies, even in the absence of interest arbitrage proper. But in situations in which arbitrageurs in the foreign exchange market would hesitate to run a risk of an open position, merchants very often leave the exchange uncovered, because, except in the case of intermediaries dealing in staple produce, their profit margins are usually wide enough to make it worth their while to assume a moderate degree of exchange risk. One of the effects of the devaluation of sterling and the franc in the 'sixties was that it weakened confidence in the permanency of existing exchange parities and made it appear expedient to a larger proportion of arbitrageurs, traders, and hedgers to cover the exchange risk on their operations.

The volume of arbitrage transactions in the narrower sense depends not only on the degree of confidence in the maintenance of the spot exchange within its support points but also in the prospects of maintaining a free foreign exchange market. If there appears to be a possibility of domestic political disturbances in a country, or if there is some other reason to expect restrictions, arbitrageurs prefer to forgo profit possibilities rather than assume too heavy commitments. Thus during the period of 1964 to 1967, when forward sterling was officially supported at an artificial level, it was, for some time, profitable to transfer funds to certain types of sterling investments, with the exchange risk covered. This was not done on a very large scale, however, because of fears entertained abroad about the possibility of additional exchange control measures in Britain.

There is, thanks to arbitrage of various kinds, a strong tendency towards the levelling out of the cost of borrowing Euro-dollars, whether borrowed direct or through the intermediary of other Euro-currencies. Even Euro-dollar rates paid or received by Communist banks tend to be equal to other Euro-currency rates, allowing for the forward exchange, though not so closely as those paid or received by other borrowers or lenders, because from time to time the Communist banks change their preference for lending or borrowing in one Euro-currency rather than another, or because they are at times prepared to borrow in whichever currency they can, without regard to rates.

We shall see in Chapter 13 that official operations, such as those carried out by the Bundesbank or by the Bank of Italy to provide their banks with swap dollars for the purpose of investment in the Euro-dollar market, are liable to give rise to profitable arbitrage opportunities if the official transactions conducted outside the market depart from the forward rates quoted in the market. The dollars thus invested in Euro-dollar deposits are liable to be used by the borrowers to acquire the currency of the country concerned.

The new market in London dollar certificates of deposits has extensive possibilities for new types of arbitrage, though at the time of writing it has not yet developed sufficiently to give rise to much interest arbitrage, and in the absence of similar markets abroad there can be as yet no arbitrage in space.

The broadening of the range of fluctuations of Euro-dollar rates during 1969 increased the scope of various types of arbitrage. So did the widening of discrepancies between rates for various maturities.

CHAPTER 7

HOW BANKS ARE AFFECTED

ALTHOUGH the development of the market in foreign currency deposits has affected banks in most countries to some extent, an examination of its effect on banks in the United States is of particular interest. This chapter is mainly concerned with the normal situation as it existed before American banks came to borrow Euro-dollars on a gigantic scale. But in view of the spectacular increase of the impact of Euro-dollars on American banking and on the American economy in the late 'sixties as a result of heavy American borrowing the subject will be re-examined in Chapter 17 in the light of that change.

Judging by the evidence given before Congressional Committees, many quarters were under the misapprehension that, as a result of the development of the Euro-dollar market, American banks had lost control over an amount of dollars representing the total of the dollar deposits that had been re-deposited in the Euro-dollar market. An increasing number of American corporations and large investors had come to follow the example of foreign holders of dollars, and this was causing considerable concern not only from the point of view of its possible effect on the dollar exchange and of the American gold reserve but also from the point of view of loss of business and of profits by American banks.

It is, therefore, necessary to state with the utmost emphasis the obvious fact that, apart from some special circumstances to be dealt with below, American banks necessarily retain the use of dollars re-deposited outside the United States. If foreign holders of dollar deposits with American banks were to withdraw their deposits in the form of dollar notes, and if they were to export the dollar notes, the result would of course be a corresponding decline of the total deposits in the United States.

Even then the bulk of the dollar notes would be sold to banks abroad and sooner or later they would be sold to, or deposited with, American banks. They would thus assume once more the form of foreign dollar balances held with American banks. Both the United States and the countries in which Euro-dollars are deposited are far too advanced for the primitive practice of keeping unnecessary amounts of notes.

Admittedly, some dollar notes are exported abroad — mostly across the Canadian frontier — by Americans anxious that their transactions should not be traceable by the U.S. fiscal authorities. Even that money, once it comes into the possession of Canadian or other non-American banks, soon resumes its original form of deposits with American banks, for there is a natural limit to the amount of U.S. dollar notes Canadian banks are prepared to hold.

As it was explained briefly in Chapter 2, the result of re-depositing dollars abroad is simply the transfer of the amount from the lender's account with an American bank to the borrower's account with the same American bank or with some other American bank. All borrowers in this highly advanced market are banks or business firms of considerable standing who are not in the habit of keeping in cash the dollars they borrow but simply add the amount to their dollar account, or to that of their non-American banker, with some American bank. In fact, as we saw in Chapter 3, the transfer of the deposit from lender to borrower simply assumes the form of an instruction by the lender to his American bank to transfer the dollars to the American account of the borrower or of a third party named by the borrower. Never for a moment does the dollar amount involved leave the American banking system.

If the borrower swaps the dollars into his own currency or into some other currency, the bank which provides the counterpart gains temporary possession of the dollars which are added to its dollar account. If the Euro-dollars are used for financing foreign trade it is the recipient of the resulting payment, or his banker, who adds the amount to his account with an American bank. The same deposit may change hands many times before the original transaction matures if it was for a period of, say, three months, but each change is only likely to mean a transfer from one American banking account to another.

As already observed, the account of the recipient need not necessarily be with the same bank. It is, therefore, quite on the cards that the bank with which the deposit was originally held loses the deposits for the duration of the transaction, and that some other American bank gains a corresponding amount of deposits. What matters is that the American banking system as a whole does not for a moment lose the amounts involved in Euro-dollar transactions, no matter how many times it may change hands.

Obvious as this may appear, it is apt to be overlooked not only by theoretical economists but even by practical bankers. This at any rate can be inferred from the evidence given by Mr. David Rockefeller before the Congressional Committee on Banking and Currency : 'This business [the granting of credits by European banks with the aid of Euro-dollars] no doubt would still be transacted in U.S. dollars, but, instead of being handled by American taxpaying banks, it would be handled by European international banks'. In fact, since the dollars remain with the American banks they are in a position to transact fully as much business — domestic or foreign — as before.

What Mr. Rockefeller may have had in mind is that European banks were enabled by the Euro-dollar deposits to lend dollars at lower rates than those at which American banks were prepared to lend to the same class of borrowers, at any rate before the rise in Euro-dollar rates in 1969. But since the volume of Euro-dollars, large as it was, did not meet all requirements by a long way, there were always sufficient foreign customers who were willing to borrow on the terms of the American bank. Considering the high level of interest rates in Japan, Latin America, and even in Europe, most borrowers were only too pleased to pay the interest charged by American banks if their requirements could not be met in full by the Euro-dollar market. The main advantage of the Euro-dollar market from their point of view was not that they could borrow cheaper but that they could borrow at all more than the amount American banks were prepared to lend. European banks do more business as a result of transfers of dollars into the Euro-dollar market, but American banks need not do any less business.

Even before the credit squeeze in the United States, customers would always gladly borrow the amount not required by foreign borrowers, so that American banks had lost no business even if the relative proportion of their foreign business to their total turnover had declined as a result of the expansion of the Euro-dollar market.

But the development of the Euro-dollar market does mean that many foreign deposits with American banks, which have hitherto been dormant, have become active as a result of their acquisition by borrowers who want to make use of the funds instead of merely leaving them on deposit. Hitherto, many of the deposits concerned were left idle for years on end, and the American banks could safely depend on it that they would not be withdrawn. They were therefore in a position to re-invest or re-lend the money for fairly long periods at a high yield. But holders of Euro-dollars are liable to sell, spend or lend them at frequent intervals, so that American banks are no longer in a position to lend those dollars for such long periods.

On the face of it the change may also mean that, since reserve requirements in the U.S. are 6 per cent on time deposits and $17\frac{1}{2}$ per cent on demand deposits, American banks may have to keep a higher proportion of reserve against their foreign-owned deposits if Euro-dollar transactions should change them into demand deposits. In a great many instances, however, Euro-dollars retain their original form of time deposits. Admittedly the use of dollars as Euro-dollars does increase the frequency with which they are apt to be transferred to other American banks. Some banks may be called upon more frequently to part with the deposits re-deposited with European banks, but, owing to the large amount of the turnover in Euro-dollars, the law of big figures is apt to come into operation. The chances are that, while sometimes one bank loses deposits and other times another bank, by and large losses and gains offset each other, more or less.

It is true, the velocity of circulation of deposits increases as a result of their use in the Euro-dollar market, but at no moment do the deposits leave the banking system. Nor has any bank particular reason for expecting that, by some freak coincidence of circumstances, it would lose substantial amounts of deposits on balance, in anticipation of which it would have to keep a larger cash reserve. From the point of view of the proportion of statutory reserves it does not matter very much if the turnover of the deposits concerned quickens, so long as the proportion of demand deposits to time deposits does not increase. Admittedly, the proportion of demand deposits is liable to increase because under Regulation Q no interest is allowed on domestic demand deposits, while interest can be earned on Euro-dollar demand deposits. But in any case the proportion of potential decline of their time deposit on that account is moderate — though it must be appreciably above the average for New York where most foreign deposits are kept.

In given circumstances the operation of the Euro-dollar system is admittedly capable of resulting in a net loss of deposits, not only by individual banks but by the American banking system as a whole. We already saw earlier in this chapter that this would occur if the deposits were withdrawn in the form of notes. It might also occur if the borrowers of dollar deposits are Central Banks who wish to use the dollars they have acquired for increasing their gold reserve. But Central Banks seldom borrow Euro-dollars, and, in any case, since they secure merely temporary possession of dollars by acquiring Euro-dollar deposits, there would be no point in converting them into gold for the limited duration of the deposit. Central Banks which are likely to borrow Euro-dollars are usually those of the financially weak countries, and from their point of view the dollar is certainly hard enough to serve as a reserve currency. Occasionally, by borrowing dollar deposits they merely anticipate seasonal or other influx of dollars, in which case they may feel justified in converting the deposits into gold. This would mean no net outflow of gold from the United States, as the transaction merely puts forward the date of the outflow which would have taken place later in any case. In view of the unofficial 'discouragement' of gold withdrawals since 1968, the importance of this factor has declined.

56

The same was true concerning losses of gold that were liable to arise through conversions by Central Banks of additional dollars acquired as a result of supporting the dollar exchange against selling pressure resulting from the sale of Euro-dollars borrowed by private firms or individuals. Sooner or later the deposits were liable to revert to their original owners, if the grand total of dollars in the Euro-dollar market did not decline. Possibly the next borrower would use the dollars in a way that would not lead to withdrawals of gold by Central Banks. In that case their repayment necessitated purchases of dollars, leading to buying pressure which, if strong enough to bring the dollar rate to upper support point, would have resulted in a recovery of gold by the United States.

There was, of course, a possibility that the unfavourable psychological effect of the temporary gold withdrawals caused by sales of Euro-dollars might induce foreign holders of dollars to realise their holdings instead of lending them in the Euro-dollar market. It might even induce American residents to transfer funds into foreign currencies. In such circumstances an expansion of the volume of Euro-dollars might have led to a net loss of gold and to a decline in the total volume of deposits in the United States.

Another situation in which Euro-dollar transactions cause a decline in total deposits held with American banks is if borrowers use the dollar deposits for the repayment of debts they owe in the United States. In view of the fact that they only gain temporary possession of the dollars, the transaction does not increase the net amount of debt repayments but merely puts the date forward. During the period of its duration the deposit used in such a way is liable to reduce the total of United States deposits, in advance of their reduction that would occur otherwise at a later date.

Disregarding the above special cases, it is reasonable to argue that the non-American banks' gain of dollars through an increase in the volume of Euro-dollars is not the American banks' loss. Nevertheless, because the system is not yet familiar to American bankers, they are naturally worried about this aspect of its operation. Hence the pressure in favour of removing Regulation Q prior to the development of heavy American borrowing of Euro-dollars. Yet those agitating for this solution ought to know that an all-round increase of deposit rates on deposits totalling well over $400 billion would be too high a price to pay for the prospects of reversing, or at any rate reducing the flow, of a small percentage of it into the Euro-dollar market. To pay an extra 1 per cent on all deposits would cost the American banking system in annual interest a high percentage of the capital amount handled by the Euro-dollar market. Moreover, it is far from certain that a removal of Regulation Q would make a really fundamental difference to the amount of Euro-dollars. In most conceivable circumstances the Euro-dollar market would be able to retain or replace a large part of the dollars withdrawn, by quoting higher deposit rates. Admittedly, if American banks were permitted to pay higher rates on domestic deposits it would reduce the need for them to borrow Euro-dollars. This has now become a strong argument for a modification of Regulation Q.

The reason why, in spite of these facts, there is a strong resistance to a complete removal of Regulation Q is that the facts are not accepted by official American opinion. Before the restrictions of 1968 a large and increasing number of American corporations and investors could transfer their deposits to the Euro-dollar market. Admittedly, there was a tendency towards the transfer of dollars owned by a certain type of American holders. Even so, since only large items were transacted in the market, the overwhelming majority of American deposits was much too small to assume the form of Euro-dollars. Even if the American funds that found their way to that market were to increase further, and even if the argument developed earlier in this chapter that American banks cannot lose any deposits through the operation of the market was completely fallacious, there would still remain the argument that the loss incurred would bear no comparison with the extra cost of interest on a much larger amount of domestic as well as foreign dollar deposits.

Even if pre-1968 conditions returned and U.S. banks ceased to borrow on a large scale, there would be no case for a removal of Regulation Q to check a drain on the American banking system through transfers to the Euro-dollar market. It would certainly not be worth while for American banks to make selective increases in their deposit rates for the sake of preventing a loss of earnings resulting from such transfers. They would not be in a very good position to discriminate between deposits which are likely to remain at home regardless of interest rates and those which are liable to be transferred unless higher interest rates are paid. They could pay better rates on large deposits, but the result would be pressure by their clients to extend at least part of such benefits to smaller deposits. Owing to inter-bank competition, they would find it difficult to resist such pressure altogether.

Even if it were possible to pay differential interest rates to foreign holders and to the class of American holders that are likely to transfer their deposits into Euro-dollars, the amount on which higher rates would be paid would be many times larger than the amount on which extra liquidity provisions have to be made in existing conditions.

In the late 'sixties the above argument became largely academic amidst the then prevailing conditions, since exchange control limited the amount of Euro-dollars U.S. residents could lend. Even if the head offices had lost some funds as a result of the operation of the market, they could regain all of the amounts lost, through borrowing in the Euro-dollar market.

One effect of the removal of Regulation Q would be the development of a market in foreign currency deposits in New York. The possibility of such a development is envisaged in an article appearing in the *Morgan Guaranty Trust Review* whose author has already invented a name for the European currency deposits to be transacted in that market, calling them 'Amero-sterling', 'Amero-franc', etc. Such a market could be created without having to repeal Regulation Q, simply by exempting deposits in foreign currencies from its provisions. This would be, however, extremely ill-advised, because the American public would acquire the habit of holding foreign currencies, and in given circumstances it might lead to heavy American buying of foreign currencies by American residents for the sake of taking advantage of higher interest rates paid on them. Whether there would be financial advantage for them to do so would depend largely on the forward rates. But during dollar scares the forward exchange would not be covered, and uncovered buying would aggravate the pressure on the dollar. At present exchange regulations prevent large American corporations from buying European currencies and re-lending them in the European markets for Euro-currencies. And such operations are clearly beyond the reach of most Americans. The creation of a market in ' Amero-currencies ' in New York would greatly simplify the flight of American capital from the dollar. It would make the acquisition of European currencies a more attractive proposition, since they would be held with U.S. banks.

Banks in the centres with foreign currency deposit markets stand to benefit greatly by the turnover in Euro-currencies. Thus, in London in particular, dealing in Euro-dollars and other currency deposits has become a very lucrative branch of banking. It is true, to some extent, this gain is offset by the decline in the use of sterling acceptances which are replaced to a large extent by the use of Euro-dollar deposits or Euro-sterling deposits for financing foreign trade transactions. It is equally true that margins of profit are not as wide on Euro-dollar business transacted on prime rates as on acceptance credits. Nevertheless, a large proportion of profits on Euro-dollars is not in place of profits on sterling credits but in addition to them. On balance, there is every reason to believe that the London banking community as a whole has greatly benefited by the development of the Euro-dollar system.

On their part, American banks which had to compete until 1969 against cheaper facilities granted abroad in their own currency greatly benefit on balance. Their London branches use part of the Euro-dollars they borrow for the purpose of financing foreign trade which their American head offices would be prevented from financing by exchange control. They have to be content with a narrower profit margin, without being compensated by profits that they would earn if a market in foreign currency deposits were in operation in New York. But the London market enables London branches of American banks to finance American subsidiaries abroad with Euro-dollars. Above all, the bulk of the Euro-dollars is re-lent to their head offices. This means that some American banks can now finance additional domestic business in spite of credit squeezes. Banks with London branches or good London connections are better placed for attracting deposits from their rivals which have no such facilities in London.

Paradoxical as it may sound, while the development of the Euro-dollar market has greatly increased the international use of the dollar and has reduced relatively the role that sterling plays in international financing, it has strengthened London's international financial role and has reduced New York's international financial rôle. This only goes to show that the international use of a currency and the international rôle played by a banking centre are not necessarily identical. There was a similar experience in the 'fifties in connection with the use of transferable sterling. It greatly increased the international role of sterling as a result of the international market that had developed in transferable sterling. The principal market in it was in Zürich, while owing to the nature of the restrictions on the use of such sterling there could be no market in it in London. As a result, the international rôle of the Zürich financial centre increased and so did the profit earned through it by Swiss banks. London banks did not benefit by the increased international role of transferable sterling. With the removal of exchange restrictions transferable sterling ceased to exist and Zürich's international rôle declined, and so did the international use of sterling. On the other hand, London's importance as an international banking centre increased, and so did profits of London banks on their foreign exchange business.

On the debit side of the development of the Euro-dollar market from the point of view of banks in general there is the trend it has brought about towards a narrowing of profit margins between deposit rates and lending rates, that had been maintained artificially wide by official restrictions or banking cartels. Banks in some countries are trying to make a stand against the trend towards narrower profit margins resulting from fiercer international competition. Generally speaking, however, the growing international competition arising from the better realisation of the new facilities is bound to force banks to abandon their attempts to maintain too rigid terms. American banks, for instance, have relaxed somewhat their formerly rigid rule under which borrowers, although paying interest on the whole amount of their loans, are expected to leave on their current account about 20 per cent of that amount.

On the credit side of the new device from the point of view of banks there is the resulting all-round increase in the volume of international business, both commercial and financial, in particular the larger profits from foreign exchange operations. Above all, in countries with scarce financial resources the banks have been able to increase their volume of lending appreciably It is true, under the influence of the increased credit supply they had to reduce their charges and were not always in a position to compensate this loss by a corresponding reduction of their interest on deposits. On balance, however, they must have stood to benefit by the larger turnover. In countries with inadequate facilities for medium-term investments banks benefited by the facilities offered by the new market. There is a great deal of borrowing of short Euro-dollars and re-lending them for medium term, which is not exactly sound banking, but it is very profitable. The centres with no adequate money markets have benefited by the provision of excellent short-term investment facilities resulting from the use of Euro-dollars.

Should the tendency towards closer margins outweigh the larger profits earned through the operation of the system it could mean that, in order to maintain adequate profits, banks would be forced to increase their charges on the multitude of their domestic bank accounts. What is really happening is that large clients are no longer prepared to subsidise small accounts by consenting to profit margins that allow for the high overheads of banks on small accounts. The Euro-dollar market gives big clients the benefit of lower overheads on their large accounts. Separation of wholesale banking from retail banking is the result of the new system.

CHAPTER 8

THE EXTENT OF RISK

THE very considerable advantages of the Euro-dollar system
are to some extent offset by actual and potential disadvantages
inherent in it. We saw in Chapter 6 that the market provides
additional facilities for speculators, and we shall see in Chapter
12 that it tends to accentuate inflationary booms and to
increase the risk to the economy arising from the duplication of
credit. In this chapter we are concerned with the commercial
risk or credit risk borne by lenders of Euro-dollars — the
risk that borrowers might be unable to repay the deposits
on maturity either owing to insolvency through overtrading or
as a result of a major crisis affecting the borrower's country
— and the risk of new exchange control measures.

Although Euro-dollars are sometimes re-lent outside the
market in the form of secured credits, within the market
Euro-currency transactions between banks are always entirely
unsecured credits. Borrowers are not required to provide
collateral securities or to surrender shipping or warehouse documents, or to assure the lenders that the transactions for which
the credit is to be used would be genuinely commercial and
self-liquidating, or indeed to inform the lenders at all about the
intended use of the deposits. No limitations whatsoever are
imposed on borrowers regarding the use they may make of the
borrowed dollars. In this sense, as in many other respects,
transactions in Euro-dollars bear much similarity to forward
exchange transactions between banks in the market, where no
information is given or asked about the purpose of the transactions and no security is offered or expected.

The system differs fundamentally from the traditional
practice in respect of acceptance credits. When a foreign bank
arranges an acceptance credit in London for its local customer

it is usually stipulated, or at any rate tacitly understood, that the credit line would be used by the latter for financing genuine self-liquidating foreign trade transactions. In the old days the bills presented for acceptance were usually accompanied by shipping or warehouse documents, though between the wars this practice was no longer insisted upon. It was a standing joke that bills were supposed to bear pinmarks, to convey the impression that they had been pinned to documents even if the documents themselves were not enclosed. But many banks and acceptance houses looked upon old-fashioned bills complete with documents as something of a nuisance, involving as they did a great deal of extra clerical labour without any extra profit.

Since the foreign banks which arranged the acceptance credits were of first-rate standing, London banks refrained from expecting borrowers to provide documentary evidence of the genuine character of the transactions which were supposed to be financed by the bills. During the late 'twenties the originally valuable safeguards of the genuine character of the transactions degenerated into meaningless pretence. Credit lines were for large round amounts and the individual bills sent to the London banks for acceptance were for relatively small broken amounts ; but sometimes by a miraculous 'coincidence' their total was exactly the large round amount of the credit line. When a lie is obviously a lie and deceives nobody by its obviousness it ceases to be a lie. The London banks and acceptance houses were fully aware that a large part of the credits were used, not for the self-liquidating short-term transactions which the bills were supposed to represent, but for credits granted by the foreign banks to their clients for longer periods. These finance bills — which in fact they were in spite of pretending to be genuine commercial bills — were renewed every three months, though in order to keep up the pretence the foreign banks kept changing the respective amounts of individual bills drawn on the credit.

It was partly the result of this system that during the crisis of 1931 the outstanding German and other Central European bills were found to be non-self-liquidating. Under the various standstill agreements between 1931 and 1939 all pretence at their self-liquidating character was discarded.

There is no hypocritical pretence whatsoever about the true character of Euro-dollar deposits that change hands within the market. No questions are asked, no information is given. A potential lender of Euro-dollars may refuse a name if he thinks the potential borrower is not of sufficiently high standing or if his limit for that name has already been reached. But no strings are attached to any Euro-dollar loan, and the borrower is not insulted by being asked for collaterals, or even for information as to his intention. It is true, strictly speaking, outright refusal of a name is even more offensive, but it can be disguised because the transaction is offered through a broker who discloses to the would-be lender the name of the would-be borrower but never gives away the name of the unwilling lender to his potential borrower if the deal does not materialise.

The same considerations do not of course arise in relation to non-banking customers, though banks would not think of asking questions or insisting on documents or collaterals when lending Euro-dollars to one of the international oil companies or other business combines of comparable standing. It is only when the Euro-dollars are re-lent to less important customers that banks may still insist on knowing the purpose for which the credit is required. They may even ask for securities, or at any rate for documents, though in this latter respect the general practice is now much slacker than it was in pre-war days. Even between importers and exporters a large proportion of payments are not made nowadays conditional on the presentation of documents to the banker who is to make the payment. Thus, it is probably true to say that nowadays the re-lending of Euro-dollars even outside the market is not always surrounded by very strict safeguards.

In the market itself, where the same amounts may be lent and re-lent a dozen times, no lender knows even whether the immediate borrower wants to use it for granting credits, short or long, to finance foreign trade or domestic trade, whether he wants it for arbitrage or speculation. He has no idea to which country and to which firm his Euro-dollar deposits will be re-lent. As for the use made of the Euro-dollars by the ultimate borrower the original lenders cannot even hazard a guess, considering that they have no means of knowing his identity.

In spite of this, the extent of the credit risk on transactions within the market is relatively small. Most participants in the market are of high standing. What is more, they are important enough in their respective countries to make it highly probable that, should they by any chance get into difficulties, other banks of their country, or their Central Bank or Government, would come to their rescue in order to safeguard the good reputation of their country's banking system. After the Creditanstalt crisis of 1931 it has come to be generally realised that no country can afford to allow one of its leading banks whose name is an international household word to get into trouble. Failure of a leading bank would be a major disaster the chain reaction to which would not be confined to the country directly concerned.

The same considerations do not of course hold good about lending to non-banking borrowers, unless it is under the guarantee of some first-rate bank of their country. For a large proportion of such transactions there is no such guarantee. But lenders take great care when selecting their non-banking customers, and they seek to safeguard themselves also by limiting the amounts lent to any particular firm and also the total lent to firms in any particular country. In this market the rules are much stricter than in foreign exchange dealings proper. Spot exchanges are usually transacted almost without limit, in view of the fact that the transaction is completed within two days. Even for forward exchange commitments the limits for good names are incomparably wider and more elastic than for Euro-currency deposits. This is because, apart from the possibility of exchange restrictions, the risk arising from the possibility of a failure to deliver or to take delivery of forward exchange is confined to the amount of the possible exchange rate difference. In the case of Euro-currency deposits, on the other hand, the risk amounts to the total of the transaction.

The safeguard by limits is purely illusory. For there is no exchange of information between banks by which they could have an idea about the total amount of outstanding credits of any particular borrower. The Bank of England and other Central Banks receive regular returns indicating the total granted by each bank to each country, so that the authorities are in a position to warn their banks if the totality of loans to a particular country appears to be excessive. There is no such method of pooling information about total borrowing by individual firms.

It is true, if a firm is very active in borrowing on the market, right, left, and centre, rumours about it get round somehow even in the absence of regular exchange of information. But this obstacle to excessive borrowing can be overcome to a large degree by borrowing simultaneously in several banking centres. While intelligence departments of banks in the same centre may informally exchange verbal information — though not nearly to the same extent as they did about acceptance credits before the war — there is practically no exchange of information between different financial centres.

In case of forward exchange transactions a name is either taken or is not taken, and no different rates are quoted according to the standing of the bank. In the case of foreign currency deposits the relative degree of confidence in the borrower's standing is expressed by the quotation of different interest rates. This recalls the practice that prevailed until the nineteenth century, described in my *History of Foreign Exchange,* under which exchange rates included interest rates, and consequently different rates were quoted according to the standing of the sellers of foreign bills. There is now only one exchange rate for each date at any given moment on the foreign exchange market for all dealers whose names are taken. On the other hand, a wide range of interest rates is quoted at any given moment in the market for Euro-dollar deposits of identical maturity. There is a standard rate for first-class names, but even that prime rate is not necessarily applied always to first-class names. When banks of a certain country borrowed too large amounts of Euro-dollars — as Japanese and Italian banks did for some time — they had to pay higher rates, even though their standing was unexceptionable. What lenders in such instances fear is not default by any individual borrower but the imposition of exchange control by their government that might prevent them from meeting their international liabilities. Whenever there is strong demand for Euro-dollar deposits by banks of any country, long before the total has approached the danger line the rate that is quoted for that country is raised. Even so, the 'insurance premium' represented by the additional rate is seldom sufficient to compensate for a real risk. Even after the unfavourable experience with some German and American borrowers towards the end of 1963, differentials remained too narrow.

The relaxation of traditional precautions against credit risk is largely due to the continued absence of a major crisis since the war. Although there were a number of recessions in every country, there was nothing comparable to the two major inter-war crises, those of the early 'twenties and early 'thirties. The number of post-war insolvencies compared very favourably with that of the inter-war period.

But it would be a mistake to imagine that we have concluded a contract with Providence ensuring the continuation of this satisfactory state of affairs for ever. In fact there are indications that the monetary policies which have ensured so far the absence of major crises in the post-war period are becoming increasingly unfashionable. The so-called 'stop and go' policy which checked booms before they got out of control came to be looked upon with disapproval and derision. Politicians, administrators, journalists, and even economists who ought to know better, appear to have forgotten the costly lessons of inter-war experience. They seem to have also forgotten the teachings of their elementary textbooks on economics which explain the causes and nature of business cycles. Human nature being what it is, the absence of a slump over a prolonged period is bound to generate increasingly unwarranted optimism about ever-lasting prosperity, and a widespread anticipation of non-stop progress at an ever-increasing rate. Continuous increase in demand is bound to create a universal sellers' market which makes it appear safe to produce almost anything. Differences between good and bad business judgement or between efficient and inefficient production methods only affect the size of the profit and the rate of the turnover. Even inefficient firms can get by. The result of such a state of affairs is a Stock Exchange boom which discounts progress many years and even decades ahead and bids up the prices of equities to a level at which its yield becomes purely nominal. The bubble is liable to be pricked sooner or later, possibly as a result of belated efforts to call a halt to the non-stop boom with the aid of drastic deflationary measures.

It is true, basic economic conditions today are much sounder than they had been during the years before 1931. We have had as yet no repetition of the Wall Street slump of 1929. There is no agriculture over-production comparable with that of the late 'twenties and early 'thirties. There is now no disturbing reparations problem. Most of the weak banks were eliminated during the 'thirties and relatively few undependable banks are now in existence. There is now a system of deposit insurance in the United States and in other countries, while in some countries such as the United Kingdom there is an unwritten rule under which any bank of standing would be supported in case of trouble, so as to ensure that depositors do not suffer any losses.

There is now much closer co-operation between banks and also between them and their monetary authorities. Since the early 'sixties there has been close international co-operation between various monetary authorities. In 1931 the Bank for International Settlements formed for promoting such co-operation was only a few months old and its usefulness was impaired not only by the inadequacy of its resources but also by political intrigues and rivalries within its board and management that paralysed its activities. Now the International Monetary Fund is securely established and has at long last really impressive resources at its disposal. Moreover, the Bank for International Settlements proved its worth during sterling and dollar scares since 1961. The monetary authorities now know that defence against an international monetary crisis is indivisible, for the collapse of one major currency would gravely impair confidence in all other currencies.

Nevertheless, it would be unwarranted optimism to ignore

the existing potential sources of trouble. The unsound pre-war practice of financing long-term operations by means of short-term credits renewable every three months or six months is once more rearing its ugly head. Before the war a high proportion of German acceptance credits was used for financing goods exported to Russia on a long-term credit basis. Today the construction of plants by German firms in under-developed countries is financed to a by no means negligible extent by borrowed Euro-dollar deposits. This practice is greatly encouraged by the ease with which renewals of six months' or twelve months' deposits can always be effected. While there may be at times difficulties to renew very short deposits over the turn of the year or for other awkward maturity dates, and those having to do so may have to pay rates that heavily penalise them, the market is on the whole highly efficient and can absorb with remarkable ease sudden withdrawals or increases of demands. That very ease is, however, liable to lull borrowers and lenders into a false feeling of security.

If a Latin American country to which Euro-dollars have been lent encountered difficulties its monetary authorities might not be in a position to handle the situation with the required degree of skill to avoid a crisis. There might be large-scale defaults, or a moratorium, or exchange restrictions might be imposed. If the amount of Euro-dollars thus affected is found to be substantial it is bound to cause large-scale non-renewals of deposits in the Euro-dollar market. Similar crises are liable to arise through a seizure of power in debtor countries by Communist Governments which would repudiate external obligations or would hopelessly immobilise them.

Yet another possible source of trouble is a recurrence of dollar scares which we experienced in the 'fifties and the 'sixties. So long as exchange rates are firmly maintained within their support points the danger of a crisis through this cause remains limited. It greatly assists confidence in Euro-dollars that the dollar has to be supported at support points by all member governments of the International Monetary Fund. This confidence would be greatly undermined, however, if there were frequent changes in parities. This conclusion emerged force-

fully from the experience of the well-meaning revaluation of the
D. mark and the guilder in 1961. Although it tended to correct
a fundamental disequilibrium, in fact it gave rise to a wave
of distrust in existing parities. The establishment of floating
rates, or of a much wider spread between support points, even
of a more flexible system under which parities would be subject
to more frequent changes, would expose borrowers or lenders
of Euro-dollars to heavy losses, unless they cover the exchange
risk, which is often costly. A fundamental change of the
Bretton Woods system would therefore greatly increase the risk
of sudden withdrawals of funds from the Euro-dollar market
by depositors who prefer to realise their holdings of dollars.

There is also the risk arising from Communist activities in
the Euro-dollar market. With the aid of subtle methods they
succeeded in establishing themselves as a major factor in the
Euro-dollar market. We saw in Chapter 5 that, to begin with,
they appeared as lenders and for the sake of establishing themselves in the market they were prepared to lend their dollars at
a shade lower rate than the current market. Once they had
established their connections they began to operate in both
ways. Banks which had borrowed Communist Euro-dollars
found it awkward to refuse to lend Euro-dollars to Communists
when they were asked to do so. By 1963 Communist banks came
to operate on a large scale both ways, but from time to time
they were on balance very large borrowers. They came to
pay by 1968 practically standard rates, so that they received at
very low rates what in fact amounts to long-term loans renewed
as a matter of form every three months or six months.

Even if this policy merely aimed at financing the trade
deficit of the Soviet Union and of other Communist countries,
the willingness of the Euro-dollar market to accommodate them
is open to criticism. 'Competitive co-existence' is all very well,
but there appears to be no valid reason why Western countries
should assist the Communist bloc to compete them out of co-
existence. Let us have more trade with the Communist bloc
by all means. But it should be on a strictly cash basis. Apart
altogether from such political considerations, from a practical
business point of view the part played by Communists in the

71

Euro-dollar market is a potential cause of trouble. Acute war scares, such as the crisis over Cuba or an open clash over Berlin, are bound to arise from time to time and the knowledge that the Communists have such a strong hold over the Euro-dollar market is liable to inspire mistrust on such occasions, leading to wholesale withdrawals of deposits, even in the absence of any deliberate Communist attempts to make trouble.

The Communists might want to fish in troubled waters by withdrawing their maturing deposits. They can do so all the more easily as they re-lend some of their three months' or six months' deposits for shorter periods — much of it at call. Even though they are on balance debtors of Euro-dollars, they are able to withdraw large amounts from the market by refusing to renew the short deposits they had lent. Amidst a war-scare, replacements of the amounts withdrawn would not be readily forthcoming, and the market might find itself in an awkward position. On top of this, in extreme circumstances the Communists might even try to trigger off a major financial crisis in the Western world by defaulting on their long-term Euro-dollar deposit liabilities, after having collected their own short-term deposits.

Suppose, for the sake of example, that during the Cuban crisis an American warship had sunk a Russian ship that refused to stop in order to submit to search. The Soviet Government would have demanded compensation and might have blocked the Euro-dollars owed by Communist-controlled banks. Such an incident could easily have occurred in 1962, and it might easily occur on some future occasion. It is of no use arguing that the record of Communist borrowers of Euro-dollars has been above reproach to date, and that, fortunately, the East-West tension has relaxed considerably. There can always be a first time. It must be borne in mind that Communists are not bound by principles of ethics and have no traditions of commercial integrity which they would feel they must uphold. They are honest merely as a matter of practical expediency. They hope to borrow more as a result of their carefully nursed reputation for honesty. But the moment considerations of expediency should make it more advantageous

for them to default they would certainly not hesitate to disregard any considerations of business ethics.

There is also the ever-present risk of some important debtor
country introducing exchange control for the sake of safe-
guarding its domestic economy against the effect of heavy withdrawals of Euro-dollar loans on the credit structure. The trend
is no longer towards a higher degree of freedom in the sphere of
international finance and trade. There is, moreover, a very
real risk that excessive use and misuse of that freedom might
create situations in which pressure in favour of reinforcing
exchange controls, which now exist in some degree in most
countries, might gain the upper hand.

All these difficulties need never materialise. A prominent
London banker remarked many years ago that if bankers
kept worrying about what *might* happen they would never have
a single night's sleep. Indeed bankers are justified in taking
calculated risks in return for adequate profit. But it was open
to question whether the drastically reduced profit margins
on Euro-dollar transactions during the 'sixties — especially
on transactions within the market — provided adequate compensation for the admittedly moderate but potentially grave
risks they have to take. A bank lending Euro-dollars for
a net profit margin of $\frac{1}{8}$ per cent per annum risked $1 million
for the sake of a gross profit of $312.50 on a three months'
deposit, not allowing for overheads. Yet some banks were prepared to operate for that profit. For shorter deposits the profit
was correspondingly smaller, although a sudden crisis might
arise even during a shorter period.

It is true, the size of the profit margin would make little
difference if the debt is defaulted upon. The market has only
been in existence for a few years, so that banks have not been
able to accumulate reserves out of their profits for stormy days.
The narrowness of the profit margin increases the vulnerability
of the system because it increases the velocity of the deposits
and makes the chain of debtors longer. If profit margins had
been kept at their original minimum figure of $\frac{1}{4}$ per cent the
number of deals might have been smaller and the system would
have been less vulnerable. This argument gained strength from

the fact that it was often banks which were not absolutely first-rate that were prepared to accept the infinitesimal profit margins for the sake of benefiting from the prestige gained through their operations on a large scale.

Although the advantages of the Euro-dollar system, both from the point of view of the banks and from that of the public interest, fully justify the taking of calculated risks, this aspect of it calls for more attention than it had hitherto received. It is true, the difficulties of the Stinnes Bank and of firms involved in the New York 'vegetable oil' scandal in 1963 showed that, even in the absence of a general crisis, heavy losses are liable to be incurred through indiscriminate lending. That lesson, painful as it was for a few lenders of Euro-dollars in London, Paris, and Switzerland, did not seem to have been sufficient to make the banks realise the need for an adequate system of exchanging information. Nor was the resulting widening of profit margins and differential rates in excess of standard rates sufficient to cover the real extent of the risk.

Some London banks decided to withdraw from the Euro-dollar market, but they resumed operations later. All lenders came to apply stricter rules concerning names and limits. As a dealer observed in 1964, the market became distinctly less light-hearted than in the old days. Even so, the Euro-dollar situation needs careful watching, not only from the point of view of its bearing on the international monetary situation but also from the point of view of credit risks.

By 1966 Communist banks came to be able to borrow at rates which were only a fraction above standard rates. By that time American banks became the chief borrowers, and the risk involved in lending them was considered to be virtually non-existent. After the near-miraculous recovery of Japan and Italy by the middle 'sixties, their banks, too, were able to borrow at favourable rates.

CHAPTER 9

INTERNATIONAL INTEREST RATES

THE spectacular expansion of the market for foreign currency deposits has brought about an institutional change of utmost importance in the monetary system by creating an international money market and by developing a structure of international interest rates. There are in fact now in existence new sets of interest rates in the Euro-dollar market and in other Euro-currency markets, which are distinct from, and to a large extent independent of, the respective structure of national interest rates that is in operation within each country in whose currency credits are granted. Outstanding among these sets of interest rates is the one operating in the Euro-dollar market. Euro-dollar rates are of considerable importance from a point of view of practice, theory, and policy, precisely because they are international interest rates distinct from those on dollar credits and deposits within the United States. Their advent constitutes a revolutionary innovation, whose very far-reaching impact on the monetary system and even on world economy came to be realised during the rise in Euro-dollar rates in 1969.

It is through giving rise to international interest rates that the Euro-dollar system has been able to influence the international allocation of active financial resources, the trend of national interest rates and that of exchange rates. Admittedly, even before the advent of Euro-dollars, interest differentials played an important part in the process of transferring surplus capital to countries short of capital. But Euro-dollar rates, precisely because they differ from interest rates in the United States, powerfully assist in that process. The higher deposit rates obtainable in London and elsewhere attract into the international economy large funds which would not have been available for those who need them outside the United States.

This innovation of first-rate importance calls for a very careful re-examination of monetary theory and of monetary policy, since they have hitherto been based on the assumption of the essentially national character of interest structures.

Admittedly, even national interest rates are far from being altogether independent of interest rates in other countries, or of various other monetary, economic, or political influences that operate outside the country concerned. There is, however, in each country a set of national factors in operation that determines, to a very large degree, the level and trend of the national interest rates structure. Even though the influence of that set of factors is often offset or reinforced by developments abroad, the monetary authorities are usually in a position to counteract such external influences if they wished to isolate the national interest structure from them. What matters from the point of view of the argument with which we are here concerned is that, while interest rates on dollar loans in the United States are determined overwhelmingly by conditions and policies within the United States, interest rates on Euro-dollar loans are apt to be influenced by a different set of conditions — by conditions prevailing largely outside the United States, and by policies pursued outside the United States.

It is true, long before the advent of Euro-dollars the operation of the forward exchange system provided an interest structure of an international character, and it provided an alternative to the national interest structure. Forward exchange offers lenders and borrowers the choice between operating in the domestic money market or in the foreign exchange market in which they are in a position to grant or secure loans in any currency by means of swap transactions. But in order that such transactions should amount to short-term credit transactions and not merely to exchanging one currency against another for a limited period, they have to be combined with a deposit arrangement, and the latter connects them up with the national credit structure. Thus when in the 'twenties a Vienna bank acquired a dollar deposit by means of a swap transaction it borrowed from the American bank the schilling counterpart.

Euro-dollar transactions, on the other hand, need not have any direct connection with the local money market or with the national credit structure either of the borrowing country or of the lending country. Even though they can have such connection, it does not constitute an indispensable part of the transaction.

What is more important, swap rates on which such transactions were based are not supposed to be basically different from domestic interest rates. They are normally determined by the differentials between the national interest rates in the two countries concerned. In theory they tend to be identical with those differentials, and any noteworthy departure from them gives rise to a tendency towards automatic readjustment. Thus, in theory at any rate, swap rates are not supposed to constitute separate international interest rates, they merely reflect the discrepancies between national interest rates. The cost or yield of a loan transaction resulting from the combination of a swap operation and a credit or deposit operation tends to be the same as that of a similar transaction executed in one of the two local markets concerned. Of course there can be marginal discrepancies over prolonged periods. But any substantial discrepancies set influences in motion towards their elimination.

Euro-dollar rates and foreign currency deposit rates in general, on the other hand, have a separate existence in theory as well as in practice. The cost or yield of Euro-dollar transactions can differ materially and over a prolonged period from the cost or yield of credit transactions in dollars in the United States. In fact the whole *raison d'être* of the Euro-dollar market is based largely on the fact that its interest rates differ from national interest rates in the United States. Admittedly, national interest rates in the United States and international interest rates on dollar loans in the Euro-dollar market also tend to react on each other reciprocally. But the influences that make for the adjustment of discrepancies between them are not sufficient to prevent their continuous separate existence.

The growing influence of international interest rates is indicated by the fact that forward exchange rates, which in the past tended to adapt themselves to their interest parities based on national interest rates, now tend to adapt themselves to the interest parities based on foreign currency deposit rates. Thus the forward sterling-dollar rate tends to adapt itself to the differential between Euro-dollar and Euro-sterling rate and tends to fluctuate largely in sympathy with that differential. Even though the relationship is reciprocal — as indeed is the relationship between forward rates and their conventional interest parities — the fact that the curve of forward rates now tends to desert that of interest parities based on national interest rates and to run more or less parallel with international interest parities has further enhanced the importance of the latter's separate existence.

When we talk about international money markets and international interest rates we have primarily the Euro-dollar market and Euro-dollar rates in mind. Markets in other foreign currency deposits are too narrow to constitute by themselves an international money market determining the trend of international interest rates. They are to a large degree satellite markets to the Euro-dollar market, and the rates of foreign currency deposits other than Euro-dollars — especially those of Euro-sterling deposits — tend to be influenced by the interplay between Euro-dollar rates and forward rates. Nevertheless, Euro-sterling rates, too, are subject to some extent to a set of international influences other than those of the Euro-dollar market, in addition to being subject to some extent to domestic influences affecting the national interest structure in Britain. The same is true about other leading Euro-currencies.

We saw in earlier chapters that there is at any given moment a wide range of interest rates quoted for Euro-dollar deposits according to the borrower's standing, the purpose for which the deposit is lent, and the estimated total of his borrowing and that of his country. To simplify matters for our present purposes, we are only concerned in this chapter with standard rates, that is, the rates paid on transactions of normal size by borrowers of first-rate standing who, in the estimation of the market, have not borrowed excessively.

This assumption is not so unrealistic as may appear at first sight. There is, after all, a set of influences that tends to affect the entire structure of Euro-dollar rates in the same sense, though not necessarily to exactly or even approximately the same extent. The differentials between the Euro-dollar rates quoted to various classes of borrowers are of course also subject to specific influences, such as changes in the relative standing of individual borrowers or in the outstanding amount of their commitments. But apart altogether from these specific influences, the differentials also tend to widen or contract under the influence of general trends influencing the market as a whole.

Whenever demand for Euro-dollar deposits in relation to their supply increases and rates tend to stiffen, lenders prefer to confine their operations to first-rate names and the differential has to widen in order to induce them to assume higher risks. Conversely, whenever demand slackens or supply increases and rates tend to decline, many lenders are inclined to lend their Euro-dollars to borrowers of inferior standing against rates which allow for narrower differentials than before.

International interest rates are not independent of national interest rates, even though usually they are affected mainly by influences outside the countries concerned. Euro-dollar rates are affected by the following American influences :

(1) Deposit rates that American banks are permitted to pay under Regulation Q, and rates at which they are prepared to lend to foreign borrowers. These two sets of rates largely determine the limits within which Euro-dollar rates can fluctuate, subject to qualification to be dealt with below.

(2) Yields on short-term investments in New York other than interest on time deposits.

(3) The forward dollar rate.

(4) The attitude of the U.S. authorities towards lending abroad and the response of American bankers and corporations to that attitude.

(5) The extent of borrowing by London branches of American banks in the Euro-dollar market. This factor, which became of decisive importance in 1969, will be dealt with in Chapter 17.

(6) The spot dollar rate, which determines to some extent the decision whether or not Euro-dollar deposits should be covered.

(7) Speculation in gold in anticipation of an increase in its official price, or of a change in its market price.

(8) The trend of the American economy, which influences borrowing and lending by American residents in the Euro-dollar market, subject to restrictions.

(9) The trend in Wall Street and in the Euro-bond market, which influences the flow of dollars to and from the Euro-dollar market.

Because few people would be willing to lend their dollars at lower rates than those paid by American banks, or to borrow at higher rates than those charged by American banks, fluctuations of Euro-dollar rates tend to remain within the limits set by statutory deposit rates in the United States and American bank loan rates. This rule is subject, however, to the following qualifications :

(a) Interest on official foreign deposits is no longer subject to restrictions. The lower limits for Euro-dollar rates to official holders are determined, therefore, by the actual rates allowed by American banks.

(b) American banks do not in all circumstances pay to private depositors the full rates that are permitted under Regulation Q.

(c) American banks are not permitted to pay interest on deposits up to thirty days, so that there is no lower limit for Euro-dollar rates on such deposits, apart from rates on loans to Wall Street which compete with rates on Euro-dollars at call.

(d) Some depositors prefer Euro-dollars to dollar deposits in the United States for considerations other than those of yield.

(e) During periods of credit squeezes availability of credits is very often more important than the level of interest rates.

(e) Since American banks are not likely ever to be willing to meet the entire foreign demand for dollar credits, many unsatisfied credit-worthy would-be borrowers may be willing to pay higher rates on Euro-dollars than those charged by American banks on dollar credits.

While deposit rates in the United States are rigid, the yields on various alternative forms of short-term investments in New York fluctuate. They respond to Bank rate changes and to other monetary policy measures. Moreover, from time to time new investment facilities with different yields come to attract foreign funds. The degree of the foreign investor's willingness to depart from first-class short-term investment naturally affects such yields. They compete with Euro-dollar rates.

The view that the foreign exchange market takes of the dollar's prospects, as expressed in forward dollar rates, necessarily affects decisions whether to borrow or not at a given Euro-dollar rate. With forward dollars at a premium the cost of covering the exchange risk has to be added to the interest, but if forward dollars are at a discount borrowers can afford to pay higher Euro-dollar rates.

Regardless of interest differentials, official measures or pressures by the U.S. authorities are liable to reduce the flow of American funds to the Euro-dollar market, or to reduce borrowing of Euro-dollars by American residents, especially by foreign branches of American banks.

If the spot dollar rate is in the close vicinity of the upper support point, borrowers of Euro-dollars may take the view that it is not likely to appreciate further, so that they are safe to leave the exchange risk on their deposits uncovered.

Speculative pressure on the dollar exchange tends to result in an increase of demand for Euro-dollars causing a rise in Euro-dollar rates, because of the advantages derived by borrowers from the wide discount on forward dollars. The same effect is produced if speculators borrow Euro-dollars and sell the spot exchange in preference to selling forward dollars, or if they finance gold or D. mark purchases with borrowed Euro-dollars in preference to buying for forward delivery.

Although changes in the extent to which American residents operate in the Euro-dollar market are at the time of writing not a major factor, an increase of the flow of American-held dollars to the market owing to a business recession in the United

81

States, and their repatriation owing to a business revival, tends to affect Euro-dollar rates to some extent. When credit is tight, high Euro-dollar rates are unable to induce American corporations to transfer their funds to the Euro-dollar market. Indeed, when domestic interest rates in the United States rise, American banks and corporations appear in the Euro-dollar market as borrowers. More is said about this in Chapter 17.

Trends in Wall Street are liable to influence the flow of funds to and from the Euro-dollar market in two ways — by affecting the flow of capital of investors and speculators to and from Wall Street and by affecting the flow of short-term funds to and from brokers' loans.

All these American domestic influences are apt to react one time or other on Euro-dollar rates to an appreciable extent. In addition to them, and largely independently of them, the following non-American influences are liable to affect Euro-dollar rates :

(1) The yield on time deposits or on other forms of short-term investments in London and other European centres.

(2) Interest charged by British banks on foreign short-term sterling credits.

(3) The domestic level of interest rates in countries borrowing their dollars in the Euro-dollar market.

(4) The strength and urgency of demand for credits in the borrowing countries.

(5) Anticipation of changes in the principal parities or exchange rates.

(6) Changes in the attitude of Central Banks towards lending their dollars in the Euro-dollar market.

(7) Changes in the volume of Euro-bond issues and in the volume and trend of operations in the secondary market in Euro-bonds.

(8) Intervention by the B.I.S.

When the London Bank rate is low, the gentlemen's agreement prevents London clearing banks from paying deposit rates that would compete with Euro-dollar rates. However, merchant banks or overseas banks are not inhibited from offering higher rates. A rise in their deposit rates or in the yield on short-term investments in London tends to cause a rise in Euro-dollar rates, because of an increase in borrowing Euro-dollars for the purpose of switching into sterling, always provided that an increase in the cost of a swap does not offset the increase in the yield. This latter consideration plays no part when a depreciation of sterling is not anticipated, so that the covering of the exchange risk is not deemed necessary.

As many foreign borrowers can choose between Euro-dollars and sterling credits, interest on the latter tends to affect the demand for the Euro-dollar loan. A decline in the cost of British acceptance credits should tend to cause a decline in Euro-dollar rates, provided that an adjustment of forward sterling rates to their changed interest parities does not offset the additional inducement to borrow sterling in preference to dollars. But the influence of sterling acceptance has diminished.

The level of interest rates in countries that borrow Euro-dollars on a large scale tends to affect Euro-dollar rates, though in the case of many countries the strength and urgency of credit requirements is more important than the cost. Until 1969 the discrepancy between national interest rates and Euro-dollar rates was so wide that it would have had to change quite considerably before affecting materially the volume of demand for Euro-dollars. Anticipation of a revaluation of some foreign currency affects speculative demand for Euro-dollars in the same way as does speculative demand in anticipation of a dollar devaluation, owing to the practice of buying and holding such currencies with the aid of borrowed Euro-dollars.

The attitude of Central Banks towards the Euro-dollar market is a major factor influencing Euro-dollar rates, not only because they control a very large proportion of the supply but also because they have the means of encouraging or discouraging lending or borrowing of Euro-dollars by banks of their countries. Changes in their attitude in respect of lending Euro-dollars to the market, or in respect of encouraging or discouraging their banks from borrowing, are liable to make an appreciable difference. Some Central Banks lend Euro-dollars and so does the B.I.S.

Supply-demand relationship of Euro-dollars is liable to

change through influences other than interest rates or forward rates. The following are some instances of such influences :

    (*a*) Discovery of Euro-dollar facilities by additional potential lenders or borrowers.

    (*b*) Development of the practice of American bank branches in London and of big American corporations to borrow or lend Euro-dollars.

    (*c*) Policy decisions by Communist Governments to lend or borrow Euro-dollars.

    (*d*) Changes in exchange control measures.

Beyond doubt, even before the advent of Euro-dollars, interest rates in the United States were influenced to some degree by extraneous changes, though the American monetary authorities were usually in a position to isolate the domestic credit structure from such influences, if they wished to do so. After all, any external supply of dollar deposits, or any external demand for dollar credits, was a mere fraction of the immense volume of domestic supply and demand. But as far as Euro-dollars are concerned, their essentially international character made them much more sensitive to international influences. They existed primarily for satisfying external requirements, so that changes in supply-demand relationship arising from such requirements were much more likely to affect international interest rates than they were likely to affect national interest rates. International influences bear on a volume of credit that has never been put higher than $35 billion even after its sharp increase in 1969, instead of bearing on the total volume of domestic American credit supply many times larger. It is no wonder Euro-dollar rates are more sensitive to international influences than national interest rates in the United States.

The relative extent of participation of American-owned dollar deposits in the Euro-dollar market did not increase considerably, but the relative extent to which Euro-dollars are re-lent in the United States rose sharply. Consequently the influence of Euro-dollar rates on American interest rates and on the supply and demand of credit in the United States increased. So long as the bulk of Euro-dollars was lent and borrowed by non-Americans, however, American domestic interest rates merely set a limit — albeit a flexible one — to fluctuations of Euro-dollar rates without necessarily determining them. American national interest rates were merely one of the many factors affecting Euro-dollar rates, not even necessarily the most important factor.

One of the basic differences between domestic dollars and Euro-dollars is that the latter are much more freely available for international purposes. Most American banks set a limit to the proportion of their resources which they are prepared to commit outside the United States. On the other hand, the entire supply of Euro-dollars, unless re-borrowed by Americans, is available for that purpose. For that reason alone, Euro-dollar rates are more exposed to international influences than American domestic interest rates.

Important amongst international influences affecting Euro-dollar rates is the yield on short-term investments in the London money market and, to a much less extent, in the money markets of other European countries. Only the London money market has a variety of investment facilities that bears comparison with those of the New York money market. Euro-dollar rates are, therefore, necessarily influenced by the relative advantages of using the London money market facilities. The extent of such advantages depends largely on the degree of confidence in sterling. If its prospects inspire sufficient confidence for investors to leave the exchange uncovered, in that case interest differentials may become very attractive. The demand for Euro-dollars for the purpose of conversion into sterling increases if no part of the interest differential has to be given away in the form of a discount on forward sterling.

To the extent to which the exchange risk is covered the level of sterling-dollar forward rates and their relation with their interest parities also affect demand for Euro-dollars for the purpose of swapping them into sterling. Demand for Euro-dollars tends to increase if interest rates on sterling credits increase without a corresponding depreciation of forward sterling. In other words an over-valuation of forward sterling, by making dollar swap cheap, tends to encourage demand for Euro-dollars. An under-valuation of forward sterling, by making dollar swap dear, tends to discourage demand for Euro-dollars. If borrowers do not wish to cover the exchange risk then demand for Euro-dollars depends on the absolute interest differential between the Euro-dollar rates and rates on comparable sterling loan facilities.

Although interest rates in the inter-bank sterling market affect primarily Euro-sterling rates, indirectly they tend to influence also Euro-dollar rates, especially as turnover in that market is often much larger than the turnover in the Euro-sterling market.

The trend of Euro-dollar rates was affected towards the end of 1963 by the coincidence of losses suffered by some lenders with the decision of some Central Banks to withdraw their dollar deposits from the Euro-dollar market. The actual effect on the rates was largely offset, however, by the increased willingness of American corporations to transfer funds into Euro-dollar deposits. On the other hand, in 1965 President Johnson's appeal to Americans to abstain from transferring their funds abroad produced a spectacular effect on the market. There was an immediate contraction in the supply of Euro-dollars and their rates rose sharply. This effect was partly due to the reduction of the time limit for American bank credits abroad which are subject to the Interest Equalisation Tax. The result was an increase in the demand for Euro-dollar deposits of over twelve months. The rise in New York interest rates during 1966, coupled with demand for Euro-dollars by American bank branches, brought Euro-dollar rates to the vicinity of 7 per cent towards the end of 1966. The fall in New York interest rates early in 1967 was accompanied by a corresponding decline in Euro-dollar rates.

In 1968–69 deflationary measures in the United States resulted in a sharp rise in American demand for Euro-dollars, causing a sharp rise in Euro-dollar rates which were for a time in the vicinity of 12 per cent. That rise, in turn, reacted on domestic American interest rates. This subject will be discussed in Chapter 17.

CHAPTER 10

IMPACT ON EXCHANGE RATES

ALTHOUGH Euro-dollar transactions are not foreign exchange transactions but credit transactions, they are in terms of a currency very often foreign to lender and borrower. This means that there is a strong likelihood of a foreign exchange transaction occurring at some stage between the conclusion of the credit and its repayment on maturity. But apart altogether from any possible direct effect of such transactions on exchange rates, the system is also liable to influence exchange rates indirectly in various ways. Indeed its operation has introduced an important new element into the foreign exchange situation. It influences, or is liable to influence, exchange rates to a considerable extent. We may say without exaggeration that no foreign exchange dealer, or Treasury or Central Bank concerned with the planning and execution of foreign exchange policy, or economist concerned with foreign exchange theory could possibly afford to ignore the impact of the market in foreign currency deposits on the foreign exchange market.

The following are the ways in which the Euro-dollar system affects the dollar rate and the other exchange rates involved :

(1) Through the actual process of increasing or reducing the volume of Euro-dollars.

(2) Through the existence of large Euro-dollar deposits.

(3) Through swapping such deposits into local currencies or into third currencies.

(4) Through the use of Euro-dollars for financing foreign trade.

(5) Through their use for covering.

(6) Through their use for hedging.

(7) Through their use for arbitrage.

(8) Through their use for speculation.

(9) Through changes in Euro-dollar rates.

Conversion of ordinary deposits held with banks in the United States into Euro-dollars, or their re-conversion into ordinary deposits with banks in the United States, produces in itself no immediate effect on exchange rates. Whether it involves a change in the nationality of the non-American residents holding the deposits, or even a transfer of dollars owned by American residents to non-residents, it involves no foreign exchange transaction. But it very frequently occurs that Euro-dollars are created not through re-depositing abroad deposits already held with banks in the United States but through the purchase of dollars in the foreign exchange market for the purpose of depositing them with a bank outside the United States.

The effect of such operations on the exchanges depends on whether the dollars are acquired through a spot transaction or through a swap transaction. If the latter is the case the favourable effect on the spot rate is somewhat mitigated, and the forward rate is affected adversely. When Euro-dollar holdings are liquidated through the sale of spot dollars the effect is of course unfavourable to the spot dollar, irrespective of whether or not the buyer uses them as Euro-dollars. For a detailed consideration of the effects of swap transactions on the spot rate and the forward rate I must refer the reader to my *Dynamic Theory of Forward Exchange*.

In a negative sense the conversion of dollars into Euro-dollars tends to affect the dollar exchange if such transactions are undertaken as an alternative to selling spot dollars in the foreign exchange market. In marginal instances the higher yield on Euro-dollars, compared with dollars held in the United States, is liable to induce holders of dollars to refrain from realising their holdings, especially if the additional yield is not offset by the cost of covering the exchange risk. The absence of sales of dollars which would have taken place otherwise tends to affect the dollar rate favourably in a negative sense. American re-borrowing of Euro-dollars mops up the supply of dollars that would otherwise be available for sale in the foreign exchange market.

The existence of large Euro-dollar deposits constitutes an

important potential source of selling pressure on the dollar. One of the reasons why the system is a potential disturbing influence in the foreign exchange market is because it carries the possibility of a duplication of selling pressure on the dollar when under attack. The same Euro-dollar deposit can be sold twice over at the same moment — by its original owner who can sell them forward for delivery on the date when the deposit is repaid if he does not wish to wait with the realisation of his holding until he has recovered possession of his dollars, and by the borrower of his deposit who can sell the spot dollars either immediately or at any time before repayment.

This argument is carried further at times. The operation of the Euro-dollar system might even be claimed to cause a multiplication of selling pressure on the dollar resulting from the repeated re-borrowing of the same deposit. Each lender has a legitimate interest in covering his exchange risk by selling the forward dollars, even though only one borrower is in a position to sell the spot dollars. It is true, if a borrower of Euro-dollars re-lends them he stands to lose nothing through a depreciation of the dollar. But he is in a position, nevertheless, to go short of dollars, by covering the exchange in his capacity as lender who has to realise in advance the dollars to be repaid to him, while leaving uncovered his liability for the deposit he had borrowed.

It is of course arguable that, after all, in the absence of exchange restrictions, anyone wishing to speculate against the dollar is in any case in a position to go short by simply selling forward dollars. From this point of view it is necessary, however, to discriminate between transactions with non-banking customers and between banks. As far as the latter are concerned, no questions are ever asked about the speculative or non-speculative character of any operation. But during the post-war period respectable banks usually decline speculative foreign exchange orders for casual clients, and most of them discourage even regular clients from engaging in purely speculative transactions. If, however, a customer has a Euro-dollar commitment his bank is prepared to provide the forward exchange cover. It seems probable, therefore, that the effect of the operation of the system is a net increase in speculative facilities provided by banks to non-banking customers.

The Euro-dollar market is liable to influence spot and forward dollar rates if borrowers swap into local currency. Swap transactions undertaken for the purpose of employing the funds in the local money market or bill market, or for the purpose of granting local credits, tend to strengthen forward dollars at the same time as weakening spot dollars. This is an important factor in view of the large extent to which Euro-dollars are swapped into local currencies. Euro-dollars can be changed also into a third currency by means of spot or swap transactions.

The use of Euro-dollars for financing foreign trade can influence the dollar exchange to the extent to which it is additional to using American bank credits and not instead of using such credits. To the extent to which such additional credits serve for financing additional American imports or trade between two foreign countries, it has an unfavourable effect on the dollar. Financing of American exports with the aid of Euro-dollars is also liable to affect the exchange if it leads to additional lags in the payments for these exports. In so far as Euro-dollars are used in the place of sterling credits their use tends to strengthen sterling. A net increase in the use of Euro-dollars for financing foreign trade necessarily means heavier pressure on the dollar during the period while the increase is actually taking place, but the pressure will level out if the extent of such use of Euro-dollars is maintained at its higher level, without further increasing it. Any reduction of the use of Euro-dollars for financing foreign trade, if not accompanied by a corresponding increase of the use of dollar credits proper for the same purpose, tends to support the dollar exchange. It is conceivable that the availability of additional dollars in the Euro-dollar market for financing exports and imports may increase exports to the United States to a larger extent than imports from the United States, or vice versa. The resulting effect on the balance of payments means additional buying or selling of dollars.

Euro-dollars can also be used for covering or hedging against depreciation of assets or against an appreciation of liabilities. To the extent to which such operations take the place of forward exchange transactions, they shift the pressure from the forward rate to the spot rate.

The use of Euro-dollars for various arbitrage transactions was discussed in great detail in Chapter 4. We saw that because of the large volume of funds available for arbitrage the use of Euro-dollars tends to keep forward rates nearer those interest parities which happen to be favoured by arbitrageurs at a given moment. That being so, arbitrage transactions arising from discrepancies between Euro-currency interest parities and other interest parities tend to divert forward rates from their conventional interest parities between national interest rates. Time arbitrage with the aid of Euro-dollar deposits for various maturities affect relationships between short and long forward rates.

By providing an alternative to forward exchange transactions, Euro-dollar operations may divert speculative pressure from forward rates to spot rates, thereby affecting both spot and forward rates. One of the results of the system is that during periods of a speculative attack on the dollar the extent to which spot rates are affected is liable to be greater while the extent to which forward rates are affected is liable to be smaller. When a revaluation of a foreign currency is anticipated, an alternative to forward buying of that currency is spot buying and lending in the Euro-currency market the foreign currency deposits thus acquired. The result is a stronger buying pressure on the spot and a reduced buying pressure on the forward.

Whenever the forward dollar is at an intrinsic discount — that is, if it is under-valued compared with its interest parities based on Euro-dollar rates — it diverts speculative selling from the forward exchange market to the Euro-dollar market. When it is at an intrinsic premium it diverts speculative selling from the Euro-dollar market to the forward exchange market.

Last but by no means least, exchange rates are affected by changes in Euro-dollar rates. Our task is to ascertain if and to what extent the effect of international interest rates on exchange rates differs from the effect of national interest rates. To that end we first propose to summarise the ways in which changes in national interest rates affect exchange rates.

(1) By influencing movements of short-term funds.

(2) By influencing borrowing and repayment of domestic credits by foreign borrowers, and of foreign credits by local borrowers.

(3) By affecting the domestic price levels.

(4) By affecting the balances of payments.

(5) Through psychological influences.

The above list concerns effects of interest rates on both spot and forward rates. In addition interest rates affect forward rates in the following ways :

(1) By changing the interest parities of forward rates.

(2) By changing the cost of the alternative method of covering exchange risk or of assuming exchange risk by means of loan transactions.

Let us now examine how changes in international interest rates affect exchange rates :

(1) An increase of Euro-dollar rates tends to attract additional funds to the Euro-dollar market while a decrease tends to divert funds from that market. We indicated above the circumstances in which the movements of funds to and from the Euro-dollar market affect spot and forward rates.

(2) If a decline of Euro-dollar rates causes forward dollars to appreciate this tends to cancel out the stimulus given by the lower interest to borrowing Euro-dollars, because the extent to which debtors benefit by the discount on forward dollars declines. The extent to which foreign borrowing of Euro-dollars responds to the increase or decline of Euro-dollar rates depends on whether the forward dollar is at an intrinsic premium or at an intrinsic discount.

(3) Unlike a change in national interest rates, a change in Euro-dollar rates does not affect the price level in the United States. Even if it attracts additional dollar deposits to or from banks in the United States it makes

no difference because, as we shall see in Chapter 17, transfers of dollars into and out of the Euro-dollar market do not affect materially the volume of credit in the United States.

(4) The effect of changes in Euro-dollar rates on the balance of payments in the United States depends on its relative effect on Euro-dollar credits used for financing American exports and American imports. There is no valid rule indicating that a change in the rate should affect imports more than exports or vice versa.

(5) While changes in national interest rates tend to produce a strong psychological effect on the exchanges, changes in Euro-dollar rates produce no such effect. A rise in national interest rates creates optimism in relation to the prospects of the dollar in anticipation of its effect on the domestic price level and on the balance of payments. Since higher Euro-dollar rates leave the American price level unaffected, and their effect on the balance of payment is obscure, there is no reason why it should produce any psychological effect.

(6) Since an increase of Euro-dollar rates tends to change interest parities against the forward dollar it tends to widen the discount on the forward dollar or, as the case may be, to reduce the premium on the forward dollar. Conversely, a decline of Euro-dollar rates tends to reduce the discount on the forward dollar or to widen its premium.

It seems that international interest rates tend to affect spot rates to a considerable extent, but not to the same extent as national interest rates. The main difference is that while national interest rates have a profound effect on the domestic price level and on the balance of payments, international interest rates leave the American price level unaffected and their effect on the balance of payments is uncertain. It is impossible to lay down definitely whether the operation of the Euro-dollar system makes on balance for more stable exchanges or for less stable exchanges. But it is probably true that, while in normal conditions the system makes for a higher degree of stability, in abnormal conditions it tends to accentuate abnormal exchange trends.

As far as forward exchange rates are concerned, they are naturally exposed to the influence of international interest rates to a higher degree than spot rates. As we saw earlier, the fashion in arbitrage changed during the early 'sixties in favour of working on Euro-currency parities. Even though the relationship between them and forward rates is reciprocal, in many instances Euro-dollar rates, and to a much less extent other Euro-currency rates, are the active factor and forward rates the passive factor.

It is essential to realise that, as a result of the development of the Euro-currency system, interest arbitrage which was hitherto two-dimensional has now become three-dimensional. Operations are determined by the interplay of three sets of rates — interest rates for short-term investment, forward margins, and Euro-currency rates. The working of the system is liable to influence forward margins to a considerable extent.

In this chapter, as in other chapters, it is assumed that the spectacular increase in one-sided American borrowing of Euro-dollars witnessed during 1968–69 is a temporary abnormal phenomenon. Sooner or later the relationship between the United States and the Euro-dollar market is certain to become once more a two-way traffic, and from time to time Americans are likely to become the chief lenders instead of being the chief borrowers.

CHAPTER 11

IMPACT ON NATIONAL INTEREST RATES

WHEN dealing with the effect of national interest rates in the United States on Euro-dollar rates, I pointed out the reciprocal character of the relationship between national and international interest rates. It is indeed essential to emphasise this, in order to avoid a repetition of history through the emergence of some one-sided theory comparable to the interest parity theory of forward exchange in its original form, which ignored the reciprocal character of the relationship. Another outstanding instance of one-sided interpretation given to reciprocal relationship in the sphere of foreign exchange was the purchasing-power parity theory, which for a long time ignored or under-rated the effect of exchanges on prices, concentrating entirely on the effects of prices on exchanges. The result in both instances was the adoption of misleading conclusions and mistaken decisions were based on them.

Admittedly, the extent of the reciprocity is not nearly so pronounced in respect of the relationship between Euro-dollar rates and national interest rates as in respect of the above instance. Yet even though Euro-dollar deposits amount to a bare fraction of the total dollar deposits, the experience of 1969 conclusively proved that Euro-dollar rates are liable to affect American national interest rates to a considerable extent.

When it comes to the effect of international interest rates on national interest rates in some other countries, however, the influence is liable to be even more pronounced. We propose to examine the impact of Euro-dollar rates on national interest rates in the United States, in borrowing countries, and in intermediary countries.

The Euro-dollar system tends to affect the national interest rates structure in the United States in the following ways :

(1) Through competition of Euro-dollar facilities with American market facilities.

(2) Through changing the volume of domestic credit.

(3) Through providing additional and alternative facilities for speculating against the dollar.

(4) Through providing additional facilities for inward or outward arbitrage.

(5) Through influencing the relationship between various maturities within the national interest structure.

(6) Through influencing official policies.

Euro-dollar facilities compete with short-term investment facilities available in the United States, especially in respect of non-resident holders of dollars. We saw in Chapter 2 the effect of this competition on Euro-dollar rates. One of the instances in which it might have produced an effect was the exodus of foreign funds from the market of U.S. Treasury bills. There was, however, no actual noticeable effect of this movement on bill rates in New York, presumably because such effect as it tended to produce was neutralised by official policies. It seems probable that in the absence of official intervention the decline in foreign demand for Treasury bills resulting from the competition of Euro-dollars would have caused an appreciable rise in bill rates.

Regulation Q prevents the competition of higher Euro-dollar rates from producing its full effect on time deposit rates in the United States. Even so, the authorised ceiling of deposit rates had to be raised repeatedly for private deposits and it was removed altogether for official deposits, largely because of representations made by American banks who complained of being handicapped in competition with the Euro-dollar market for deposits. There was mounting pressure in favour of a total repeal of Regulation Q, not so much for the sake of preventing foreign deposits from being transferred to the Euro-dollar market as on account of the growing interest taken by American residents in Euro-dollar rates. Should the Washington Administration yield eventually to this pressure it would mean that Euro-dollar rates might force up deposit rates in the United

States. Meanwhile, they do affect to some slight extent the rates quoted in the newly developed market for deposit certificates.

The extent to which Euro-dollar rates influence or are likely to influence deposit rates in the United States is kept down, not only by official policy but also by the desire of American banks to maintain a reasonably wide profit margin between deposit rates and lending rates. It is safe to assume that even if Regulation Q were repealed American banks would not raise their standard deposit rates to a level at which the profit margin would become much narrower, though they might raise their rates on large deposits.

Euro-dollar facilities to American borrowers tended to affect the interest charged by American banks on credits to large corporations which had access to the Euro-dollar market. Rather than lose valuable accounts, the American banks were willing to reduce to some extent their profit margins on their transactions with that type of client. The Euro-dollar market and the extent of the American participation in it had to expand, however, very considerably before Euro-dollar rates could influence the standard lending rates of American banks directly, in addition to their effect through influencing deposit rates. In specific instances American banks compete for foreign business by lowering their interest charges on foreign credits. But their interest charges on the bulk of domestic credits, and even of foreign credits, remained unaffected until the sharp increase in Euro-dollar rates paid by their London branches. It is of course very difficult to decide whether, and to what extent, the rise in prime rates and in Treasury bill rates in New York was the cause or the effect of the sharp rise in Euro-dollar rates during 1969.

Situations are liable to arise in which additional speculative pressure against the dollar resulting from borrowing Euro-dollars and selling the spot exchange might force the United States authorities to raise interest rates. If, as a result of heavy borrowing of Euro-dollars by speculators for the purpose of selling spot dollars, Euro-dollar rates should rise sharply, it might become more profitable for speculators to borrow dollars in the United States instead of borrowing Euro-dollars. Any such trend would induce the United States authorities to take counter-measures in the form of raising domestic interest rates or tightening their exchange control measures.

Since forward rates tend to adjust themselves to interest parities based on Euro-currency rates, discrepancies between these parities and interest parities based on national interest rates are able to cause unwanted inward or outward arbitrage. Should this movement assume considerable dimensions it might tend to affect interest rates in New York. To prevent such unwanted movements of funds, or to counteract their effect, the authorities might have to adopt measures to influence interest rates or to restrict transactions.

Within the interest structure in the United States, relationship between rates quoted for long and short maturities is liable to be influenced by changes in Euro-dollar rates, mainly through their effect on the cost of very short loans. The sphere in which Euro-dollar rates are most likely to make themselves felt is that of the market for call money. But situations did arise in which a sharp rise in short Euro-dollar rates caused rises in rates on longer maturities.

Developments in the Euro-dollar market are liable to produce other results which might impel monetary authorities to adopt policies affecting interest rates. With a further substantial expansion of the Euro-dollar market, and more especially with an increase of the participation by American residents in it, the effect on American policies aiming at influencing interest rates is likely to increase.

Let us now examine the effect of Euro-dollar rates on interest rates in borrowing countries. Such effect is liable to be produced even if countries which borrow Euro-dollars re-lend abroad part of the amount borrowed so long as a substantial part of it is used at home. Interest rates in borrowing countries are affected for the following reasons :

(1) Competition of Euro-dollar facilities with other credit facilities.
(2) Competition between banks.
(3) Use of Euro-dollars for speculation.

(4) Use of Euro-dollars for arbitrage.

The total of Euro-dollars represents a very small percentage of the total volume of credit in the United States or even in Britain. On the other hand, the amount of Euro-dollars borrowed by Japan and by Italy represented for some time quite an appreciable proportion of their total domestic borrowing. In such situations the national interest structure of such borrowing countries is naturally affected by Euro-dollar rates to a larger extent than that of the United States. Even allowing for the extra premium that Japanese banks had to pay in the market, Euro-dollar rates remained very considerably below national interest rates, and the fact that it was possible to borrow at international rates tended to lower the national rates. The trade expansion witnessed in Japan during the late 'fifties and in the 'sixties would have caused a considerable rise in local interest rates had it not been for the availability of cheaper Euro-dollar facilities. Latin-American countries, too, received extensive credits which would not have been available had it not been for the expansion of the Euro-dollar market. The result was that domestic interest rates did not rise as much as they would have risen in the absence of Euro-dollar credits. In all these instances it was not so much the Euro-dollar rates as the availability of additional credits that tended to reduce or keep down national interest rates.

Another way in which Euro-dollar rates have contributed towards lowering national interest rates in borrowing countries has been the triggering off of fierce competition between banks. This may not be a permanent part of the system. The cut-throat competition is largely the natural consequence of the appearance of an additional supply of credit, but is partly due to the appearance of an entirely new line of business with considerable possibilities. It is only natural that each bank should endeavour to secure for itself the largest possible share in the allocation of the new credit supplies.

Moreover, the lending and borrowing of Euro-dollars was not covered by the various cartel arrangements under which banks were under an obligation not to compete with each other in respect of deposit rates they allow and/or loan rates they charge. Nor was it even controlled by conventions under which banks of standing abstain from poaching on each other's recognised preserves. There were, and are, no generally adopted codes of conduct — not even unwritten ones — to regulate the behaviour of banks in the Euro-dollar market. 'Free for all' prevailed therefore in that sphere. Even in London, where banks by long-established tradition considered it ungentlemanly to go out of their way to poach on each other's preserves, fierce competition developed for business arising from the Euro-dollar system.

Competition between banks resulting from the Euro-dollar system is not confined to within the borders of the borrowing countries concerned. If it were, it might be possible for the banking communities within a country to extend cartel arrangements so as to prevent rate cutting with the aid of Euro-dollar deposits. Because of the essentially international character of the Euro-dollar market, however, large borrowers in each country are in a position to obtain credits abroad over the heads of their local bankers. The latter have to compete not only against each other but also against their foreign rivals. For this reason, to the extent to which Euro-dollar credits are made available, local lending rates are apt to come under pressure.

The interest structure in the United Kingdom was affected to no slight degree by Euro-dollar rates. The total swapped into sterling for loans to local authorities and hire-purchase finance houses in 1964–69 mitigated the drain on the reserve. But for this, the Bank rate might have had to be kept even higher. As a large proportion of the Euro-dollars is invested in Lombard Street in money at call, changes in day-to-day Euro-dollar deposit rates are apt to influence from time to time interest rates in Lombard Street to an appreciable degree. Another large proportion of Euro-dollars swapped into sterling is lent to local authorities or hire-purchase finance houses. Consequently, rates on such credits must have been influenced by Euro-dollar rates. It is true, in theory, changes in Euro-dollar rates should be offset by corresponding adjustments of forward rates to their interest parities in relation to Euro-sterling. In practice, however, forward rates are often subject to other influences and are not adjusted altogether to changes in their Euro-dollar parities. In that case it is Euro-sterling rates, and through them London interest rates, which tend to change.

Speculation and arbitrage brought about by the use of Euro-dollar facilities is apt to give rise to situations in borrowing as well as lending countries in which official action becomes necessary to resist an unwanted movement through influencing interest rates. Such influences are also liable to affect interest rates in countries which act as intermediaries between lenders and borrowers of Euro-dollar deposits. For instance, since Euro-dollar deposits handled in London compete with sterling acceptances their rates tend to affect national interest rates in Britain. Moreover, Euro-dollar facilities give rise to a variety of triangular arbitrage and speculative operations liable to affect sterling in a sense as to call for intervention which in turn affects interest rates.

A remarkable instance of the impact of Euro-currency rates on local interest rates was provided by London's experience during the sterling scares of 1964–67. Demand in Paris for Euro-sterling for speculative purposes pushed up its rates, and this in turn reacted on inter-bank sterling rates and on rates on Local Authority funds and on hire-purchase finance house deposit rates.

The main effect of the Euro-dollar system on national interest rates is produced not so much through the level of Euro-dollar rates or through changes in Euro-dollar rates as through the effect of the operation of the system on the availability of credit. In addition to its obvious direct effect, the Euro-dollar system affects interest rates also through providing a basis for credit expansion, both national and international. This subject will be dealt with in the next chapter.

CHAPTER 12

EXPANSIONARY EFFECTS

WE already saw in Chapter 7 that unless Euro-dollar deposits are used by the borrower for withdrawing gold or notes or for repaying a liability in the United States they do not reduce the volume of deposits held with the banking system in the United States. American banks as a whole retain possession of the dollars re-deposited abroad. Such deposits are liable to change hands more frequently, but what matters is that they are bound to remain within the American banking system. It is one of the paradoxes of modern banking that it enables us to eat our cake and keep it. The same dollars which are lent abroad by their foreign owners can be used simultaneously by American banks for lending to the United States or abroad. The result of a transfer of a deposit to the Euro-dollar market is that the volume of dollars lent by non-American banks increases without corresponding reduction in the volume of dollars lent by American banks. This means an increase in the grand total of the international volume of credit resources.

This peculiarity is by no means special to the Euro-dollar system. A comparable instance, this time in the domestic sphere, is provided by deposits with financial intermediaries such as hire-purchase finance houses. Even highly competent commentators are under the misapprehension that deposits attracted to hire-purchase finance houses by their high deposit rates are necessarily lost by the banks. They fail to realise that, since the former are bound to pay the cheques received from their depositors into their banking account, the total deposits at the disposal of the banking system as a whole remain unchanged in spite of the increase in the amount of deposits at the disposal of the hire-purchase finance houses. This means that their deposits, instead of replacing bank

102

deposits, are additional to them. What happens is that the transaction increases the velocity of circulation of the bank deposits. While the original holders of bank deposits that are now held by hire-purchase finance houses would have left their money at the disposal of their bank, the new holders lend it to industrial firms to finance goods sold on hire-purchase; the deposits remain in the banking system even if their ownership changes and even if in the course of the changes in ownership they are transferred from one bank to another. A larger volume of business transactions is financed with the same amount of bank deposits as a result of the increasing velocity of deposits.

The same applies to deposits with American banks that are converted into Euro-dollars. In fact, while part of the deposits transferred to hire-purchase finance houses may temporarily leave the banking system when the industrial borrower pays wages to employees who have no bank accounts, all those concerned in Euro-dollars in any capacity have bank accounts so that the dollars are bound to remain all the time with American banks.

Although one of the results of the operation of the Euro-dollar system is an increase in the volume of dollar credits used for financing abroad, this does not mean that to that extent less credit is available for American domestic requirements. As we already pointed out, the increased velocity of deposits might make it expedient for banks to keep larger cash or liquid resources, and to that extent the amount available becomes reduced. In existing circumstances, however, the extent of such reductions would be purely marginal.

The volume of credit in a country which receives Euro-dollar deposits tends to increase in the following ways :

(1) Dollar reserves of the Central Bank increase if Euro-dollar deposits are swapped into a national currency and if such transactions lead to selling pressure on the spot dollar, providing an opportunity for intervention by the authorities who thereby acquire additional dollars.

(2) A Central Bank may reinforce its dollar reserve by

means of borrowing Euro-dollars to cope with temporary pressure. Owing to the availability of facilities by which such contingencies can be met, the authorities may feel safer to expand credit in between critical dates of heavy pressure, instead of having to keep an idle reserve to be available for such occasions.

(3) In a negative sense, Central Banks may be able to abstain from curtailing credit as a result of a temporary decline of their reserves by borrowing Euro-dollars.

(4) A Central Bank may put its idle dollar reserves to productive use by lending them to the banks of its country in the form of Euro-dollar deposits.

(5) The accessibility of Euro-dollars enables banks to keep their reserve ratios or liquidity ratios near the statutory or conventional minimum, in the certain knowledge that extra requirements could be covered with the aid of Euro-dollars.

(6) Banks may secure in the Euro-dollar market additional credits for themselves or their customers, and the latter may secure direct credits in the Euro-dollar market in addition to those obtainable from banks in their own country or from the United States.

(7) Owing to the existence of Euro-dollar markets in several financial centres, banks and business firms can borrow to the limit simultaneously in more than one of these centres.

The expansionary effect of borrowing Euro-dollar deposits and using the proceeds in the borrowing country's currency is obvious. It calls for closer examination, however, when the borrowers are American banks. We saw in earlier chapters that London and Paris branches of American banks have become systematic borrowers of Euro-dollar deposits, largely for the purpose of lending them to their own head offices. On the face of it such transactions may simply appear to restore the *status quo* that existed prior to the transfer of dollar deposits from American banks to the Euro-dollar market. This is certainly the case if the deposit that had been transferred into Euro-dollar deposit is re-borrowed by the same bank which held it before the change and which in fact still holds it in the absence of a transaction involving the transfer of the deposit to some other American bank. If, however, the London branch of an American bank borrows a Euro-dollar deposit which was originally deposited with some other American bank, it means an addition to the deposits of the borrowing bank and a deduction from the resources of the original holder. The American banking system as a whole does not gain or lose dollars through the transaction.

Nevertheless, the situation is liable to be affected to some slight extent if a deposit which was formerly repayable on demand or at short notice is re-deposited in London for a longer period and is re-borrowed by an American bank for a longer period. The result is a change in the liquidity structure of the American bank concerned. Part of its liabilities now matures at a later date. Conversely, if a former time deposit with an American bank is re-deposited in Europe in the form of a deposit at call or at short notice and is re-borrowed in that form by an American bank, the latter's liquidity structure is altered in the opposite sense. But in June 1969 the Federal Reserve authorities, in order to discourage American banks from borrowing Euro-dollars through their London branches, imposed reserve requirements on new borrowing from branches abroad.

If the borrower of a Euro-dollar deposit, whether American or non-American, uses it for the purpose of financing foreign trade in the form of a dollar credit this leaves the volume of American deposits unaffected. The dollars may change hands but they remain all the time within the American banking system. In so far as such credits are additional to dollar credits which American banks themselves grant for financing foreign trade, they may increase the reserves of the exporting country or they may prevent a reduction of the reserves of the importing country. An increase of the amount of Euro-dollars lent for financing foreign trade means a once-for-all change of the reserves of the countries concerned. So long as the amount of the Euro-dollars so employed is not reduced, this increase does not become reversed.

If a Euro-dollar deposit is lent to a non-American borrower

who sells the dollars instead of using them in the form of dollar credits, the reserves of the country against whose currency the dollars are sold stand to benefit by the transaction. The extent of the resulting credit expansion depends on whether the forward exchange is covered. If so, it relieves part of the selling pressure on spot dollars and reduces the extent to which the authorities of the country concerned are enabled to increase their dollar reserves.

There are very few known instances of direct Central Bank borrowing of Euro-dollars for the purpose of expanding credit. Indirectly, however, Central Banks might encourage the banks of their country to borrow Euro-dollars in order to be able to acquire the dollars when they are swapped into national currency. More will be said about this in the chapter dealing with the attitude of Central Banks. Likewise we shall examine credit expansion encouraged by Central Banks lending dollars to their banks without requiring the latter to surrender the equivalent in local currency. The opposite effect is produced if Central Banks swap their dollars against local currency, thereby mopping up domestic credit resources.

With or without official encouragement, banks may expand credit by borrowing Euro-dollars. The same effect is produced if non-banking clients obtain Euro-dollar credits direct from banks abroad. The Euro-dollar system provides opportunities for additional borrowing, and therefore for additional credit expansion, by enabling banks and large firms to borrow simultaneously in several markets.

We saw in Chapter 7 that as a result of the Euro-dollar system the same dollars which are used abroad for financing trade can be used by banks for financing domestic trade. There can be no doubt that the result of this duplication of credit is an increase in the total international volume of credit somewhat similar to the increase resulting from the practice of the gold exchange standard under which the same gold serves simultaneously as a basis for currency or credit expansion in the two countries. It has been suggested that the effect of the Euro-dollar system is in fact much more expansionary, because it leads not merely to a duplication of credit but to its multiplication. This view was put forward by Mr. Robert D. Roosa in his evidence before the House of Representatives Committee on Banking and Currency in the course of its hearing on the Bill to permit banks to pay interest on time deposits of foreign governments at rates different from those applicable to domestic depositors.

In answer to a request by a member of the Committee to explain how the Euro-dollar system operates Mr. Roosa said that, because Euro-dollar deposits can be re-lent again and again, 'we get a multiplication of dollar claims on the basis of one initial dollar transfer. It might build up so that you would have a sequence of five or six or maybe more interrelated claims, all on the same initial deposit. . . . In this interrelated structure you have none of the control and none of the systematic regulation of banking practice which leads to the multiplying of bank deposits that occurs inside the commercial banking system of this country or any other country. Thus you have a kind of loose form of international monetary expansion which can go on and on building up a pyramid of claims which is vulnerable.'

Mr. Roosa's theory appears to imply that, just as in domestic banking an increase in the banks' holding of cash or of liquid resources can form the basis of a credit expansion several times larger than the amount of the increase, so an increase of Euro-dollar deposits can give rise to an expansion in the volume of international credit several times its amount. In considering this theory we must distinguish between the peculiarity of the modern credit system under which credit may be created to several times the cash reserve and the multiplier effect of any addition to the volume of credit.

Whether the Euro-dollar system enables banks outside the United States to expand the total volume of their credit by more than the actual amount borrowed depends on their statutory or conventional rules regarding cash ratio and/or liquidity ratio. Under the British system clearing banks are not supposed to allow their cash ratio to decline below 8 per cent and their liquidity ratio below 30 per cent. If a British clearing bank re-lends Euro-dollar deposits to another bank it includes the amount among its deposits with banks which form part of its liquid resources. This means that, if its assets and liabilities increased equally by the amount of the Euro-dollar deposit borrowed and re-lent, the increase on its liquid resources should enable it to increase its liabilities more than threefold the amount. If it borrows and re-lends a deposit of $1 million it should be able to increase its liabilities by the equivalent of $3.3 million — that is, in addition to re-lending the $1 million it can create additional deposits to the equivalent of $2.3 million, by means of increasing its advances to customers. There is, however, a snag. Clearing banks cannot include Euro-dollar deposits lent to other banks among their 8 per cent cash reserve which must consist of cash and balances with the Bank of England. They prefer, therefore, to leave operations in Euro-currencies to their affiliates which are not bound by the rule concerning cash ratio.

Affiliates, and also merchant banks, overseas banks, and foreign branches operating in London, while observing the rule regarding liquidity ratio, are under no obligation to observe the rule regarding cash ratio. They are, therefore, in a position to increase their Euro-dollar lendings to a larger extent than clearing banks, because they can make profitable use of the addition of Euro-dollar assets to their liquid resources.

Under other banking systems a liquidity ratio has to be maintained in the form of certain definite assets such as Government securities, so that assets held in the form of Euro-dollars may not qualify for inclusion. The position varies from country to country. In some instances there are special provisions under which reserves have to be kept against Euro-dollar and other foreign currency liabilities. It is therefore difficult to give a definite answer whether and to what extent the operation of the Euro-dollar system leads to an additional expansion of credit over and above the direct expansion resulting from the borrowing of dollars and the indirect expansion resulting from the increase of dollar reserves by their Central Bank.

However, this is not what Mr. Roosa appears to have had in mind. He is concerned with the multiplication of credit resulting from Euro-dollar deposits being passed from one borrower to another. From this point of view there seems to be no basic difference between credit expansion due to an increase of Euro-dollar deposits or to any other loan transaction. Some borrowers use the dollars in ways that are liable to produce multiplier effects on the volume of credit — if they spend the dollars and the recipient re-lends them. If the dollars are re-lent by the borrower there is no multiplier effect because the lender relinquishes the lending or spending power represented by the dollar deposit. It is only if the borrower spends the dollars that they become available for re-lending or re-spending. Apart from the original duplication of the use of the same dollars, the only expansionary effects Euro-dollar transactions are apt to produce are identical with those of any kind of credit expansion.

It is true, if the same Euro-dollars are re-lent again and again the international credit structure tends to become more vulnerable. This is not, however, because, as Mr. Roosa appears to believe, the process of the repeated re-lending of the same dollars builds up a 'pyramid' of credit expansion. A deposit of one million dollars does not grow into a deposit of ten million dollars if it is re-lent ten times. It is still only one million dollars.

Mr. Roosa is none the less right in saying that the repeated re-lending of Euro-dollar deposits creates a vulnerable situation, because it creates a chain the strength of which depends on that of its weakest link. Moreover, in so far as the borrowing banks are subject to liquidity rules similar to those of British merchant banks, each one of them is in a position to expand credit to an extent well in excess of the amount of Euro-dollars it has re-lent. On the other hand, the use of the dollars for increasing the Central Banks' dollar reserves cannot have a pyramiding effect, because only one Central Bank can be in possession of the dollars at any given moment.

To the extent to which Euro-dollars lead to an increase of the banks' liquid resources and to the extent to which that increase is actually used for serving as a basis for additional credit expansion in excess of its amount, the comparison with the pyramid is correct. Apart from that, to the extent to which the original amount changes hands the credit chain thus created will become longer and possibly more vulnerable with each additional transaction, but the total volume of credit will remain unaffected.

Even so, the expansionary effect of the system should not be under-rated. It has powerfully contributed towards increasing international liquidity to meet the requirements of international trade and finance. For many years it has now been the perennial complaint that, because the dollar price of gold has not changed since 1934 and the increase in the monetary supply of gold has been lagging considerably behind that of international requirements for liquid resources, there is not enough gold available for meeting these requirements. It is concluded, therefore, that inadequacy of international means of payments has been handicapping a further expansion of international trade. Moreover, since inadequacy of liquid international resources is blamed for the frequently recurrent balance of payments crises which compel governments to restrict credit for domestic purposes, that inadequacy is held responsible for the unsatisfactory rate of expansion of domestic production and for the slow rate of economic growth.

The expansion of the Euro-dollar system has gone a long way towards meeting increased liquidity requirements for routine financing of international trade in normal conditions. Even if the total of Euro-dollars employed in a way as to add to the liquid international resources is smaller than the total annual value of foreign trade, owing to the easy availability and high velocity of Euro-dollar deposits the extent to which they contribute towards meeting requirements is well in excess of the proportion suggested by the bare amount. More dollars are now available for financing international trade than the amount which American banks themselves would be prepared to lend, this in spite of the fact that a high proportion of the Euro-dollars is now used for financing domestic trade in the United States and not for financing international trade.

The most striking effect produced by the Euro-dollar system in the form of credit expansion occurred within the domestic economies of countries which, though possessing a very advanced economic system, did not possess during the post-war period sufficient liquid financial resources to enable them to expand production to an extent anything like their capacity. They were enabled to do so to a very large extent by borrowing Euro-dollars. The expansions of production known as the 'German miracle', the 'Italian miracle', and the 'Japanese miracle' were greatly facilitated by the influx of Euro-dollars.

But in Germany, Italy, Japan and other countries the monetary authorities adopted measures compelling banks and non-banking borrowers of Euro-dollars to reduce their liabilities. The resulting disinflationary effect was, however, offset and more than offset by heavy American borrowing in the Euro-dollar market, assisting American business expansion to some extent in spite of the credit squeeze.

Apart altogether from the effect of the Euro-dollar system on the volume of credit, it also tends to make for expansion through increasing the velocity of circulation deposits. Formerly idle deposits become active deposits. By changing hands more frequently they finance a larger volume of trade.

Having said all this, we must admit that the Euro-dollar system has contributed nothing towards the solution of the problem of increasing international liquid resources for meeting abnormal requirements during periods of acute crises. On the contrary, by increasing the volume of international transactions and by making the international credit system more vulnerable, the Euro-dollar system has increased requirements for reserves to meet such emergencies. Because it provides additional facilities for speculation and for disturbing arbitrage, the Euro-dollar system has created new problems relating to international liquidity. Above all, the possibility that some international crisis is liable to bring about a sharp contraction in the volume of Euro-dollars and in the volume of credit based on them, must be borne in mind.

CHAPTER 13

ATTITUDE OF CENTRAL BANKS

W E saw in Chapter 2 that Central Banks were among the first holders of dollar deposits to re-lend their dollars in what were the early beginnings of the Euro-dollar market. A number of them were not slow in seizing upon the opportunity provided by its facilities to increase the yield on their dollar reserves. But for their participation in the new market, its progress would have been much less spectacular. Earlier estimates, according to which some two-thirds of Euro-dollars had been provided by Central Banks, are no longer valid, but there can be little doubt that ever since 1957 many Central Banks have largely contributed towards the development of the new market by supplying it with ample funds.

Notwithstanding this, Central Banks could not really claim credit for the initiation and progress of the new system. They had not employed their funds in the Euro-dollar market deliberately as a matter of major policy on the basis of any conclusion that the development of such a market would be to the advantage of their countries or to the international monetary system. They simply drifted into it as a matter of immediate expediency doing the right thing for a wrong reason, or at any rate for an inadequate reason. They helped to build up the new system simply for the sake of higher yield — which should surely be regarded as a consideration of secondary importance compared with the major objectives of monetary policy.

Admittedly, for Central Banks the difference between deposit rates permitted under Regulation Q and those obtainable in the Euro-dollar market may have been tempting. In particular it is to their advantage to invest in Euro-dollars that part of their reserve which has to be available at a moment's notice. For while no interest is allowable by American banks on sight deposits, in the Euro-dollar market deposits at call have a reasonably good yield. There is, however, no justification for Central Banks to determine their attitude towards Euro-dollars wholly, or even mainly, by their desire for higher yields. Even though it is understandable if they, like the rest of us, should want to increase their earnings, that consideration should not have determined their decision whether to help, or to abstain from helping, or indeed to hinder the development of an important institution such as the Euro-dollar market.

Central Banks ought to have made up their minds at an early stage of its development whether or not, from the broad point of view of public interest, the Euro-dollar market would be on balance worth having. There is no reason to suppose that this was done by all of them. They ought to have decided on the merits of the issues involved whether it was worth while to put up with the disadvantages and to assume the risks with their eyes open.

One is permitted to wonder if, and to what extent, and at what stage, some of the monetary authorities which have greatly assisted in the expansion of the Euro-dollar market by supplying it with funds came to realise that the spectacular development of the new device had in fact greatly weakened their control over the monetary system. Possibly some Central Banks or Treasuries are to this day blissfully oblivious that, for the sake of a relatively modest additional yield on their dollar holding, they have greatly increased the difficulty of their own main task of defending their currencies and of controlling their money markets and their domestic credit structure.

The control of the monetary system by Central Banks is liable to be weakened by the development of the Euro-dollar market and of other foreign currency deposit markets in the following ways :

(1) Monetary authorities have less control over the volume of the liquid resources in their money market.

(2) They have less control over the supply of credit available to their economy.

(3) They have less control over the structure of national interest rates.

(4) They have less control over the financing of unwanted imports.

(5) They have less control over the influx and efflux of short-term funds.

(6) Surviving or restored exchange controls can be circumvented more easily.

(7) Gold purchases for hoarding or speculation are made easier.

(8) The exchanges have become more vulnerable, because speculation is facilitated by the new devices.

(9) Discipline within the banking communities is less firm.

Liquid resources of the money market can now be more easily expanded or reduced independently of the policy of the monetary authorities. As far as Lombard Street is concerned this consideration is of secondary importance, because the Bank of England is always well in a position to counteract very speedily and very effectively any unwanted changes in the supply of money brought about by foreign exchange or Euro-dollar operations. This is a great advantage, because the foreign exchange department of the Bank can be allowed a free hand to operate with the sole object of maintaining spot and forward rates at figures that suit the purposes of foreign exchange policy. It does not have to feel itself handicapped in its foreign exchange operations by the requirements of regulating the supply of money and credit.

Other monetary authorities are not so well placed, however. They have to resort to forward exchange manipulations or other devices in order to prevent unwanted flows of Euro-dollars into and out of their money market or to neutralise their effect on the supply of liquid funds in accordance with the objectives of their policy. This involves the pursuit of foreign exchange tactics for purposes other than foreign exchange policy, which complicates the tasks of those in charge of that policy.

The trend of Euro-dollar operations often influences the supply of credit available to the economy in a sense contrary to the objects of the official monetary policy. For instance, in 1968–69 the United States authorities found that their policies aiming at tighter credit were frustrated by the heavy influx of funds borrowed by their banks in the Euro-dollar market. The West German and Swiss authorities, too, found it more difficult to resist an unwanted inflationary influx of moneys, owing to the operation of the Euro-currency system. It became necessary to resort to the elaborate policy measures to counteract the unwanted trend, or at any rate the extent of official intervention had to be much more drastic because of the new device.

Because of the existence of an alternative source of credit, Bank rate changes are apt to produce a less marked effect on the national interest structure and are less able, therefore, to influence the trend of the domestic economy. Dear money policy is liable to be frustrated. In any case, although high domestic interest rates are likely to discourage domestic credits on which national interest rates are charged, these credits may be substituted by Euro-dollar loans bearing lower international interest rates. It is true, a rise in the British Bank rate, for instance, tends to cause Euro-dollar rates to rise through causing an additional demand for Euro-dollar loans, but the resulting rise in Euro-dollar rates need not necessarily be more than a fraction of the Bank rate increase.

From the point of view of sterling's international position, Bank rate increases tend to be effective, because more Euro-dollars will be borrowed and swapped into sterling. But the long-range effect of the Bank rate change will be weaker, as we explained in Chapter 10. One of the ways in which high Bank rate produces its effect is through the confidence it inspires in sterling, in anticipation of its deflationary material effect on the domestic economy. If as a result of the operation of the Euro-dollar system that deflationary effect is less pronounced then the high Bank rate is likely to inspire less confidence. What is even more important in the long run, if the high Bank rate does not reduce domestic demand to the same extent as it did before the advent of Euro-dollars, then it will not contribute to the same extent as before towards correcting the balance of payments.

Now that physical controls have been greatly mitigated and exchange transactions for current requirements of imports are practically free, selective credit restrictions are among the most effective weapons in the armoury of many Central Banks to discourage unwanted imports. It is all the more essential, therefore, from the point of view of efficient monetary policy, that the authorities should exercise effective control over the volume of credit used for financing imports. Owing to the alternative facilities provided by the Euro-dollar market this control has greatly weakened. The control of movements of hot money, too, has become more difficult, because there is an important additional source of arbitrage funds.

Exchange control on short-term capital transactions has been weakened as a result of authorising banks to borrow or lend in the Euro-dollar market. In Britain, for instance, where each bank has a maximum limit fixed for its external commitments, Euro-dollar deposits are not included in that limit. In this instance the British authorities assumed with their eyes open the risk involved in relaxing their control over the movements of capital, for the sake of encouraging deliberately the development of the Euro-dollar market in London.

Private hoarding of gold affects primarily the United States authorities, because any substantial increase in buying pressure on the free market as a result of increased demand for hoarding and speculation means an increase of the free market price over the official American price. Should such an increase become self-aggravating, it might revive dollar scares of the kind we witnessed before the establishment of the two-tier system in 1968. So long as the American authorities are determined to defend the existing dollar parity, an increase in the free market price of gold as a result of increased hoarding demand stimulated by the availability of Euro-dollars is against their policy. This is a matter of considerable importance from the point of view of the United States. Doubtless, these facilities stimulate buying of gold by speculators which is also financed with the aid of Euro-dollars, and the evidence of speculative pressure stimulates hoarding demand.

We saw in Chapter 10 that the exchange position ha become more vulnerable as a result of the development of the Euro-dollar market, owing to the availability of additional facilities for speculation and outward arbitrage. The dollar is the only currency that is directly affected by Euro-currency markets, but to a lesser extent speculative pressure can increase against other currencies. For instance, speculative buying of D. marks is encouraged by the possibility of earning abroad interest on D. mark deposits in spite of the German ban on interest on foreign deposits. Central Banks which feed the Euro-dollar market out of their dollar reserves in times of dollar scares do not appear to realise that by providing ammunition for attacking the dollar they indirectly endanger the stability of their own currency.

Euro-dollar facilities have been used extensively not only for speculation against a currency but also for speculation in favour of a currency. This was done, for instance, in 1969 when Euro-dollars were borrowed and sold against D. marks and Swiss francs in anticipation of a revaluation of these currencies, rather than a devaluation of the dollar.

The German monetary authorities, by supplying the Euro-dollar market with dollar deposits through the intermediary of German banks, increased the difficulty of their own task in resisting the pressure for a second revaluation. In fact they initiated and maintained a vicious circle when lending their unwanted dollars to the German banks and through them to the Euro-dollar market, for much of the self-same dollars were sold by the borrowers against D. marks, so that they found their way back into the Bundesbank's reserve, only to be re-lent again to the Euro-dollar market through the German banks.

The main reason why Central Banks are in a position to enforce discipline in their respective banking communities is that they are the main source from which banks can receive assistance in case of need. As a result of the development of the Euro-dollar market, banks in many countries are now in a position to raise funds to tide them over difficult dates without having recourse to their Central Banks. For this reason they no longer feel the same necessity to submit to discipline. Central Banks have only a limited control over lending and borrowing operations through the Euro-dollar market. Although they may be in a position to reassert their authority if, as occurs from time to time, sudden withdrawals of Euro-dollars from the day-to-day loan market cause a scramble for funds, during most of the time the market runs itself and debtors have no difficulty in obtaining the renewal of their maturing commitments.

It has been suggested that Central Banks, by abstaining from feeding the Euro-dollar market, could reassert their control over the domestic credit system. But it seems reasonable to assume that even if Central Banks stopped supplying the market altogether it would not make a fundamental difference. Now that the system is firmly established all that would happen if Central Banks were to withdraw their deposits would be that Euro-dollar rates would rise to a level at which they could attract more privately-owned dollars. The substantial amount of Central Bank funds withdrawn as a result of the suspension of the Bundesbank's swap transactions with German banks and of the modification of Regulation Q for the benefit of official deposits left the market unaffected.

There are some undoubted advantages in the system from the point of view of Central Banks, in addition to its undoubted direct advantages from the point of view of banks, industrialists, merchants, and investors of short-term funds. We saw above that the operation of the Euro-dollar system tends to reduce the effect of Bank rate increases on a domestic economy. In given situations this may be a point of favour in the Euro-dollar system. If the object of the Bank rate increase is purely to reverse an unwanted outflow of the short-term fund, and the authorities do not deem it necessary to deflate the domestic economy, then the existence of the Euro-dollar system tends to assist in a policy of strengthening the exchange without inflicting deflation on the economy. But in some situations no lasting improvement can be achieved without deflation.

The Euro-dollar market enables monetary authorities with inadequate reserves to increase their reserves by borrowing Euro-dollar deposits. They can do so either as a stopgap measure to tide over some awkward date or as a more or less permanent expansion. This is believed to have been actually done by some of the weaker Central Banks, though not by any of the leading Central Banks which are always lenders and never borrowers of Euro-dollars.

As pointed out in Chapter 3, the Belgian Treasury has been a frequent borrower of Euro-dollars, as an alternative to increasing the ceiling of its advances from the National Bank of Belgium during lean periods. From the point of view of sound finance, the borrowing of Euro-dollars was distinctly the smaller evil.

A question of highly controversial character is whether Central Banks — or for that matter Treasuries — are entitled to include the Euro-dollars they hold in their published foreign exchange reserves, considering that the possession of such dollars is purely temporary and that their value as a reserve is greatly reduced by the fact that when the deposits expire they have to be repaid. The principle involved was argued out in great detail in connection with the inclusion of foreign exchange re-sold by Central Banks for forward delivery. On balance, expert opinion deprecates the inclusion of such foreign exchange, and the same principle applies to Euro-dollars. Yet there is no consistency in the attitude of those opposed to the inclusion of Euro-dollars. After all, the authorities usually include in their published reserves dollars or other currencies borrowed from the International Monetary Fund, even though the possession of such currencies is no more permanent than that of borrowed Euro-dollars. Both dollars are borrowed and their retention depends on the renewal of the facilities.

Central Banks are inclined to be more strictly purists than Treasuries in their attitude on this matter. But it is extremely difficult to know where exactly to draw a line. After all, if a Central Bank buys dollars sold in connection with the selling pressure on dollars that develops from swapping Euro-dollar deposits into the local currency, the possession of these dollars is apt to be just as temporary as the possession of Euro-dollars borrowed by the Central Bank themselves. Indeed, while they are in a position to decide whether to renew their maturing Euro-dollar deposits, continued possession of their dollars derived from the sale of Euro-dollars borrowed by banks depends on the decision of the banks concerned whether to renew their commitments. It is true, Central Banks are able to influence such decisions with the aid of various policy measures, but it is not the same as being able themselves to decide whether to renew the arrangement that secures for them the temporary possession of dollars.

Yet nobody would suggest excluding dollars bought as a result of swapping Euro-dollars into national currency — apart from any other reasons, because it would be very difficult for Central Banks to know which dollars offered in the market originate from Euro-dollar transactions. For one thing, some Central Banks do not as a rule provide the counterpart of the actual swap transactions originating from Euro-dollar transactions, but merely intervene to steady the spot dollar rate against the adverse pressure caused by the swaps.

While the Euro-dollar system means some additional headaches to Central Banks, it also provides them with a very flexible device of monetary policy and foreign exchange policy. This device can assist them in their task of regulating the liquidity of the national economy and the inflow and outflow of short-term funds. To that end there is no need for them directly to intervene in the Euro-dollar market, but merely to offer to their banks dollar swaps on favourable terms, on the assumption that most of these dollars would be invested in Euro-dollar deposits. An alternative device at their disposal is to influence forward rates in a sense as to encourage or discourage the swapping of Euro-dollars into or out of the local currency.

Both the West German and the Italian monetary authorities systematically resorted to tactics in which the Euro-dollar market played an important if indirect part. We saw earlier that it is a recognised part of the Bundesbank's monetary policy to offer to German banks dollar swap facilities at par with spot rates or at rates more favourable to them than the prevailing market rates, on the condition that the dollars would be reinvested abroad. Even though Euro-dollar deposits were never actually prescribed, they were for a long time the most attractive form of investments for such purposes, and the bulk of the swap dollars were employed in that form. In

Italy the Ufficio dei Cambi provided Italian banks with similar swap dollar facilities. The Bank of France, on the other hand, often influences swap rates by direct intervention in the foreign exchange market, and in doing so it can influence the flow of Euro-dollars and of other Euro-currencies.

The rates quoted for official German transactions aiming at influencing the flow of Euro-dollars were adjusted from time to time according to whether the authorities wanted to encourage or discourage transfers of short-term funds abroad or their repatriation, and according to whether they wanted to tighten or ease domestic monetary conditions. The Italian monetary authorities, in an effort to increase the liquidity of the Italian banks, left with them the lire equivalent of the dollars, but later they discontinued the practice and sought to mop up lire by parting with their dollars only against the surrender of lire. They even resorted to devices to discourage the influx of Euro-dollars. From August 1960 the Italian banks were ordered to balance their external liabilities with equivalent external assets. On the other hand, from November 1962 they were permitted to borrow Euro-dollars not only for financing international transactions but also for financing domestic transactions.

The German authorities, too, came to realise eventually that the new device of providing dollars for use in the Euro-dollar market had its disadvantages, because it set into motion the circular process described above, under which the funds diverted into Euro-dollars found their way back to Germany over and over again. By 1962 the futility of this process became obvious. Later the Bundesbank made it a condition that the dollars must be invested in U.S. Treasury bills.

The United States authorities, on their part, resorted to tactics to discourage the use of Euro-dollars for the purposes of covering or hedging against a change of parities during the period of pressure against the dollar that followed the revaluation of the D. mark and the guilder. To that end, during the spring and summer of 1961 they supported the forward dollar rate systematically, thereby making it less costly to cover, hedge, or speculate by means of selling forward dollars. But

121

for this measure there might have been much more borrowing of Euro-dollars for the purpose of selling spot dollars.

In March 1965 the U.S. Government sought to persuade American residents voluntarily to withdraw their funds from the Euro-dollar market. In 1968 official restrictions replaced voluntary restraint.

Other methods by which the flow of funds was regulated included the demand that the proceeds of Euro-dollars should only be used for international purposes or that a certain percentage of the deposits used for domestic purposes should be kept in liquid form. In the case of Japan this percentage was fixed at 20 per cent towards the middle of 1962, by which time the amount of Euro-dollars used by Japanese banks for the requirements of the domestic economy rose to something like one billion. As a result of this measure that amount became gradually reduced. The Bank of Japan sought to regulate the volume of borrowing by fixing the maximum interest which Japanese banks are permitted to pay for Euro-dollars. This was done by fixing the maximum differential in excess of the prevailing standard Euro-dollar rates. In Germany the reserve requirements from all external short-term liabilities of the banks are as high as 30 per cent if the proceeds are used for domestic financing, but lower if they are used for foreign financing.

In 1964 the Swiss authorities adopted a measure requiring banks in Switzerland to place abroad in foreign currencies the counterpart of any new Swiss franc deposits on non-resident accounts, as an alternative to sterilising them at the Swiss National Bank. The object of this measure was to prevent an influx of foreign funds from producing inflationary effects. It created additional demand for Euro-currencies.

The use of Euro-dollars in the service of foreign exchange policy or of monetary policy is still in its experimental stage. As the system itself has not yet settled down to its definite form, its evolution will give rise to new problems from time to time, and it will provide new responsibilities and new opportunities for the authorities.

In Italy official policy in respect of Euro-currencies was somewhat contradictory. On the one hand Italian banks were encouraged to borrow such currencies by the fact that their minimum reserve requirements did not apply to their foreign currency liabilities. On the other hand they were not free to convert Euro-currency deposits into lire without special permit. From January 1961 to November 1962 they were required to balance their foreign currency assets and liabilities in relation to non-residents. The removal of this restriction resulted in a sharp increase in Italian borrowing of Euro-dollars at the end of 1962 and early in 1963. In September 1963 a limit was imposed on Italian bank borrowing abroad, and the official policy arrived at inducing the Italian banks to repay their Euro-currency loans. Excessive borrowing of Euro-dollars is also discouraged by the rule that non-banks can only borrow through the intermediary of banks in Italy.

In 1969 the United States authorities, in a half-hearted attempt to discourage American banks from borrowing Euro-dollars through their London branches, applied reserve requirements to amounts borrowed in excess of those outstanding in May 1969. This measure defeated its object, because the banks borrowed in London the amounts they needed in order to comply with the reserve requirements.

In France banks could borrow Euro-currencies abroad but were not allowed to convert them into francs. They were entitled to lend Euro-currencies to French residents for financing foreign trade.

Modifications of the Central Banks' attitude towards borrowing and lending Euro-currencies have become an important instrument of foreign exchange policy and monetary policy. The technique of this device is still in a state of evolution, however.

CHAPTER 14

EURO-STERLING AND OTHER
FOREIGN CURRENCY DEPOSITS

THROUGHOUT this book we have focused our attention on
Euro-dollars, making only occasional references to other foreign
currency deposits. This chapter will examine briefly the
operation of the system as it relates to these other so-called
'Euro-currencies'. This collective name for deposits in terms
of various Western European currencies re-deposited outside
the respective countries concerned, and the names of 'Euro-
sterling', 'Euro-Swiss francs', 'Euro-D. mark', etc., are of
course even more absurd than the name of 'Euro-dollars'.
As it was pointed out in the introductory chapter, sterling
deposited in London is held in Europe, so that from that point
of view it makes no difference if it is re-deposited in Paris.

Since, however, the terms have found their way into usage
in the foreign exchange markets and in the financial Press —
though perhaps not so universally as 'Euro-dollars' — they
might as well be accepted, if only for want of better terms
that would be equally suitable and equally brief. There is
much to be said for using a term as brief as 'Euro-sterling'
instead of having to say 'non-resident sterling deposit re-
deposited with a continental bank', each time we refer to the
subject. What matters is that the reader should know what
we are talking about, and even the sternest opponents of the
terms could not contend that the meaning of the terms 'Euro-
sterling', etc., is not absolutely clear.

In the Euro-currency market Euro-sterling was for a long
time easily next in importance to the Euro-dollar market. It
was much more important than the markets in either Swiss franc,
or D. mark, not to speak of guilder, or French franc, or Italian
lira deposits.

Until the relaxation of exchange control in 1958, transferable sterling was an important international currency. Its exchange rate differed from the ordinary sterling rate, even though the disparity tended to disappear during the late 'fifties. Transferable sterling, though inconvertible outside the transferable area, was freely accepted in international payments between countries within that area. A very active market developed in transferable sterling, especially in Zürich. When at the end of 1958 transferable accounts were abolished, sterling owned by residents outside the sterling area became, broadly speaking, one uniform type of sterling on non-resident account — with the exception of 'security sterling', which also disappeared, in 1967. In spite of the limitations maintained on the use of sterling on resident account there was never any separate quotation of exchange rates for the two categories of sterling, and there was no disparity between them.

From the very outset a distinction arose, however, between resident and non-resident sterling as a result of the development of a market in non-resident sterling deposits, which can be lent and borrowed at international interest rates, as distinct from the national interest rates at which resident sterling has to be lent and borrowed.

While the development of the Euro-dollar market was largely due to the limitations of interest rates allowed on deposits under Regulation Q, in Britain there have been no statutory regulations limiting interest rates since the abolition of the anti-usury law more than a hundred years ago. On the other hand, since before the war a gentlemen's agreement has been in operation among clearing banks, fixing a maximum limit to deposit rates at 2 per cent below the Bank rate and a rather less rigid minimum limit to standard lending rates at 1 per cent above the Bank rate. Foreign commercial bank branches in London have followed the tradition of applying the same rates as the British clearing banks. Even though the gentlemen's agreement does not apply to merchant banks or British overseas banks, by far the largest volume of sterling deposits are held by the clearing banks. The rule could be circumvented, however, for the benefit of non-resident holders of sterling whose deposits came to be allowed higher deposit rates in foreign financial centres, especially in Paris.

The artificially low level of deposit rates in London was not, however, the main reason for the emergence of the Euro-sterling market. After all, with the Bank rate between 6 and 7 per cent for a long time, deposit rates were reasonably attractive even under the terms of the gentlemen's agreement. What was mainly responsible for the adoption of the practice was the restrictions imposed in 1957 on sterling credits to finance trade between two foreign countries and to re-finance trade beyond the conventional period. It is true, Euro-dollars were available for those purposes, but in many instances sterling was the prescribed currency of payment or the traditional currency in which certain types of transactions were financed. Or it was found for some reason more convenient to use sterling. Or the covering of forward sterling at a heavy discount was profitable to borrowers. As a result, a demand for sterling facilities developed and was met — at a price — by non-resident holders of sterling deposits on transferable or American account. The practice continued after the unification of non-resident sterling types in 1958.

There are ample non-resident sterling deposits held outside the Sterling Area and available for supplying the needs of the Euro-sterling market. In March 1969 their total was £1,711 million — not counting the £425 million belonging to Central Banks and Treasuries. While there is no absolute reason why such official sterling deposits should not be lent in the Euro-sterling market in the same way as official dollar deposits are lent in the Euro-dollar market, there is no evidence that this was in fact ever done on any appreciable scale. Even so, the possibility was certainly there. But even if we disregard official balances, the amount of sterling held by private residents outside the sterling area and qualified for being lent in the Euro-sterling market could be increased out of the proceeds of Treasury bills and other short-term assets, and even out of the proceeds of long-term assets, especially of British Government stocks. After each run on the pound it is asserted that foreign-owned sterling available for speculation or for re-lending has now become reduced to a minimum — a remark which could and should be included in the list of 'famous last words'.

Admittedly a large part of such deposits is required for keeping alive accounts of a large number of foreign banks with their London correspondents, or for maintaining normal working balances needed for current commercial or financial purposes. But anything that is above the rock-bottom figure to which the balances often declined may be considered to be available for Euro-sterling transactions. Even some of the indispensable sterling holdings retained could be converted into Euro-sterling deposits at call, in which form funds could be conveniently held for the purposes of working balances in London.

Moreover, it would be a mistake to imagine that the amount of sterling held on non-resident account constitutes the absolute limit to the potential amount of Euro-sterling deposits. As we shall see later, it is a widespread practice for non-residents to buy sterling for the sole purpose of using it in the Euro-sterling market. Thus, even though the potential limits of the market are narrower than those of the Euro-dollar market — because the amount of non-resident sterling is much smaller than that of non-resident dollars, and because resident sterling does not qualify for being used as Euro-currency deposits while resident dollars are eligible for that purpose in given circumstances — they are indeed very wide and flexible.

Very active markets developed during the 'sixties in Paris and to a lesser extent in Switzerland and Amsterdam. There is also a fairly active market in London — second only to the Paris market — in spite of the fact that London banks cannot and do not transact business in it on their own account. Some clearing banks, merchant banks, and British overseas banks have subsidiaries or branches abroad and the sterling deposits of these subsidiaries or branches with their parent institutions are treated as non-resident sterling for the purposes of exchange control, so that they can be used for Euro-sterling transactions. The same is the position regarding sterling balances of foreign banks with their London branches.

Moreover, there is nothing to prevent London banks, if

asked by a continental bank, to quote simultaneously their Euro-dollar lending rate and a swap-and-deposit rate for the conversion of dollars into a Euro-sterling deposit. In practice such a combined quotation amounts to a quotation of a Euro-sterling rate. As a result, there can be, and there is, an active market in Euro-sterling also in London. But it is a one-sided and restricted market. For the moment a Euro-sterling deposit is borrowed by a London bank or the London branch or subsidiary of a non-resident bank, it becomes a resident sterling deposit pure and simple. While the borrower is of course entitled to repay it to the non-resident lender, he is not entitled to re-lend it to non-residents, so that the deposit has to be held in sterling or invested in the United Kingdom until it matures. United Kingdom residents are not entitled to lend sterling deposits in the Euro-sterling market without obtaining license, which is only granted exceptionally. Most Euro-sterling business in London is done direct with continental centres. Relatively little is done within the market.

Likewise, there is a very limited one-way market in Euro-sterling in New York. American banks are entitled to lend abroad their sterling deposits but they are prevented by Regulation Q from paying for sterling deposits the high rates quoted in the Euro-sterling market.

In Paris, banks of all types are active in the Euro-sterling market. Euro-sterling rates are subject to more erratic movements than Euro-dollar rates, because the market is narrower and more sensitive, and because it is more likely to play a passive part in the interplay between Euro-dollar rates on the one hand and forward sterling-dollar rates, and certain London interest rates on the other. When there was an hour's difference between business hours in Paris and London from October till April of each year, forward sterling often tended to drift downward during the first hour of business in Paris while London was closed, and such temporary depreciation of forward sterling tended to affect Euro-sterling rates. This effect ceased of course since the perpetuation of Summer Time in the United Kingdom.

As in the case of the Paris market in Euro-dollars, the

favourite type of deposits in the Paris market in Euro-sterling are those for two days' notice. Whenever there is speculative pressure on sterling such deposits are in good demand and their proceeds sold, in preference to selling spot sterling to be delivered in two days, because it is easier to renew such deposits every other day than to cover spot sales by buying for 'value today' and re-selling the spot on the day of delivery.

To some extent Euro-sterling credits have taken the place of sterling acceptance credits, with the difference that it is not London banks who grant them. But normally the bulk of the Euro-sterling operations is in connection with arbitrage. There is indeed a great deal of very active arbitrage between Euro-dollars and Euro-sterling, and very often Euro-sterling is acquired for that purpose. It can be acquired not only as a result of an export surplus or an increase in the volume of hot money in London but also through the purchase of sterling for the sole purpose of using it in arbitrage. As already noted earlier in this chapter, non-resident holders of dollars or of any foreign currency can acquire unlimited amounts of Euro-sterling by simply buying spot sterling, or by engaging in swap transactions. If the counterpart of persistent demand for sterling for this purpose is not forthcoming automatically the Exchange Equalisation Account provides it in order to add dollars to its reserve. In any case it would intervene if sterling appreciated to its upper support point, to prevent its appreciation above $2.42.

As we saw in Chapter 6, the Euro-dollar–Euro-sterling parities have become the most important interest parities affecting interest arbitrage. Continental holders of idle funds have the choice between investing in either currency, according to the relative yield determined by the interest differentials and the forward rates.

Whenever there is a speculative attack against sterling — such as there was on a great many occasions during the 'sixties, especially since the advent of the Labour Government in 1964 — instead of assuming the form of forward selling it can assume largely the form of borrowing Euro-sterling and selling spot sterling without covering the forward exchange. This is done when the discount on forward sterling widens to such an extent that it would be costlier to go short in sterling by selling it forward. Such demand for Euro-sterling for speculative purposes tends to raise Euro-sterling rates, thereby attracting additional funds to the market. These operations have, however, a natural limit, for when sterling is under adverse pressure the discount on short forward sterling is apt to become wide, and few people would on such occasions buy spot sterling for the purpose of lending it without covering the exchange risk. Holdings of non-resident sterling available for the purpose, though substantial, are far from inexhaustible. In this respect sterling is at an advantage compared with the dollar, precisely because resident sterling deposits cannot be converted into Euro-sterling deposits. Even so, as we saw above, many hundreds of millions of privately-owned non-resident sterling are available, and there is a possibility of the market being supplied also by some official holders if the rates become attractive.

Precisely because of the continued existence of exchange control on sterling on resident accounts, British banks are not faced with the dilemma of the Federal Reserve — whether to remove the artificial ceiling to deposit rates on the entire volume of domestic as well as foreign sterling deposits, for the sake of preventing the transfer of part of the latter to the Euro-sterling market. Although the proportion of Euro-sterling deposits to total sterling deposits may be as high as the proportion of Euro-dollar deposits to total dollar deposits, the potential increase of the former is incomparably smaller than that of the latter. Whatever arguments there may be in favour of discontinuing or relaxing the gentlemen's agreement, they are not reinforced, as in the case of the dollar, by fears of an exodus of resident deposits into the Euro-currency market.

In the late 'sixties Euro-sterling became overshadowed in importance by D. marks and Swiss franc deposits. The market in both of them developed as a result of the ban imposed on the payment of interest on foreign deposits in West Germany and Switzerland in an attempt to discourage the influx of unwanted hot money. In both countries a negative interest of $\frac{1}{2}$ per

cent (commission) was charged on foreign deposits. This ban
came to be circumvented by offering the non-interest-bearing
Swiss deposits or low-interest-bearing German deposits to
borrowers abroad who are willing to pay reasonable interest on
them. Markets in these two Euro-currencies become very
active whenever there is an influx of hot money on a large
scale.

The market in D. mark deposits was supplied from time to
time with funds indirectly by the Bank of France. On occasions
when it had to sell D. marks in order to prevent its appreciation
against the franc, it secured the maintenance of its holdings
by means of swap transactions, just as the Bundesbank
unloaded unwanted dollars, with the difference that the Bank
of France announced no official rates for the purpose but simply
sold the D. marks in the foreign exchange market with the
forward exchange covered. The French banks in turn employed
the D. marks bought from the Bank of France mostly for
lending them in the Euro-mark market.

There is a much smaller turnover in the market for deposits
in Euro-guilders and Euro-French francs, in spite of the ban
on interest payment to non-residents on French franc deposits.
Even though it is possible to obtain quotations of rates also
for deposits in other currencies, their turnover is limited. Most
of the transactions in foreign currency deposits other than Euro-
dollars take place in Paris or Switzerland. There is a fair
demand for various Euro-currencies whenever exchange rates
are trusted, for the purpose of selling the spot exchange borrowed, without covering the forward exchange. Whichever
Euro-currency is lent at the lowest rate is borrowed and, by
selling the spot against, say, sterling, the borrower is able to
secure Euro-sterling well below the current Euro-sterling rate.
This is, of course, impracticable when it is necessary to cover
the forward exchange.

The existence of markets in Euro-currencies other than
Euro-dollars has greatly broadened the basis of the system
created through the development of the Euro-dollar market.
Between them these foreign currency deposits have a fairly
large turnover and play their part in the new international

money market. Their interest rates are largely determined by
Euro-dollar rates and forward rates, though in respect of the
latter the relationship is reciprocal. While even Euro-sterling
rates are hardly ever able to influence Euro-dollar rates, they
are very often able to influence the forward sterling-dollar
rate. They are largely influenced by British interest rates —
especially by rates on loans to local authorities or on deposits
to hire-purchase finance houses — but they in their turn are
able to influence those rates. For the most part, however,
Euro-sterling rates are just calculated, as a matter of simple
arithmetic, from Euro-dollar rates on the basis of the prevailing
forward sterling-dollar rates.

The variety of Euro-currencies gives lenders and borrowers
a wide choice. There is very often a fractional advantage
— and at times rather more than a fractional advantage — in
favour of preferring to invest or borrow in one Euro-currency
rather than in others, allowing or not allowing for the forward
exchange as the case may be. The possibility of choosing
between operating in half a dozen Euro-currencies further
accentuates the essentially international character of the
system.

The predominant position held by Euro-dollars among
Euro-currencies has far-reaching theoretical and policy implications. The rates of Euro-currencies other than Euro-dollars
are determined to a considerable extent by Euro-dollar rates
and by forward rates, while the extent to which either Euro-
dollar rates or forward rates are affected by Euro-currency
rates is usually very moderate. This is apt to give rise to
anomalous situations in which Euro-currency rates move in
the opposite direction to that of the trend of the national
interest rates in the countries of the currencies concerned. An
illustration is provided by the B.I.S. report for 1963–64.
During the first three quarters of 1960 interest rates in Germany rose sharply, but the rate for three months' Euro-D.
marks in London declined from $4\frac{1}{2}$ to $2\frac{1}{2}$ per cent. This was
largely due to the appreciation of the forward D. mark. After
the middle of 1961 interest rates in Germany were declining,
but Euro-D. mark rates in London rose by 2 per cent, because

Euro-dollar rates were rising while the discount on forward dollars against D. marks narrowed from $2\frac{1}{2}$ to just over $\frac{1}{2}$ per cent p.a.

The dependence of Euro-currencies other than Euro-dollars on Euro-dollar rates and on forward rates makes them even more independent of their respective domestic interest rates than Euro-dollar rates are of U.S. domestic interest rates. The fact that the German money market was not freely accessible to non-residents accounts for the extent and duration of anomalies which are, however, inherent in the system so long as the volume of any Euro-currencies other than the Euro-dollars remains a mere fraction of the volume of Euro-dollars.

Whenever there was a rush to buy D. marks in anticipation of its revaluation, there was an increase in activity in the Euro-D. mark market. It was, however, a very one-sided activity with many would-be lenders and few takers. During the revaluation scare of May 1969, and again on the eve of the revaluation in September 1969, Euro-D. mark rates declined to purely nominal figures. In spite of the increases in the turnover, it was not a good market. Nevertheless, the possibility that some day Euro-D. marks might attain an importance comparable to that of Euro-dollars cannot be ruled out.

There is also a possibility of the development of a Euro-yen market. After the revaluation of the D. mark the yen became the most revaluation-prone currency. But the existence of various exchange restrictions and trade restrictions in Japan discouraged a large-scale influx of foreign funds and the emergence of a market in non-resident yen deposits. Isolated deals in such deposits in London, borrowed by Japanese firms, were a matter of negotiation.

133

CHAPTER 15

IMPACT OF EUROPEAN DOLLAR BONDS

SINCE the publication of the original edition of this book the evolution of the European market in foreign long-term loans issued in terms of dollars, D. marks, composite units of account and other currencies has made considerable progress. While the Euro-currency market has created a system of international short-term interest rates, the European market in foreign currency bonds has brought into being a system of international long-term interest rates. Admittedly it has not reached the same advanced stage of evolution as the Euro-currency market. Nevertheless, it is an institutional change which deserves close attention. I tried to explain its various implications in my recently revised book on *The Euro-Bond Market*, which contains a chapter dealing with the impact of such loans on Euro-dollars. Although it is outside the scope of this book to deal at length with international long-term interest rates, I propose here to give a brief summary of the relevant facts and conclusions in so far as they have a bearing on the Euro-dollar system.

Differences between Euro-dollars and foreign dollar bonds issued in Europe are not confined to length of maturity. When Euro-dollar deposits change hands their nominal amount is fixed and it is only the deposit rates that are subject to market influences. On the other hand, interest rates of European dollar bonds are fixed and it is the prices at which they change hands that are subject to market influences. In the case of Euro-dollars the ultimate debtor is necessarily one of the American banks with which the dollars are held on deposit, while in the case of European dollar bonds the ultimate debtor is very often a resident outside the United States, even though payment is due to be made by the American agents of non-American debtors in dollars payable in the United States, unless the bondholder prefers it to be made in some other country. Euro-dollars are unsecured, while dollar bonds may be secured. In the case of bonds there is only a single debtor — the original borrower — while Euro-dollar deposits may have gone through the hands of many intermediary debtors.

Foreign dollar bond issues in Europe are financed partly by means of borrowed Euro-dollars. They are acquired in many instances by holders of Euro-dollars. They are often issued in order to repay existing Euro-dollar debts or to avoid having to borrow Euro-dollars. In either case Euro-dollar rates are liable to be influenced by the extent to which Euro-dollars play an active or passive part in the transaction. They are also liable to be influenced to some extent by the issue terms of, or subsequent yield on, European dollar bonds.

In Britain the authorities encourage the use of Euro-dollars for financing the issue of dollar bonds, because it obviates the necessity of a temporary use of sterling for that purpose. Issuing houses and underwriters, being of high standing, can easily borrow Euro-dollars on favourable terms. For this reason alone, Euro-dollar rates are affected by the volume of dollar bond issues. If their flow is more or less continuous a certain amount of Euro-dollars is almost permanently employed in the temporary financing of each issue as they follow each other in close succession. If there is an interval between the issues or if their amount declines, repayments of the Euro-dollars borrowed will exceed new borrowing. If there is an increase in the volume of dollar bond issues the amount of new borrowing of Euro-dollars will exceed that of repayments.

There is reason to believe that subscribers to new bond issues include many lenders of Euro-dollar deposits, especially during periods when a decline of Euro-dollar rates is expected to take place in the long run. On the other hand, Euro-dollars are not likely to be borrowed systematically on a large scale for the purpose of permanent financing of investments in European dollar bonds. Even during periods when a decline in Euro-dollar rates is expected, the risk involved in such operations would deter most people.

Potential borrowers who have the choice between borrowing

Euro-dollars or issuing bonds do not decide exclusively according to the prevailing interest differential, or even according to the view they take of the future trend of interest rates. In many instances one form or the other is more convenient for other reasons. Nevertheless, the ups and down of interest rates on bonds do tend to affect the demand for Euro-dollars. Borrowers' decisions, once made, cannot be changed until they want to raise additional funds or re-finance maturing loans. Holders of Euro-dollar deposits, on the other hand, are in a position to decide to change over to bonds each time their deposits mature, whenever the differential between deposit rates and bond yields makes long-term lending appear to be to their advantage.

The issue of European dollar bonds tends to cause a rise in Euro-dollar rates in the following circumstances :

(1) If the volume of Euro-dollars used for financing the new issues exceeds the repayments of Euro-dollars used for the financing of previous issues.

(2) If bonds offer high enough yields to tempt holders of deposits to risk immobilising their capital for longer periods.

(3) If on the basis of the views holders of deposits take about prospects of interest rates they expect a capital appreciation on bonds or a fall in Euro-dollar rates.

Issues of European dollar bonds tend to lower Euro-dollar rates in the following ways :

(1) By repayments of borrowed Euro-dollar deposits out of the proceeds of bond issues.

(2) By reduction of demand for Euro-dollars by borrowers who prefer to borrow through bond issues.

(3) By causing a decline in interest rates in New York as a result of diverting foreign borrowing from that market.

On balance an increase in issue of dollar bonds probably tends to cause a fall in Euro-dollar rates, in so far as the bond issues are additional to the amount of long-term capital that would have been lent by the U.S. in the absence of facilities for these bond issues. Although in 1969 Euro-dollar rates increased in spite of the decline in Euro-bond issues, this was because this factor was more than outweighed by other factors.

In my book on *The Euro-Bond Market* I attempt to examine in detail the question of the impact of dollar bond issues on the supply of Euro-dollar deposits. On the face of it, bond issues tend to reduce the turnover in the Euro-dollar market, because some deposits are immobilised through their temporary or permanent use for financing bond issues, and many deposits are repaid out of the proceeds. But I arrived at the conclusion that the resulting reduction in the supply need not be more than purely temporary so long as there is no reduction in the insistent demand for Euro-dollars. For if the contraction of the supply should raise Euro-dollar rates the market is likely to attract additional dollars into the Euro-dollar market.

From this point of view, as indeed from various other points of view, it is essential to bear in mind that there exists a very large volume of foreign-owned dollar assets which are not Euro-dollars but which are liable to be attracted into the Euro-dollar market by a rise in Euro-dollar rates. Apart from deposits, foreign holdings of U.S. Treasury bills and other short-term investments, and even of American long-term securities and direct investments, constitute potential sources of Euro-dollars.

Euro-dollar rates and the turnover are liable to be affected by the issue of foreign bonds in Europe in terms of foreign currencies other than the dollar in substantially the same way as they are liable to be affected through the issue of dollar bonds.

European dollar loans are often referred to as ' Euro-dollar loans '. This is entirely unjustified. As I pointed out in Chapter 1, such loans can also be paid for through buying ordinary dollars or investment dollars.

CHAPTER 16

THE ECONOMIC CONSEQUENCES OF
EURO-DOLLARS

HAVING examined the impact of the market in foreign currency deposits on exchange rates, national interest rates and
the supply of credit, and the resulting attitude of Central Banks
towards Euro-dollars, there remains to be considered the main
question — whether on balance the changes brought by the
new device are in the right direction or in the wrong direction.
Accordingly we have to try to sum up the economic consequences of Euro-dollars and to arrive at a conclusion whether
their advent is for better or for worse. We must try to make up
our minds whether or not its unquestionable advantages are
outweighed by its equally unquestionable disadvantages, and
whether the balance, if any, in its favour is sufficient to outweigh the risk of an aggravation of the disadvantages as a result
of some acute crisis.

The following are the main changes that the operation of
the system produced in the economies of the countries directly
concerned and in world finance :

(1) The Euro-dollar market has produced a structure of
international interest rates distinct from, and largely
independent of, the national interest rate structures.

(2) It makes for a more even international allocation of
financial resources.

(3) It tends to reduce discrepancies between the levels of
national interest rates in various countries.

(4) In normal conditions it assists towards overcoming the
disadvantages of inadequate international liquidity.

(5) It technically facilitates foreign short-term lending and
borrowing.

(6) It provides opportunities for lending and borrowing in

those currencies in those markets in which it is possible on the most favourable terms.

(7) It has made the levels of national interest rates more dependent on international influences, and therefore more interdependent.

(8) It tends to eliminate artificially rigid terms for loans and deposits by providing means for their circumvention.

(9) It reduces profit margins between deposit rates and lending rates.

(10) It increases the volume of funds available for arbitrage.

(11) It provides additional inducements for international movements of funds through arbitrage.

(12) It facilitates monetary expansion by means of duplicating the use of the same deposits.

(13) It increases the velocity of circulation of deposits by transferring idle deposits to those more willing to make active use of them.

(14) It tends to stimulate international monetary co-operation.

(15) It tends to mitigate the restrictive effects of exchange control.

(16) It tends to mitigate discrepancies between interest rates on credits for various maturity dates.

(17) It creates a wider variety of short-term investment facilities.

(18) It provides means for spreading the risk involved in lending abroad and for specialising in the risk the lender is willing to assume.

(19) It provides monetary authorities with a new device for influencing the international flow of funds.

(20) It tends to mitigate the discrepancies between forward rates and their interest parities.

(21) By increasing the range of interest parities it reduces the possibility of achieving and maintaining equilibrium between forward rates and all interest parities.

(22) It creates an additional technical device for speculation in exchanges.

(23) It provides additional liquid resources easily available for speculation and gold-hoarding.

(24) It increases medium-term credit facilities and bridges the gaps between short credits and long-term loans.

(25) By creating additional uses for dollars it increases the inducement for retaining liquid resources in the form of dollars.

(26) It tends to increase the potential instability of the inverted pyramid of international credit structure.

(27) It tends to increase commercial credit risk assumed by banks, and also the risk of the possibility of exchange control.

(28) It increases temptation for banks and business firms to over-trade.

(29) It provides facilities and temptation for lending for long-term against borrowing for short-term.

(30) While in normal times it tends to increase international liquidity, in times of crisis it is liable to produce the opposite effect.

(31) It weakens discipline within banking communities, and is apt to lead to excessive reduction of profit margins.

(32) It weakens the power of monetary authorities to make conventional monetary policies effective.

(33) It has inspired the creation of the inter-bank sterling market which provides additional facilities for banks to lend cash out without security.

(34) It exposes economies to shocks of sudden large-scale withdrawal of credits.

(35) It provides a channel through which Communist governments can borrow on a large scale.

(36) It provides these governments with a means for causing or aggravating any crisis.

All the above points were covered in detail in the foregoing chapters, and I propose to confine myself here to some general observations in an attempt to weigh the relative advantages and disadvantages of the system.

The development of a system of international interest rates which are in a large measure independent of domestic interest rates is a structural economic change, the fundamental importance of which has not been adequately realised. All theories of monetary policy assume the essentially national character of interest rates, and on the basis of this assumption they take it for granted that the interest structure is controlled by the national monetary authorities in each country. The new situation created through the appearance of international interest rates calls for a re-examination of the operation of the whole monetary system and for a far-reaching re-thinking of monetary theories and policies. It may take some time before experience would enable us to appreciate the full significance of this fundamental change, and to assess the definite balance sheet of its advantages and disadvantages.

The more even allocation of liquid financial resources is beyond doubt in accordance with the interests of mankind. Three of the world's leading countries, gravely handicapped by a scarcity of liquid resources, were enabled by the new facilities to recover from their post-war difficulties and achieve spectacular progress leading to far-reaching adjustments in the international economic balance of power. Under-developed countries, too, can be financed extensively with the aid of resources raised in the Euro-dollar market. This is done in Latin America, also in India. Apart from the use of Euro-dollars for assisting in the progress towards levelling out fundamental discrepancies in the allocation of financial resources, they can be used also for levelling out temporary discrepancies in balances of payments, and even more temporary discrepancies due to seasonal and other fluctuations in money market or foreign exchange market requirements.

The international re-allocation of liquid resources tends to reduce discrepancies between levels of domestic interest rates resulting from an international maldistribution of capital. Moreover, international interest rates quoted in markets for foreign currency deposits compete with domestic interest rates, and the fact that borrowers have a freer choice to borrow in the cheapest market and in terms of any major currency is bound to affect national interest rates in countries where interest rates are high for lack of adequate capital resources.

Where discrepancies between levels of domestic interest rates are due not to an international maldistribution of capital, but to buying or selling pressures on currencies, the operation of the Euro-currency system does not tend to restore equilibrium but tends to widen the abnormal discrepancies. It produces this effect by providing additional facilities for speculation. For many non-resident holders of sterling, for instance, who do not wish to sell their holdings during a sterling scare, are tempted by high Euro-sterling rates to lend their sterling to speculators. In 1965 and in 1969 heavy borrowing of Euro-sterling for the purpose of carrying forward short positions resulted in a sharp rise in Euro-sterling rates which, in turn, caused a more moderate but none the less substantial rise in rates for Local Authorities in London.

A great deal has been written in recent years about the inadequacy of gold and other international liquid resources to meet the growing requirements of international trade and finance. The additional resources provided by the Euro-dollar market have gone a long way towards meeting the deficiency, at any rate in normal conditions. Even though some of the facilities obtained through the Euro-dollar market simply replace facilities that would have been granted in dollars, sterling, or other currencies by American, British, and other local banks, to a large extent the new facilities are additional to the previously existing ones.

Euro-dollars facilitate international financing, owing to the technical simplicity of transactions in them. There are obvious advantages to borrowers to be able to conclude credit transactions in a matter of minutes instead of having to engage in lengthy and often difficult negotiations — during the course of which many questions are asked and rigid terms are insisted upon. The advantage of the Euro-dollar market is that it enables banks of first-class standing to raise large amounts as a matter of routine with the least possible delay. The other side of the picture is that the ease with which credits can be raised and renewed in normal conditions is liable to encourage excessive borrowing.

The above remarks apply also to the inter-bank market in sterling which owes its existence largely to the inspiring example of the Euro-dollar system. London banks, having acquired

the habit of lending each other unsecured foreign currency
deposits, came to apply the practice to sterling deposits.
During the middle 'sixties such deposits came to be lent and
borrowed on a very large scale. During the abnormal conditions caused by the rise in Euro-sterling rates during sterling
scares, the turnover in inter-bank sterling assumed spectacular
dimensions, running into many hundreds of millions of pounds
on a single day. This new device has much to recommend it.
Although its extensive application does entail increased risks,
this market, even more than the Euro-currency market, is confined to dealings between banks of very high standing. The
fact that it is confined to one market reduces the possibility
of over-borrowing, which is an ever-present risk in the case of
Euro-currencies that can be borrowed simultaneously in half a
dozen markets.

Dealing in Euro-currencies entails the transfer of liquid financial resources from holders reluctant to take risks on foreign
credits beyond a certain limit to holders willing to take such
risks. It spreads the risk among a larger number of banks. As
Altman pointed out, the Euro-dollar system enables various
banks to assume specific kinds of risks attached to international financing while leaving it to other banks to assume
other types of risks. The overall risk is reduced through this
specialisation, and also because European banks are more
familiar with the credit rating of European borrowers.

Thanks to the market in Euro-dollars and other foreign
currency deposits, borrowers can now borrow in terms of
currencies in which their loan operations are the cheapest or the
most convenient. Although in the past they had been in a position to borrow in foreign currencies, the new facilities present
obvious advantages. National interest rates for loans in foreign
currencies are very often not so advantageous as international
interest rates obtainable by borrowers in those currencies outside the countries in whose currencies they borrow.

Because of this competition of international interest rates,
domestic interest rates have become more interdependent of
each other. In the past the compensation of interest rate discrepancies by forward rates tended to perpetuate and accentuate

the gross differentials rather than reduce them. On the other hand, the Euro-dollar market tends to influence domestic interest structures by attracting funds to markets with high interest rates, thereby reducing the gross differential between them.

Markets in foreign currency deposits owe their existence and expansion largely to artificial situations created by interference with normal trends of interest rates by governments or bank cartel arrangements. One of the main effects of the new device is a circumvention of the rigid statutory, monopolistic, or conventional artificial interest rates. Normal market influences are now given a better chance to produce their effect and to operate the free interplay of the market mechanism. There is now an active market in loanable funds, in which fractional changes in supply-demand relationship are immediately expressed in fractional changes of rates.

The competitive character of the Euro-dollar market has reduced the banks' profit margins between their deposit rates and lending rates, as far as large transactions are concerned. Their overhead expenses are, proportionately, incomparably lower on large transactions than on the multitude of small transactions for whose sake they have to employ large staffs. It was not until the advent of the Euro-dollar market that a method has been devised to discriminate adequately between large and small transactions by reducing profit margins in favour of the former. This change admittedly increases the unfair disadvantages of smaller firms, but it is arguable that from a purely economic point of view this is an advantage, at any rate in spheres in which large size makes for a higher degree of efficiency.

Competition also induced banks to be more adaptable in their terms to the requirements of their customers. Hitherto, they were inclined in each country to lay down their hard-and-fast rules to which their customers had to adapt themselves willy-nilly. Now that they have to contend with competition of foreign banks they feel impelled to make allowances to their customers' requirements. In Chapter 3 I quoted the instance of the rule enforced by American banks that borrowers are to retain on current account some 20 per cent of the amount lent to them. As no such rule exists in London or in some other centres, American banks relax in given circumstances their rule rather than lose clients who can borrow Euro-dollars without submitting to that rule.

Another way in which abnormal discrepancies are kept within bounds is through the provision of large additional resources available for arbitrage. The main reason why lasting and substantial discrepancies are liable to arise is that the resources available for arbitrageurs are not sufficient to take full advantage of profit possibilities arising from discrepancies. The operation of the interest parity theory can only continue so long as there are arbitrage funds available. Thanks to the Euro-dollar market such resources have been greatly expanded and are less likely to become exhausted before the discrepancies are removed. This goes some way towards mitigating frictional discrepancies. It must be borne in mind, however, that in given circumstances an increased volume of arbitrage can produce disequilibrating effects.

The new system has resulted in a considerable increase in the velocity of circulation of deposits. Formerly idle deposits — that is, dollar deposits whose owners left the fund idle with American banks, leaving it to the latter to make active use of the funds — have become converted into active deposits. Moreover, owing to the peculiarity of modern banking systems the American banking system as a whole is not deprived of the use of the deposits by the fact that they are now employed more actively by their new holders.

The duplication of the use of the same deposit provides the means for considerable additional credit expansion. By transferring funds from countries where there is plenty to countries where there is not enough, without reducing thereby the resources of the lending country, the international grand total of credits is increased.

The system goes a long way towards making expert and official opinion realise the full extent of the interdependence of national monetary policies. It is now widely realised that monetary policies of sovereign states are liable to react on each other and that their co-ordination is to the interest of every country. The Euro-dollar market provides an inducement as well as a means for international monetary co-operation.

During the late 'sixties there has been some evidence of concerted action by the monetary authorities of the countries whose currencies are used in Euro-currency markets to influence the trend in those markets, beyond efforts that have been made to co-ordinate statistical and other information relating to the subject. There is much scope, however, for more co-ordinated intervention on lines similar to those of interventions to influence forward exchanges. The Bank for International Settlements, by its increasingly frequent intervention during 1968–69, has prepared the ground for future developments in that direction.

Most exchange restrictions on movements of short-term funds belonging to non-residents have been removed, and the markets in foreign currency deposits tend to mitigate the restrictive effects of those that are still in force. This, of course, is to the disadvantage of countries trying to protect their exchanges through maintaining exchange restrictions which are now more easily circumvented than before.

Owing to the incessant flow of time arbitrage in the Euro-dollar market discrepancies between interest rates for short and long periods tend to be evened out. Precisely because more funds are available for time arbitrage this is now done more effectively than in the past. Nevertheless, concentrated demand for, or supply of, certain maturities is apt to create wider discrepancies in given situations. In particular rates for very short maturities are liable to become grossly distorted.

The markets in foreign currency deposits have created a number of new interest parities that differ materially from those based on domestic interest rates. Since the forward rate for a given maturity can only be at equilibrium with one interest parity, this multiplication of interest parities is bound to provide additional possibilities for arbitrage, leading to additional movements of short-term funds. 'Hot money' has increased in volume, also — to carry the popular metaphor further — in temperature. This is, however, a price that has to be paid for the tendency of levelling out discrepancies between national interest rates.

The Euro-dollar market has created additional opportunities not only for arbitrage but also for speculation. Hitherto, speculators had to choose between operating in forward exchanges or borrowing from the country whose currency was under attack. Now they have a third alternative. They also have additional facilities for financing speculation in gold and hoarding of gold.

The markets in foreign currency deposits provide not only the technical device for speculation but also the additional means for it. There are billions of Euro-dollars and of other foreign currency deposits that are available, or can be made available at short notice, for that purpose. The system helps speculators to overcome the reluctance of banks to finance them in their effort to go short in a currency under attack. The extent to which this is liable to aggravate selling pressure on a currency was illustrated by the experience of the sterling-scares in 1964–69. Short positions in sterling were created or renewed to a very large extent with the aid of borrowed Euro-sterling. The high interest rates that speculators were prepared to pay on Euro-sterling borrowed for very short periods must have increased considerably the amount of foreign-owned sterling lent to that market and must have greatly weakened the effect of the official ban on British credits granted for that purpose. The development of this new practice which has drawn upon hitherto untapped resources went a long way towards upsetting the confident calculations of the British monetary authorities who had relied upon buying pressure on sterling resulting from bear covering on various occasions when speculative forward sales of sterling were expected to be covered as the forward contracts were due to mature.

Another point against the new system is that it tends to increase the vulnerability of the international credit structure. This would be, however, broadly speaking, the effect of any expansion of international liquidity unless based on an increase in the volume of monetary gold supplies, whether through an increase of output, de-hoarding, or a writing up of the monetary value of gold through devaluation. The increase of liquid resources through the operation of markets in foreign currency deposits does not entail greater economic risks, as distinct from commercial risks, than the creation of fictitious international liquid resources by means of the new device of Special Drawing Rights.

The expansion of international resources through the Euro-dollar system differs from expansion that is expected to result from the extended application of S.D.R.s., in that it increases the extent of commercial risk and also the risk of default as a result of new exchange restrictions. Such risks are increased by the repeated re-lending of the same Euro-dollar deposit which creates a chain of debtors often extending over a number of countries.

Because of the ease with which banks can add to their resources by means of borrowing in the Euro-dollar market that device offers to banks additional temptation and additional opportunities for over-trading. Business firms, too, finding it easier to borrow in several markets and in several currencies, might be tempted to over-trade. The ease with which maturing short-term deposits can be renewed as a matter of form makes it tempting for borrowers to re-lend them for long-term.

Should a crisis arise in a country with heavy Euro-dollar debts there would be wholesale withdrawals of funds from the Euro-dollar market. This would aggravate conditions within the economy affected ; it might even disturb the entire international monetary structure and would constitute an additional strain on liquid resources. It might lead to a repetition of the crisis of 1931.

The amazing degree of complacency that prevails on this subject is strikingly illustrated by the remarks of Mr. Henry N. Goldstein in his review of the first edition of this book, appearing in the *Journal of Finance*. He dismisses my warning about the possible repercussions to the adoption of exchange restrictions in any one of the borrowing countries that forms part of a chain of borrowers, on the ground that, since some of the biggest banks are among those who borrow and re-lend Euro-dollars, the existence of a chain of intermediaries between the

original lender and the ultimate borrower actually increases the
degree of security for the benefit of the former.

If this view were correct it would be very difficult to explain
the well-known fact that American bank branches in London
are often able to borrow Euro-dollars at rates that are fractionally lower even than those paid by first-class British or
other Western European banks. American banks are at an
advantage precisely because in their case it is inconceivable
that the dollars required for the repayment of maturing
deposits should ever become unavailable.

That European banks of equally high standing are not
deemed to be in the same happy position is shown by the stern
warning issued by the Bank of France after the Stinnes Bank's
difficulties. Incensed by the extent to which one of the leading
French banks was involved, the Bank of France warned all
French banks not to take it for granted that permit for the
replacement of Euro-dollars lost through a default of their
debtors would necessarily be granted. This incident should
provide a reminder that, no matter how sound an intermediary bank may be, it is possible and advisable to envisage
situations in which it might be prevented by exchange restrictions from meeting its Euro-dollar commitments if its Euro-
dollar debtor should default.

This danger is duly realised in banking circles. Hence the
attempt of the International Forex Club — an association of
the local group of foreign exchange dealers in the principal
countries — to elaborate rules concerning the clearing of commitments that might become frozen as a result of some major
international crisis. Even if losses resulting from isolated bank-
ruptcies could be shrugged off, it would be unwise to be com-
placent about the very real if remote possibility of wholesale
default by all debtors in one of the countries which have
borrowed a high proportion of Euro-currency deposits. Such a
default might have easily occurred during recent years when
lenders of Euro-dollars placed too many eggs in the same
national baskets by lending freely to first-class banks of the
countries concerned. The fact that successful efforts have been
made by the Bank for International Settlements to collect and

co-ordinate national statistics about Euro-currency commitments specified according to the borrowers' countries shows that the monetary authorities at any rate are alive to the risk even if Mr. Goldstein is blissfully oblivious of its existence.

Owing to its highly competitive character, the new system tends to reduce co-operation and increase cut-throat competition within banking communities. Although this was quoted above as an advantage from the point of view of an increase in the flexibility of terms to depositors and borrowers, it is not without disadvantages. An excessive reduction of profit margins, which are necessary to enable banks to fulfil their constructive function, is not to the public interest. From this point of view the reversal of the tendency towards excessive reduction of margins, following on the losses suffered in 1963, was a change for the better.

What is much more important, Central Banks and Treasuries find that they are less favourably placed in imposing their policies on the banking community. As the banks are able to secure additional resources they do not depend to the same extent on the goodwill of their Central Banks and are at times tempted to disregard or circumvent the latter's policies. As a result, official monetary policies are apt to be less effective.

Since banks of Communist countries are able to borrow on a large scale in the Euro-dollar market they are able to contract a large short-term indebtedness in the Western countries. This possibility carries considerable disadvantages. Apart from assisting the Communist bloc in competing successfully against the free world, it enables Communist governments to aggravate and even initiate at a suitable moment a major crisis by suspending the repayment of such credits. Likewise, by accumulating large amounts of dollars concealed behind the façade of Euro-dollar deposits, they are able to accentuate any selling pressure on the dollar that is liable to develop at a time of a major political crisis.

In spite of all these dangerous possibilities, the conclusion that seems to emerge from the above balance sheet is that, pending the acquisition of further experience, the advantages appear to outweigh the disadvantages by a fair margin. In any case it is well worth remembering that anything that contributes towards increasing prosperity tends to increase the risk of a relapse. An economist once observed that the main cause of economic crises is prosperity. It would be a sad day for mankind if it were ever to decide to renounce progress for the sake of avoiding the risk attached to it.

Once this is admitted the only question to decide is whether progress that may reasonably be expected to result from the new system is likely to be an adequate compensation for the long-term disadvantages it entails and the unknown extent of the risk it involves. Time alone can give the definite answer. So far we are only familiar with the operation of the system in fair weather. Even so, the results which have already been achieved are substantial and their extent justifies the taking of further risk — within reason.

A limitation of the degree of risk has been achieved by the more cautious attitude adopted by most banks in lending Euro-currencies, also by the more active interest taken by the monetary authorities in the operation of the system. There is, however, scope for improvement in both directions.

CHAPTER 17

AMERICAN BORROWING OF EURO-DOLLARS

ALTHOUGH frequent reference has been made throughout this book to the role of American banks as borrowers in the Euro-dollar market on a large and increasing scale, the accelerated increase in the volume of their borrowing operations in the late 'sixties makes it necessary to deal with the subject in greater detail. The changes brought about by that increase were not merely a matter of degree. The greatly increased amount of American borrowing of Euro-dollars and the increased importance of its effects has created a new situation which calls for a closer examination.

The increase in American borrowing operations and the resulting expansion in the volume of Euro-dollars has far exceeded all expectations. Although I have always believed in the immense possibilities of the new device, I must admit that I had not expected such a degree of expansion until much later, and I had expected it to be much more gradual. My explanation, if not excuse, is that the acceleration of the growth in the volume of Euro-dollars has not been a logical result of tendencies inherent in the Euro-dollar system. It has been the result of an unpredictable inconsistency in the monetary policy of the United States authorities. While it may be possible to foresee reasonable and logical official measures and predict their effects, when it comes to muddle-headed measures utterly divorced from logic and common sense there is no possibility even for guessing them in advance.

The speeding-up of the expansion in the volume of Euro-dollars and the accompanying steep rise in Euro-dollar rates through the greatly increased amount of American borrowing was admittedly due to some extent, at any rate in its earlier phases, to policy measures logically arising from the situation created by the balance of payments deficit of the United States. But in its later stages its acceleration was the result of sheer incompetence.

The following is a list of the causes, predictable or otherwise, which were responsible for this unexpected development:

(1) President Johnson's measures to strengthen the balance of payments of the United States by inducing American firms to cover abroad the credit requirements of their foreign branches and affiliates.

(2) President Johnson's measures inducing American banks to finance credits to non-residents by means of funds borrowed abroad.

(3) Realisation by American banks of the necessity to defend their deposits from being depleted through the borrowing of Euro-dollars by other American banks.

(4) The discovery of the advantages of covering even purely domestic credit requirements with the aid of borrowed Euro-dollars.

(5) The accentuation of the domestic credit squeeze in the United States in 1968–69 which increased the extent to which the American banks endeavoured to cover their domestic requirements in the Euro-dollar market.

(6) The increased popularity of dollar Certificates of Deposits issued in London by American banks.

(7) The policy of expanding industrial interests abroad financed with the aid of capital and credits raised abroad.

(8) The increased use of borrowed Euro-dollars for speculative buying of D. marks.

President Johnson's guidelines, which were reinforced in stages and were eventually given statutory power in 1968, required foreign branches and subsidiaries of American corporations to finance their credit requirements outside the United States. At the same time lending by American firms in the Euro-dollar market became restricted. The result was that the United States gradually became the largest borrower of Euro-dollars.

Originally the measures aimed at discouraging the American banks from granting conventional credits to foreign borrowers were confined to credits in excess of twelve months. Later they were extended to shorter maturities.

American banks realised that, unless they became active borrowers of Euro-dollars, borrowing of Euro-dollars by other American banks was liable to deplete their deposits. This aspect of the subject was already mentioned in Chapter 7. Growing realisation of the need for defending their deposits, and the growing desire to show an increase in their resources at the expense of their rivals, resulted in the creation of a large number of American bank branches in London with the main purpose of gaining direct access to the Euro-dollar market. The cost of running such branches is considerable, especially as expert staffs have to be attracted from British banks by paying much higher salaries. But American banks deem it worth while for the sake of the advantages of direct access to the London Euro-dollar market.

In due course American banks came increasingly to realise the advantages of being able to increase their credit resources for domestic purposes by borrowing in the Euro-dollar market. At first such borrowing aimed mainly at tiding them over brief periods of tight money. Later, American banks drifted into the habit of using the Euro-dollar market also for providing funds for the domestic requirements of their customers. This practice was encouraged by the fact that dollar deposits borrowed from branches abroad were not subject to reserve requirements. Nor were they subject to Regulation Q, so that American banks were able to attract additional deposits by paying higher deposit rates than those allowed under Regulation Q. Above all, they attracted deposits up to 30 days on which they are not permitted to pay interest to U.S. residents.

The use of the device of covering domestic requirements in the Euro-dollar market through borrowing from branches abroad increased considerably as a result of the reinforcement of the credit squeeze in the United States towards the end of 1968 and during 1969. The efforts of head offices of American banks to satisfy the requirements of their customers led to Euro-dollar operations in London on a really large scale. London branches of American banks came to borrow considerable amounts systematically, and American banks without London branches borrowed through their London correspondents. The amount of individual transactions increased to a multiple of their former standard amounts. Until 1968 transactions of $10 million, or even smaller amounts, were a matter of negotiation. By 1969 it became possible to transact items of $100 million and more. The largest single item I have come across was $150 million. As a result it became well worth while for banks operating in the Euro-dollar market to reduce their profit margins for the sake of participating in transactions of such amounts.

The increasing popularity of London Dollar Certificates of Deposits provided American banks with additional opportunities for borrowing Euro-dollars, especially when it became practicable to issue such certificates for periods exceeding twelve months. Although non-American banks are also active in this market, London branches of American banks have the lion's share of it.

What is much more important is that the policy of expanding abroad pursued by American industries — with the full approval of the United States Government in so far as it does not result in additional pressure on the dollar — continued unabated during 1968–69. American industrial concerns are permitted to acquire foreign firms or to establish branches or affiliates abroad, provided that the operations are financed abroad. Although the capital required for the purpose is raised mostly through the issue of Euro-bonds, the resulting current credit requirements are covered to a large degree through the intermediary of American bank branches or of other banks, through borrowing Euro-dollars.

During periods of dollar scares Euro-dollars were borrowed for the sake of speculating against the dollar by selling the proceeds. The same practice was also pursued during periods of speculative buying of D. marks in anticipation of a revaluation. Banks from every country took an active hand in such operations, and American banks themselves did not keep aloof from them.

The combined effect of these influences was an expansion of

the Euro-dollar market at an accelerating rate. The total amount of Euro-dollars was estimated to have risen to around $34 billion by the middle of 1969, and practically the whole of the increase was borrowed by the United States. Although even borrowing on such a scale represented a relatively small fraction of the total volume of domestic credit the ' syphoning ' of deposits by borrowers from other American banks forced the latter to draw more extensively on other domestic resources. This reduced the effectiveness of the credit squeeze pursued by the United States authorities in an effort to protect their reserves against the effect of the adverse current balance of payments. Monetary measures to resist the expanding trend of credit were adopted with the utmost reluctance. The opponents of such measures were able to secure the maintenance of loopholes through which it was possible to mitigate the credit stringency by borrowing Euro-dollars.

The policy pursued by the United States authorities in permitting American borrowing of Euro-dollars to continue was absurdly self-contradictory. On the one hand they aimed at improving the balance of payments by curtailing the volume of credit. On the other hand they abstained completely right until June 1969 from any action that would have weakened the influx of Euro-dollars, an influx which went some way towards frustrating their policy of credit squeeze.

The explanation of the strong resistance to the adoption of effective measures is probably the official desire to reduce the volume of dollars abroad which their non-resident owners might sell otherwise, thereby increasing selling pressure on the dollar. If such dollars were bought by local Central Banks in order to prevent an appreciation of their currencies above maximum support point, the resulting increase in their dollar reserve might induce them to replace their dollars by means of purchases of gold in the open market.

Although American borrowing of Euro-dollars may appear therefore convenient to the United States authorities, it produced highly disadvantageous effects in the international sphere. American borrowing mopped up a large proportion of the Euro-dollar supplies and forced up the Euro-dollar rates to over

12 per cent for three months' deposits by the middle of 1969. The result was an all-round increase in interest rates throughout the free world, to unprecedented levels. Bank rate increases followed each other in close succession.

High interest rates meant heavy falls in government loans and other fixed-interest-bearing securities, inflicting heavy losses upon investors. There was a sharp setback in the Euro-bond market. This was most disappointing, because the remarkable expansion of Euro-bond issuing activity during 1968, and the increasing amounts of such bonds taken up by German investors, had given rise to hopes that it might be possible to consolidate the excessive volume of international floating debts and to improve the official reserves of deficit countries. This setback in Euro-bond issues also delayed the financing of a great many productive schemes of public-works industrial expansion.

In order to mitigate the effect of American borrowing on interest rates, the B.I.S. increased the extent of its intervention in the Euro-dollar market during 1969. It lent Euro-dollars on a large scale, partly with the aid of Euro-dollars which many Central Banks were anxious to lend for the sake of the tempting yield, but largely through acquiring dollars from the Federal Reserve for the purpose. To that end it made increased use of its swap arrangement with the Federal Reserve. To a very large extent the dollars lent by the B.I.S. to the Euro-dollar market were provided by the Federal Reserve. A vicious circle thus came to be created. Dollars borrowed by American banks from the Euro-dollar market were re-lent by the Federal Reserve to the Euro-dollar market through the intermediary of the B.I.S. The resulting increase in the supply of Euro-dollars — to be precise, the replacement of the supplies borrowed by American banks — enabled American banks to borrow even more.

Largely as a result of this intervention by the B.I.S., interest rates in the Euro-dollar market declined to below 10 per cent for some time after June. This provided some degree of relief to countries by mitigating the internationally rising trend of interest rates. On the other hand it tended to encourage American borrowing, which might otherwise have become discouraged by prohibitive interest rates. It is no wonder that the half-hearted measures adopted by the Federal Reserve failed to produce the effects they were aimed at. And later other ill-advised measures raised the rate once more.

One of the disadvantages of the expansion in the volume of Euro-dollars resulting from increased borrowing by American banks from an intervention by the B.I.S. was that it increased the potential amount available for going short in dollars or for going long in D. marks. Admittedly there was no danger of a run on the dollar during the period of accelerated increase in American borrowing of Euro-dollars. The technical position of the dollar became stronger in 1968–69 through an increase of the gold reserve. There was also a demand for dollars in the foreign exchange market for the purpose of lending them in the Euro-dollar market. The rise in the price of gold came to a halt and became reversed to a considerable extent. Exchange controls in the United States, though far from fully effective, went some way towards reducing the selling of dollars on capital account. But even in the absence of any acute danger of dollar scares, the possibility of increased selling pressure resulting from the increased volume of Euro-dollars ought to be borne in mind, even allowing for the amount re-borrowed.

Was it really necessary to assume such a risk in addition to weakening the effect of the credit squeeze and inflicting hardship on other countries? If the United States authorities did not wish the credit squeeze to produce its full effect on American business conditions, it would have been a simple matter for them to mitigate the extent of their domestic squeeze instead of allowing it to be mitigated by an influx of Euro-dollars.

The self-contradictory policy of allowing the credit squeeze to be partly neutralised by permitting American banks to circumvent it on a large scale carries some very obvious disadvantages. For one thing it reduces the extent to which the credit squeeze will lead to an improvement of the American balance of payments.

The direct effect of borrowing Euro-dollars on a large scale was that the extent to which the credit squeeze tended to reduce or keep down domestic consumer demand was less than it would have been in the absence of an increase of such borrowing. Its indirect effect was that the sharp rise in interest rates abroad tended to reduce or keep down domestic consumer demand in other countries, so that the balance of payments of the United States could not derive unilateral benefit from the American deflationary policy. Yet without an elimination of the American deficit there can be no hope for a consolidation of the international monetary situation.

What is perhaps even worse, the sharp world-wide rise in interest rates means a danger of a world-wide slump. There must surely be a limit beyond which producers and merchants all over the world would cease to be prepared to finance their activities with the aid of money borrowed at 10 per cent and more. The moment they begin to fear that they might not be able to pass on the increased costs of financing to buyers of their goods, they would feel impelled to curtail their production or their purchases. This might result in a disastrous all-round setback in production and trade.

It is in the vital interest of the United States and the rest of the free world that such a setback should be avoided. The upward trend of interest rates could, of course, be reversed by a sensible re-alignment of parities involving a drastic increase in the official price of gold. But even in the absence of such far-reaching measures the upward trend could and should be reversed with the aid of measures preventing further American borrowing of Euro-dollars and enforcing a repayment of a large proportion of the Euro-dollars borrowed by American banks. In the absence of some such measures the free world is exposed to grave immediate inconveniences and to incalculable future dangers.

To avoid misunderstanding, let me repeat once more that the American borrowing of Euro-dollars does not increase directly the volume of deposits in the United States. It merely reallocates the deposits amongst American banks. But American banks which do not borrow Euro-dollars and which lose deposits as a result of borrowing Euro-dollars by other American banks are usually in a position to make good their deficiency to a considerable extent. The net effect of the exercise is therefore a reduction of the effectiveness of the credit squeeze in the United States.

CHAPTER 18

FUTURE OF THE EURO-DOLLAR SYSTEM

As I pointed out in the introductory chapter, expert opinion was until recently divided on the prospects of Euro-currency deposits. Many quarters firmly believed that the system had come to stay and that, apart from inevitable temporary ups and downs in its turnover, it was bound to expand further in the long run. It was assumed that its institutional expansion was more or less complete, but that there was nevertheless ample scope for more gradual expansion in sympathy with the trend of economic growth in general, and with the expansion of international trade and finance in particular. But in other quarters the opposite view was held with equal firmness. They were convinced that the new device was purely temporary and that, as soon as the set of largely accidental circumstances which have been responsible for its appearance and its expansion ceased to operate, the whole system would disappear. Or at any rate it would cease to play the part of a major influence in the foreign exchange market and in the credit system.

Ever since the Euro-dollar system emerged from its infancy there have always been prophets predicting its early demise. But, instead of disappearing, it has been going from strength to strength throughout the late 'fifties and the 'sixties. On repeated occasions it had its setbacks, but each one of them was followed by a revival of its activities which reached new peak levels after each temporary relapse. Notwithstanding this experience, many experts — bankers, financial editors, and Treasury and Central Bank officials — persisted until recently in their firm conviction that sooner or later the volume of Euro-dollars would decline to a fraction of its present figure. They based their opinion on one or several of the following anticipations :

(1) Higher deposit rates in the United States as a result of a repeal or further relaxation of Regulation Q.

(2) Higher national interest rates in the United States, due to a policy of dear money.

(3) Lower special lending rates to big customers in order to retain or regain the business lost to the Euro-dollar market.

(4) Decline of interest rates in London, making sterling acceptance credits cheaper than Euro-dollar deposits.

(5) Abolition of the gentlemen's agreement among London banks that would enable London deposit rates to compete with Euro-dollar rates.

(6) Removal of the remaining British exchange restrictions on financing foreign trade.

(7) Contraction of interest differentials between London and New York to an extent that would not leave an adequate margin for the market to operate profitably.

(8) A substantial improvement of the American balance of payments that would reduce the amount of dollars available for the market.

(9) Reduction of American export of capital and repatriation of American capital abroad, leading to a scarcity of dollars.

(10) Conversion of official dollar balances into gold.

(11) A substantial deterioration of the American balance of payments that would inspire distrust in the dollar and would cause the withdrawal of a large proportion of foreign dollar balances.

(12) A financial crisis that would frighten the majority of depositors into withdrawing from the market and keeping aloof from it.

Euro-sterling, too, was predicted to disappear, mainly as a result of a termination of the gentlemen's agreement and the removal of the remaining exchange control in Britain. As for the market in Swiss franc deposits and in D. mark deposits, they were predicted to disappear as soon as the Swiss and

West German authorities gave up their efforts to keep out unwanted 'hot money' by means of restricting interest payment on foreign funds.

In fact there is much more to the system than was assumed by those who regarded it as being a purely temporary outcome of fortuitous circumstances. What they failed to realise is that it fulfils very important requirements and that its development is in keeping with the basic trend of progress. The international integration of the money markets, the elimination or reduction of rigidities in deposit rates and loan rates, the circumvention of artificial obstacles, the freeing of competition between lenders, and the improvement of the automatic functioning of market-mechanism, had long been overdue. What is strange is not that it arose and developed during the late 'fifties but that it had not come into being many years earlier.

The foregoing chapters show that the Euro-dollar system is the answer to many problems. They lead to the conclusion that if it were not already in existence it ought to be invented. Having brought the system into existence, the international banking community is not likely to abandon it lightly. It is, of course, easy to imagine circumstances in which the turnover in foreign currency deposits might suddenly or gradually contract temporarily to a fraction of its volume attained in the middle 'sixties. But no change in the situation could conceivably deprive the City and other banking communities of the know-how they have acquired. They are now thoroughly familiar with the operation of the new system and they appreciate its advantages. Should changes in the circumstances cause a sharp contraction in the volume of deposits available in the market they would doubtless await the opportunity for expanding it once more.

The system has become familiar and popular among Central Banks and Treasury officials, bankers, merchants, and investors all over the world. Most of them are very keen on maintaining it. The difficulty had been to establish the system. Once it had come into existence and had become a going concern, no extraordinary influences were needed for its maintenance in existence.

Needless to say, the mere fact that those operating the system wish to maintain it would not in itself ensure its continued existence, unless its facilities continued to offer tangible advantages to those in a position to avail themselves of them. The question is whether any of the causes listed above are likely to cancel the advantages the market offers to investors or borrowers and check or reverse the flow of dollars to the market, or divert the demand for dollar credits from the market.

(1) There is beyond doubt a possibility that the United States government might repeal Regulation Q altogether, having already exempted official foreign deposits from its provisions. Or the statutory limits of deposit rates on privately owned foreign deposits might be raised further. In that case the Euro-dollar market would simply have to bid higher rates in order to attract dollar deposits. This could be done, because many of the ultimate borrowers of funds lent in the Euro-dollar market are quite prepared to pay even higher interest rates than the rates prevailing in 1969, so that the market is well in a position to pay higher rates to depositors and still lend at a profit. In any case, if American banks were to pay higher deposit rates, they would also want to raise their lending rates, so that they would not be in a much better position to compete with the Euro-dollar market for foreign business than they are now.

(2) The same argument would apply to a situation in which Euro-dollar rates would rise in consequence of a stiffening of national interest rates on credits in the United States as a result of a policy of dear money. Such a policy failed to affect the market in the 'sixties.

(3) Conceivably, American banks, in order to retain their big customers, might drastically reduce their profit margins for the benefit of favoured big customers who would be able to borrow well below the standard lending rate. This is actually happening already to some extent, but, in order to be able to compete with the Euro-dollar market, American banks would have to make

much more drastic reductions. Since they would be
unable to confine such concessions to the firms who
have actually borrowed in the Euro-dollar market but
would have to extend them under pressure to a widening
circle of borrowers who could conceivably borrow in
that market, the cost would be too high to make it
worth while.

(4) Admittedly, a decline of interest rates in London would
reduce the cost of sterling acceptance credits, and this
might induce many foreign borrowers to revert to that
method of financing. But there are many important
types of operations at present financed with the aid of
Euro-dollars which could not conveniently be financed
with the aid of sterling acceptance credits, or of any
acceptance credits. A decline of demand for Euro-
dollars resulting from the diversion of business to
sterling acceptance credits would tend to reduce Euro-
dollar rates, which again would stimulate demand for
other purposes.

(5) The abolition of the gentlemen's agreement in Britain
might attract more deposits into sterling, but the
chances are that it would also mean higher lending rates,
so that it would not mean a fundamental difference to
the Euro-dollar market. In any case, the gentlemen's
agreement only affects clearing banks and London
branches of commercial banks. Other institutions are
already in competition with the Euro-dollar market
without being able to compete it out of existence.

(6) If a decline of deposit rates and lending rates in London
were to coincide with an increase of deposit rates and
lending rates in New York, the resulting contraction,
disappearance, or reversal of the interest differential
might make it more advantageous to borrow sterling —
provided that the cost of covering of the forward
exchange would not wipe out the benefit. In that case
there might be an increase in the demand for Euro-
sterling facilities, so that the relative part played by
sterling in the market for foreign currency deposits

would increase. But it would not mean the end of the system, it would only reduce — possibly temporarily — the predominant part played in it by Euro-dollars.

(7) There are at the time of writing still some restrictions on British credits to finance foreign trade. Foremost amongst them is the ban imposed in 1957, and never repealed, on re-financing exports beyond the period in which the transactions could normally be expected to liquidate themselves. Demand for Euro-dollars arising from this restriction represented a substantial proportion of the total demand in 1957, but today it represents a bare fraction, so that its cessation would in itself hardly affect the market.

(8) It is the height of absurdity to suggest that an improvement of the American balance of payments, through reducing the volume of foreign dollar deposits, would bring the Euro-dollar market to an end. While an export surplus would tend to reduce the foreign deposits, the resulting strengthening of confidence in the dollar would attract more funds ranging from speculative 'hot money' to official reserves. Above all, an appreciation of forward dollars would lead to demand for spot dollars through inward arbitrage, and the dollars thus acquired might find their way to the Euro-dollar market because of the higher yield it offers. In any case foreign-owned long-term dollar assets can always be realised and the proceeds converted into Euro-dollars. Their supply was replenished from that source in 1969. The setback in Wall Street induced foreign holders to sell their equities and keep the cash in Euro-dollars.

(9) The reduction in the volume of Euro-dollars in the spring of 1965 resulting from the response of American lenders to President Johnson's appeal to abstain from exporting capital and to repatriate their funds was widely looked upon as a foretaste of things to come, and a return of the 'dollar gap' came to be freely predicted. As a result of pressure of a substantially unchanged demand for Euro-dollars on a reduced

supply, there was a sharp rise in Euro-dollar rates, and this tended to attract more foreign-owned dollars to take the place of American-owned dollars withdrawn. Any improvement in the dollar position, by enabling the American authorities to keep down interest rates in the United States in face of rising Euro-dollar rates, would divert more foreign-owned dollar deposits into the Euro-dollar market. It also might tempt Americans to evade the ban on American lending.

(10) Large-scale conversions of official dollar balances into gold might have made much difference to the Euro-dollar market during the period when a very large proportion of the official dollar reserves was employed directly or indirectly in Euro-dollars. But in the late 'sixties the American authorities ' discouraged ' such conversions. In any case, the ups and downs of dollars held by foreign Governments or Central Banks failed to prevent the expansion of the market.

(11) Moderate dollar scares resulting from a deterioration of the balance of payments position would not bring the Euro-dollar market to an end. Demand for Euro-dollars for speculative purposes would raise Euro-dollar rates to such an extent that the higher rates would attract deposits in spite of the increase in the cost of covering the exchange risk. Borrowers for commercial requirements could afford to pay high rates, because they would have the benefit of the discount on forward dollars. Nothing short of a sweeping dollar scare would induce so many holders to sell rather than lend their deposits that it would affect the volume of dollars available to the Euro-dollar market to a considerable extent.

(12) The only real danger to the Euro-dollar market lies in the possibility of major defaults on Euro-dollar deposits, or their freezing through exchange control or moratorium, which would result in a wholesale withdrawal of funds when possible. This problem was discussed in detail in Chapters 8 and 15. There can be no doubt

that after some such a blow it would take a long time for lenders in the Euro-dollar market to recover their confidence. But sooner or later they would return to the market, just as the granting of the new acceptance credits was resumed a few years after the bulk of outstanding acceptance credits became frozen in 1931.

The following are some of the main reasons why the Euro-dollar market has come to stay :

(a) Profit margins between deposit rates and lending rates are a bare fraction of the differentials that prevail in American banking practice.

(b) Borrowers find it much easier and more convenient.

(c) They can raise dollar credits in excess of what is obtainable from American banks.

Regulation Q maintains the differentials between deposit rates and lending rates artificially wide. But even if it were repealed, American banks are not likely to be content with a standard profit margin less than, say, 2 per cent. They are most unlikely to reduce their profit margins to below 1 per cent even for the benefit of their most highly favoured clients. Since the differentials in the Euro-dollar market are of the order of $\frac{1}{4}$ per cent, London banks and continental banks would always have a fair margin in hand, out of which they would always be able to bid higher rates than those which are likely to be allowed by American banks, and they would always be able to lend at lower rates. It is true, as was pointed out above, American banks might grant favourable terms to clients who are important enough to get alternative facilities in the Euro-dollar market. But they are not likely to reduce their profit margin to anything like $\frac{1}{4}$ per cent even to foreign banks of first-rate standing. These banks would find it to their advantage to lend or borrow in the Euro-dollar market.

Moreover, other things being equal, most banks would prefer to borrow Euro-dollars. The negotiation of a large credit in New York is apt to be a slow cumbersome process, in the course of which the borrower is expected to state the purpose for which the credit is required and the lender has to decide whether it is a sound purpose. On the Euro-dollar market he can raise the credit in a matter of minutes, with no questions asked. While the credit obtainable from New York would be for three months, possibly with one renewal, in the Euro-dollar market deposits for twelve months are easily obtainable and the borrower may safely rely on being able to renew the deposit, or borrow similar amounts, again and again.

Finally, American banks are not likely to be prepared to satisfy all foreign requirements of dollar credits. Borrowers whose requirements are not met would turn to the Euro-dollar market even if rates were higher than in New York.

In any case, as we saw in Chapter 2, apart altogether from considerations of interest rates there may be a variety of geographical, legal, political, etc., considerations for which holders of dollars may prefer to hold them with banks outside the U.S. European banks are open when New York is closed.

The development of the Euro-dollar system constitutes a great improvement of the monetary mechanism, and for this reason alone it is in keeping with the basic trend. It represents a most important step in the progress towards overcoming national barriers that divide the international financial system into separate compartments. Thanks to the new device, those compartments are now much less isolated than they had ever been before. While it is of course conceivable that a revival of economic nationalism might cause a temporary reversal of this progress, taking a long view it seems likely that the basic trend will move towards the growing internationalisation of the financial system.

The development and progress of the Euro-dollar market is in keeping also with the general trend towards increasing competition between banks. While that trend can be suppressed within a particular country by means of official regulations or cartel arrangements, banks outside cartels are able to compete with the aid of borrowed Euro-dollars. It would be difficult to visualise any cartels being adopted on an international scale. In the course of his evidence before a Congressional Committee Mr. Roosa was asked whether there would be a possibility of adopting some form of 'international Regulation

Q'. He replied that on the basis of his experience with international negotiations he would not like to be the one to try to negotiate such an agreement.

The rigidities imposed on the community by uniform banking terms, which are only adjusted reluctantly in response to infrequent basic changes, tend to give way to a more adaptable system. Borrowing and lending terms are more flexible under the new system, and they are subject to the same fluctuations through ever-changing supply/demand relationship as money rates or discount rates in Lombard Street, or exchange rates, or insurance rates at Lloyd's. There have been such developments recently also in the sphere of domestic finance. There is now a market in deposit certificates in the United States, and a market in loans has been created in Amsterdam. Both markets are in their infancy, but their initiation itself indicates the trend of evolution. The latest development has been the creation of a market in dollar certificates of deposits in London during 1966. It is described in detail in Appendix I.

The Euro-dollar system constitutes an improvement precisely because it reduces friction which handicaps the smooth operation of market mechanism. The theoretical ideal is that any excess of demand over supply of credit in one country should produce its automatic correction by attracting additional supplies of credit from other countries. The existence of international interest rates in an international money market goes a long way towards ensuring progress towards this ideal. Flexible national interest rates tend to ensure the balancing of credit supply and demand in the national economy. Flexible international interest rates are meant to perform the same task in the international economy.

There is of course another side to the story. Cut-throat competition is liable to reduce profit margins to a level at which it certainly would not cover the risk involved. The view was widely held that this stage had already been reached, and it only needed the experience of a crisis, which would immobilise part of the Euro-dollars and might lead to some losses, insolvencies, or eleventh-hour rescues of banks in difficulties, to make banks realise that the game was not worth the candle, any more

169

than it was worth while before 1931 to grant acceptance credits at a commission of $\frac{1}{2}$ per cent per annum. Any such experience is liable to bring about a setback in the expansion of the market for foreign currency deposits. It would mean that, in order to induce banks and others to lend their deposits, deposit rates would have to rise and borrowers would have to be prepared to pay high enough rates to leave sufficient margins for intermediaries.

Actually the tendency towards unduly narrow margins became reversed towards the end of 1963 even in the absence of a major financial crisis, as a result of some substantial but far from disastrous losses suffered by some lenders of Euro-dollars through the difficulties of some isolated borrowers. But it is a matter of opinion whether even a margin of $\frac{1}{4}$ per cent is really wide enough, and it seems probable that profit margins will have their ups and downs in accordance with supply/demand relationships and with the changing extent of risk.

Simultaneously with the widening of profit margins there was a tendency in the opposite direction in respect of interest rate differentials according to the borrowing banks' countries. Rates quoted to Italian or Japanese banks, and even those quoted to Communist banks, are now only fractionally above standard rates. The conflict between the two trends may be due to the effect of losses through difficulties of individual firms in countries of first-rate financial standing, such as the United States and West Germany. Lenders arrived at the conclusions that the commercial risk is higher than the exchange control risk, and they prefer, therefore, to lend to first-class banks in any country rather than to less dependable borrowers in 'safe' countries.

An important question is whether the system will continue to exist for the sole benefit of the 'rich', owing to the high minimum figure of the units transacted in the foreign currency market. If so, the small depositor and the small businessman will be at a permanent handicap from the point of view of the yields on deposits and the cost of borrowing. Indeed it is conceivable that the banks may want to recoup the losses they suffered through having to work with a very narrow margin in respect of Euro-dollar deposits by charging more or paying less to their small customers. On the other hand, perhaps growing competition among banks will induce them to extend the facilities to smaller investors or borrowers. But while it is possible to visualise a reduction of the standard unit from $1 million to, say, $100,000, or even $50,000, it is impossible to visualise the Euro-dollar market dealing in tens of thousands or hundreds of thousands of small deposits and loans. The overhead cost would rise to such an extent that margins between deposit rates and lending rates would have to be raised considerably.

In any case the market will always remain confined to dealing between banks. It would be technically impossible to let loose in it a multitude of relatively small transactions in broken amounts for odd maturities. As in respect of foreign exchanges, dealings between banks and their customers must remain outside the market proper. While it is conceivable that differences between Euro-dollar rates quoted in the market and those quoted to first-rate customers outside the market may become narrower in the course of time, the presence of the risk element, which is higher than in the case of foreign exchange transactions, will always prevent the margins from shrinking to the level of differences between exchange rates quoted within and outside the market.

Conceivably, the D. mark or some other currency might gain in popularity and the dollar might lose in popularity, in which case the foreign currency deposit market would not remain so overwhelmingly a Euro-dollar market. At the time of writing, however, it is difficult to see which currency could possibly replace the dollar as the favourite currency in the market. Sterling is even more likely to come under a cloud from time to time than the dollar. The Swiss franc owes its strength to the increasing volume of hot money, but its inherent strength might be affected if the balance of payments remained persistently adverse. Until the concluding months of 1966 the French franc was inherently sound and was regarded as the ' hardest ' of all currencies, but, owing to the maintenance of certain exchange controls until 1967, it was not popular

internationally. Troubles in 1968 and new exchange controls
did not help. As for the D. mark, official measures against the
influx of money deterred its widespread use as a currency of
the foreign deposit market, except when there were revaluation
rumours and speculative purchases of D. marks. For want of
better, the dollar is likely to remain the ruling currency.

What changes in the structure of the market in foreign
currency deposits are likely to occur in the future ? Possibly
in the long run a market in longer maturities will develop.
This is in keeping with the long-range trend in forward exchanges and, given international stability, it is likely to make
progress. But the trend is liable to become reversed from time
to time, as a result of defaults or of uncertainty about the
prospects of the dollar, or a rising trend in interest rates. Such
uncertainty did in fact develop in 1964–65, with the result that
the time-limit for negotiated transactions, having risen to five
years, declined temporarily to two years. Even Arab oil
royalty recipients came to prefer to lend their dollars for six
months and renew the deposits.

Conceivably, the United States authorities may reach the
conclusion that the disadvantages of preventing the development of an active market in New York in European currency
deposits outweigh its advantages. The main obstacle is the
application of Regulation Q to all deposits, regardless of the
currency of their denomination. This could be corrected, independently of the future of Regulation Q in general, by confining
its application to dollar deposits. But, as I pointed out in
Chapter 8, there are strong arguments against such an arrangement.

Another possible development might be the regulation of
the London market in short Euro-dollar deposits to avoid the
scramble that recurs frequently when notice is given for the
withdrawal of large amounts of day-to-day deposits. There is
no reason why the Bank of England should not look after this
market in London in the same way as it looks after Lombard
Street to smooth out awkward shortages or surpluses of funds
on the eve of week-ends, holidays, or the turn of the year. The
Euro-dollar market for short-term facilities has become so

closely integrated with the money market proper that sooner or later the authorities are bound to come to realise that it is part of their duties to ensure its smooth functioning.

A regular forward market in Euro-dollars beyond its present limit of seven days may reasonably be expected to develop sooner or later. Such facilities serve a genuine purpose, because borrowers or lenders naturally wish to safeguard themselves against suffering losses through a change of foreign currency deposits rates to their detriment. In this respect, too, uncertainty of prospect caused a setback in 1965, and arrangement of forward transactions is still a matter of negotiation.

Progress is likely to be made towards the codification of the rules adopted in practice in the market for foreign currency deposits. The institution is of too recent origin for its rules to have become crystallised, although the practice tends towards assuming a high degree of uniformity.

Some system of exchanging or pooling information about the amounts lent to various borrowers is bound to develop between banks, if not before the first Euro-dollar crisis, at any rate immediately after it. Apart from exchanging information on amounts actually borrowed, the banks could usefully exchange information about the rules they follow in respect of limits, if not for individual borrowers, at any rate for types of borrowers.

A further considerable expansion of the market is liable to be prevented by an exhaustion of the limits placed by each bank on the amount to be lent to any bank. The aggregate of these limits constitutes the maximum limit of the total turnover in the market. If it is deemed advantageous to ensure an expansion of the market without imprudently extending the limits, a solution would be for Central Banks and Treasuries to be borrowers as well as lenders of Euro-dollars. Apart from the Belgian Treasury, which has been a systematic borrower of Euro-dollars for years, and the various Communist governments which, through the Communist banks, have become borrowers on a large scale, major monetary authorities abstain from borrowing and confine their participation in the market to lending. Yet two-way operations by Central Banks

173

in Euro-currencies could provide a flexible alternative to the system of reciprocal assistance established under the Basle arrangement between a number of Central Banks, or to the reciprocal swap arrangements operating between the Federal Reserve and a number of monetary authorities. What would matter is for Central Banks to abstain from lending any currency which is under adverse pressure.

No standardised rules have emerged as yet concerning arrangements to ensure liquidity. In some countries there are statutory rules, but in their absence banks are left very much to their own devices. They ought to be given in every country definite guidance as to the proportion of cash and liquid reserves they should keep against foreign currency deposits they have borrowed. Their present policy is to synchronise maturities of borrowed deposits with those of lent deposits.

While it would be a pity if competition between banks in the new sphere were curtailed in the same way as in respect of conventional banking transactions, official discouragement of cutting margins too fine would be a step in the right direction. It is difficult to imagine, however, a formula which could sail between the Scylla of cartellisation and the Charybdis of unrestricted cut-throat competition. As in other trades, new-comers or banks on the margin of eligibility to participation in the market are likely to be inclined to cut margins.

Finally, it is conceivable that some formula for providing security for foreign currency deposit transactions might emerge in the course of time. The completely unsecured character of these loans is the main cause of the unduly low limit to their total. As I pointed out above, since there is a limit to the amount any bank is prepared to lend to any other bank, the sum total of these limits constitutes a ceiling. It is admittedly a flexible ceiling, but it is by no means impossible that it has already been approached, if not reached. This would mean that even if the supply of Euro-dollars tended to expand their re-lending to borrowers other than Central Banks would encounter difficulties unless a formula were to be worked out to provide security for loans in excess of the limit for unsecured loans.

No doubt the monetary authorities have their plans ready

to face a Euro-dollar crisis if and when it should arise. Presumably they would advise the government concerned to adopt some form of moratorium or exchange restrictions, and open positions in each country would be offset against each other by means of clearing arrangements within the country, similar to those adopted about outstanding foreign exchange contracts during the second World War.

There is, of course, no way of preventing a political crisis, but the risk attached to the new system could be greatly mitigated by sensible economic policies. Perhaps those concerned will realise in due course that it is safe to accelerate expansion so long as it is not exploited by excessive wage demands. It is the inflationary exaggeration of the natural effect of expansion which is the source of the danger of an inflationary boom of a kind that is liable to lead to a Euro-dollar crisis. But that would not be the new system's fault. In Japan and Italy, two of the principal beneficiaries of the new system, it became necessary to renounce part of the benefit from it, because of the wage demands which made further expansion risky.

In any case, risk is not special to the extensive use of Euro-currencies. Any expansion would entail similar risks. A boom triggered off by a drastic devaluation of all currencies in terms of gold is just as liable to get out of control as any conceivable boom resulting from the increased use of Euro-dollars. The creation of additional international liquidity through extensive allocation of S.D.R.s entails similar dangers. Any international currency serving that purpose can be very useful in normal conditions but its excessive use increases the danger of a crisis. The reason why Euro-dollars compare favourably with the various devices suggested is because their development is less artificial than that of the suggested devices.

It is worth noting that many official quarters do not share the widely-held fears about the possible dangers through excessive lending of Euro-dollars. The Bank for International Settlements considers such fears as exaggerated. 'There is no evidence', its report states, 'that Euro-currency business has occasioned widespread departures from the canons of prudent banking. . . . Some of the comment which the market has attracted no doubt reflects the element of novelty as well as the growing prominence of Euro-currencies in short-term capital movements during recent years. So far, in fact, the market does not seem to have given rise to policy problems of a different order from those of other movements of short-term funds.'

On its part, the Bank of England states in its *Quarterly Bulletin* of June 1964 that, although there are risks involved, the U.K. authorities have not discouraged London banks from participating in this business, relying on their good judgement in the way they conduct their operations. 'The market has shown that it has a useful part to play although, if the pause in growth during the past few months reflects a more cautious approach, this may not be wholly a bad thing.'

There is, of course, the danger of the system being misused by the Soviet Government for political purposes. The Communists could throw a spanner into the works both as borrowers and as lenders in the Euro-dollar market. That situation certainly needs watching, especially since there is evidence that the Communist bloc borrows much more than it lends, and that it lends for short-term while borrowing for long-term. But the relaxation of the East-West tension has reduced the likelihood of deliberate attempts to engineer a crisis in the West.

We have now an international money market with a structure of international interest rates. It seems that there is a strong case for its regulation in some measure by international monetary authorities, in a sense somewhat similar to the regulation of national money markets by the national monetary authorities. The Bank for International Settlements has assumed that task, albeit to a limited extent. It has direct experience in dealings in Euro-currencies and it is geographically closer to their markets. It intervenes to regulate the trend in the Euro-dollar market. Such an arrangement is a rudimentary beginning to a world-wide monetary policy which should be the ideal to be pursued, even if its full attainment may at present appear to be Utopian. Only under a World Government could there be an effective international monetary policy. But the effort of the B.I.S. to influence the Euro-dollar market is a step in that direction.

APPENDIX I

LONDON DOLLAR CERTIFICATES OF DEPOSITS

THE new market in London dollar certificates of deposits came into existence only in May 1966, and its development during 1966–69 was satisfactory. It is impossible at the time of writing to form very definite conclusions about its scope, techniques and broader implications. Nevertheless it is essential to examine at this relatively early stage the new device, and the facilities available for dealing in it, on the basis of the limited experience that is at our disposal. For I am convinced that we are witnessing the early phases of a major innovation which is likely to affect extensively the Euro-dollar system and the whole system of international finance.

I doubt if there had ever been any previous ten years' period in international financial history during which so many important institutional changes had occurred as during the past ten years. During the late 'fifties we saw the evolution and spectacular expansion of the Euro-currency markets which have revolutionised the foreign exchange markets and money markets. Systematic official intervention in forward exchanges and close collaboration between Central Banks for the mutual defence of their currencies have created a new foreign exchange system during the 'sixties. The operation of the support points mechanism — the present-day equivalent of the gold points mechanism under the gold standard — came into full effect towards the end of the 'fifties. The emergence of credit cards is yet another institutional change whose international implications have yet to be ascertained. Although the new markets for certificates of deposits and for Federal funds in New York, and for inter-bank sterling, for Local Authority loans and for hire-purchase finance house deposits in London, concern primarily the two money markets, they have created important new scope for international arbitrage. There is also the new European market for bonds issued in terms of dollars or of composite units of account.

The initiation in London of a market in dollar certificates of

177

deposits is one of the most recent of these innovations. It is a combined outcome of two separate institutional developments which converged into one another in May 1966 — the development of the Euro-dollar market in London and the almost simultaneous development of the market for negotiable certificates of deposits in New York.

One of the disadvantages of Euro-dollar deposits — as indeed of any kinds of time deposits — from the depositor's point of view is that he has to relinquish the use of his money for a definite period. Since Euro-dollar rates are almost always higher for longer periods, it is tempting for owners of liquid funds who do not expect to need their money for some time, and who do not anticipate a rise in interest rates, to commit themselves for longer periods. In doing so they of course run the risk that they might need their money before their deposit matures, or that they might be unable to take advantage of more profitable investment opportunities that are liable to arise.

Attempts to deal with this dilemma by means of option contracts under which the depositor is entitled to reclaim his money at any time after a certain date, or by means of break clauses under which he can withdraw his deposit at any time at the cost of a penalty — usually of the order of $\frac{1}{4}$ per cent — have failed to satisfy requirements. For one thing, the cost of such provisions usually wipes out most, if not all, of the additional yield obtainable on long-term deposits. Moreover, the device is rather involved and is usually available to favoured clients only. It is too clumsy to be convenient from the point of view of the speedy transaction of business as a matter of routine, which is one of the great advantages of the Euro-currency system. In any case, the Euro-currency market is an inter-bank market in which individual transactions are too large for non-banking clients.

In order to attract into Euro-dollars additional funds which have hitherto been deterred by the considerations indicated above, bankers in London had been considering for some time the possibility of issuing Euro-dollar certificates and creating a market in them. The idea was inspired by the outstanding success of the market in certificates of deposits that developed in the United States during the early 'sixties and has been expanding uninterruptedly ever since. Such certificates have been in use for a long time in several countries, but they had no adequate markets. An experiment in New York in 1960 to offer them to foreign holders of dollar deposits without providing for them a secondary market met with scant response.

London Dollar Certificates of Deposits

In 1961, however, one of the leading banks of New York initiated the issue of certificates of deposit to corporations and other depositors, while at the same time the Discount Corporation of New York created a secondary market in these certificates by buying and selling them out of its own holdings. The New York bank's example was soon followed by a large number of other American banks, and the Discount Corporation's lead was followed by several firms of Government security dealers. In a short time the new device became very popular, and today it is regarded as the largest sector of the New York money market, overshadowing in importance the markets in U.S. Treasury bills, commercial paper and bank acceptances. The amount of outstanding certificates of deposits rose to $17 billion by March 1966.

The temptation to emulate the New York experiment in London became increasingly stronger with the sharp increase of American demand for dollar deposits in the London Euro-dollar market. American branches in London were anxious to increase the borrowing of Euro-dollars without bidding up unduly the rates which were rising in any case as a result of the rising trend of interest rates in New York. One of the ways to that end was to attract depositors from outside the market and for that purpose the idea of issuing negotiable certificates of deposits had obvious advantages. American banks had been, therefore, exploring the possibilities of initiating that device. The big commercial bank of New York, which was responsible five years earlier for the initiation of the New York market for certificates of deposits, was first in the field also in London. Apart from dealing with legal problems, technical problems and taxation problems, it had to obtain the consent of the British authorities to the introduction of the new device.

Fortunately for the success of the scheme, the Bank of England adopted a very liberal attitude towards the proposed innovation. This was in keeping with its enlightened policy in respect of the development of the Euro-currency market itself which, so far from being hampered, was actually encouraged in official quarters. Although the use of Euro-dollars for international financing was bound to reduce sterling's role as an international currency, the Bank took the line that the advantages of having another important international market in London would more than outweigh the disadvantages of a decline in the international use of sterling. Thanks to this attitude, and to the enterprise and technical knowhow of London banks, London has succeeded in increasing her importance as an international banking centre through the expansion of the

Euro-dollar market, in spite of having been handicapped by the need for defending sterling against frequent attacks.

The Bank of England's willingness to extend this broad-minded treatment also to the proposed London dollar certificates arose logically from its original favourable attitude towards the Euro-dollar market. Limitations arising from exchange control regulations that are applied to the certificates of deposits are by no means too severe. They are substantially identical with those applied to Euro-dollar deposits in general. United Kingdom residents are under the same restriction in respect of acquiring and holding such certificates of deposits as they are in respect of acquiring and holding Euro-dollar deposits. Neither deposits nor certificates can be acquired against sterling on resident account. They can only be acquired by United Kingdom residents with the aid of dollars which they are authorised to hold for limited periods and for specific approved purposes, or with the aid of investment dollars. It is evidently not worth their while to buy investment dollars — whose premium ranged between 15 and 28 per cent during the last two years — for the purpose of acquiring dollar certificates of deposits. But if they want to hold investment dollars in any case, the certificates offer the highest yield compatible with liquidity. As the attractions of the certificates cannot increase selling pressure on sterling through United Kingdom demand for dollars, and does not even increase the demand for investment dollars, the Bank of England felt it could afford to be liberal in authorising their issue even during the difficult year of 1966 when the trend was towards a tightening of exchange control.

The idea of creating yet another international market in London must have been looked upon with favour in Threadneedle Street. The fact that London alone was chosen not only by an increasing number of American banks but also by several continental banks as the only centre for the issue of their certificates of deposits implies a recognition of the importance of the role the City still plays in international finance in spite of the chronic troubles of sterling.

At the time of writing, over thirty banks are now engaged in issuing dollar certificates of deposits in London. They now include a number of British banks — international subsidiaries of clearing banks, merchant banks and British overseas banks — which have been active in the Euro-dollar market. The number of British and foreign banks engaged in the issue of such certificates is likely to increase, because those banks which keep aloof from it are liable to lose Euro-dollar deposits as and when the practice becomes increasingly popular among depositors.

London Dollar Certificates of Deposits

London dollar certificates of deposits are issued in multiples of $1,000, with a minimum amount of $25,000 with the exception of one bank which fixed the minimum at $100,000. Although many certificates of between $25,000 and $100,000 are in circulation, units of $500,000 and $1,000,000 are not infrequent. As far as I know the largest single certificate issued to date was for $5,000,000. Certificates are mostly for standard maturities — 30, 60, 90, 120, 150, 180 days, twelve months and, since 1967, for several years — but there have been instances of issuing certificates for odd dates. The issue of certificates for periods exceeding twelve months was made possible by the repeal of the provision under which banks had to deduct income tax from interest payments on deposits for longer periods. But for this change no non-resident would have deemed it worth while to have to reclaim income tax on his interest receipts.

The certificates are issued by London branches of American banks against the payment of their dollar amounts to their offices in New York. Upon receiving advice from their New York offices that payment has been effected the London branches issue the certificates to banks nominated by the depositors. In a great many instances the certificates are left deposited with the issuing bank itself. Maturing certificates are repaid with interest at the New York office of the issuing bank concerned, upon the surrender of the certificates by the depositor to the London branch. Payments are made through the medium of a bank representing the depositor. All certificates are bearer certificates unless otherwise stipulated by the depositor.

No taxes are charged or deducted by the issuing bank. Certificates are not subject to any U.S. taxes, unless depositors are citizens of, or residents in, the United States. The only United Kingdom tax is the 2d. stamp duty on each certificate, which is paid by the issuing bank. There is no United Kingdom stamp duty on the transfer of certificates or on their presentation for repayment. If the certificates are actually held in the United Kingdom at the time of the owner's death, however, they are treated as part of the United Kingdom estates of non-residents for the purpose of death duties.

The text of the certificates makes it clear that the obligations of the issuing bank are subject to the laws of the United Kingdom. This provision may become important in the event of the adoption of new exchange control measures that would place a ban on the repayment of these dollar liabilities. The ban would then apply to American branches in London in the same way as to British banks, in spite of the fact that the head offices of the former would be well in a position to meet the liabilities of their London branch. However, that contingency is so remote that it may safely be ignored at present.

That the U.S. Government recognises the special status of London dollar deposits — or, for that matter, Euro-dollar deposits in general — is shown by the fact that they are not covered by Federal Deposit Insurance, and neither Regulation Q fixing maximum interest rates for deposits nor the statutory reserve requirements apply to them.

The issuing banks fix the interest rate on certificates every morning before 10 a.m. They fix their rates independently of one another. Once fixed, the rate is usually left unchanged for the day, in spite of the fluctuations of Euro-dollar rates in the course of the day. This practice has been adopted to attract non-banking depositors who are not in sufficiently close touch with the market to follow its fluctuations. It is not an absolute rule, however. While it is observed for small transactions, when large amounts are involved or when Euro-dollar rates move sharply during the day, the basic rule that no quotation is binding unless it is accepted immediately is apt to be observed.

The interest rates are based on the current Euro-dollar rates for corresponding maturities. Broadly speaking they are about $\frac{1}{8}$ per cent lower, which is justified on the ground of the extra advantage of marketability. Actually the differentials vary between $\frac{1}{16}$ and $\frac{3}{16}$ per cent. They tend to be wider for longer maturities than for shorter maturities, but this depends on the issuing banks' view on future tendencies of interest rates, on its relative commitments in Euro-dollars for various maturities, and on the relative demand for certificates for various maturities. If a bank has over-lent Euro-dollars it may be anxious to offset its commitments by borrowing more, in which case it may reduce the differential in order to attract more deposits. Conversely, if it has over-borrowed Euro-dollars it would widen the differential because it has no immediate desire to attract more deposits.

Interest rates are also affected by the day of the week on which the certificates are issued and on which they fall due. Issuing banks are naturally anxious to receive deposits on Thursdays or Fridays, and even more so on the eve of window-dressing dates, and are prepared to reduce the differentials for the sake of attracting more deposits for such dates. But then the basic Euro-dollar rates themselves are already affected by such considerations.

On the basis of the New York experience of 1960, the American banks deemed it essential to ensure the creation of a secondary market simultaneously with the initiation of the issue of certificates. It would not have been sufficient to rely on the spontaneous development of a natural market. The new London device came, so to say, out of the blue, because the scheme was kept a closely-guarded secret until the moment of its public announcement. In order to attract deposits, it was essential to be able to give positive assurance that they would encounter no difficulty if and when they should wish to dispose of their certificates.

As in the case of certificates of deposits issued in the United States, there can be no question of redeeming the certificates before maturity. This would merely have amounted to an option clause or a break clause in a new form. The alternative was to make a definite arrangement, following on the precedent of New York in 1961, for a financial house to be prepared to buy and sell securities of its own account, playing a part similar to that of firms of jobbers on the London Stock Exchange. This was in fact done. The announcement made by the New York bank on June 23, 1966, that as from June 26 it was to issue London dollar certificates of deposits, was followed immediately by the announcement by an international financial house of New York that its London branch was prepared to deal in such certificates.

While the Euro-dollar system came into existence very gradually, and was for a long time hardly noticed by anyone except those directly concerned (who went out of their way to avoid publicity), the system of Euro-dollar certificates was initiated with the maximum of publicity. This difference was due to the fact that while Euro-dollar dealing was between banks, certificates were intended to appeal to a wider public.

If finance houses had merely offered their services as brokers it would not have helped very much, for the certificates were bound to have a very limited market during the early phases of their existence. Until their circulation attained fairly substantial proportions would-be sellers could not be expected to rely on the chance of finding a counterpart at reasonable rates. But several firms were prepared to act as principals and to buy on their own account certificates offered for sale. They were prepared to retain them and to meet demand for certificates out of their own supply.

Before very long several other firms were also prepared to provide a secondary market in certificates. Attempts were made by some London firms at the early stages of the development of this market to act exclusively as brokers, but owing to the smallness of the initial turnover this has proved to be rather difficult. Nevertheless,

several firms of bill brokers applied for, and received, permission
from the Bank of England to operate in London dollar certificates of
deposits.

Firms which provide a secondary market quote regularly their
buying and selling rates at which they are prepared to deal, with a
spread of $\frac{1}{8}$ to $\frac{3}{16}$ between them for short maturities and up to $\frac{1}{4}$ for
longer maturities. As in the case of issuing banks, the rates quoted
vary not only in sympathy with the corresponding Euro-dollar rates
but also according to supply and demand and according to the commitments of the firms for the various dates. While issuing banks
issue mostly certificates for standard dates, most of the turnover in
the secondary market consists of certificates for odd dates sold by
depositors some time after having obtained them. But since the
market houses have a wide international clientele they also receive
orders for certificates for standard dates, in which case they buy
new certificates from the issuing banks.

The terms of settlement are identical with those applying in the
foreign exchange market and the market for Euro-dollar deposits —
delivery and payment two clear business days after the conclusion
of the transaction. Payment is to be made in clearing house funds
in New York. The certificates are delivered free of charge in London,
and a charge is made for delivery costs if the depositor prescribes
delivery outside London.

As most deposits reach the issuing banks through the intermediary of banks, they have no means of knowing whether the depositors act as agents or as principals. The size of the individual amounts
is practically the only indication. If it is large, the assumption is
that banks buy the certificate for their own account, though large
corporations or Middle East oil millionaires are well in a position to
deposit $1 million or more. If the demand is for certificates of small
amounts then it is safe to assume that the depositors are non-banking
clients of the intermediary banks. Although the original intention
behind the scheme was to be able to secure hitherto untapped non-
banking sources of dollar deposits, there is reason to believe that a
high proportion of the certificates is held by banks. They find the
certificates very useful liquid assets whose yield compares usually
favourably with that of Euro-dollars at call, even though the marketable certificates are just as liquid.

Switzerland is one of the main sources of demand for certificates.
Holders of foreign accounts with Swiss banks may want to employ
their liquid balances in that form. In particular, if they are awaiting
a favourable moment for investing in Wall Street they naturally

prefer to acquire liquid assets which secure for them yields usually considerably above those obtainable through investment in U.S. Treasury bills or bank acceptances.

Having regard to the advantages offered by the certificates, during the three years' existence of the new market the increase of their volume has been remarkably slow. Estimates of the outstanding total varied, but even the highest figure did not exceed $2 billion in the middle of 1969, compared with the estimated total of Euro-dollar deposits of $34 billion. The turnover in the secondary market is not very active. There is a great deal of inquiry because all issuing banks are anxious to keep in touch with the market, but actual transactions are few and far between. The main reason for this, apart from the novelty of the device, is that during most of the time of its existence Euro-dollar rates have been rising. If depositors anticipate a further rise in interest rates the marketability of the certificates offers no attraction for them, since they assume that, should they wish to recover their deposits before maturity, they would only be able to do so at a loss. For this reason they may prefer to employ their funds in Euro-dollars at call. It seems reasonable to assume that the market will expand during a period of declining interest rates.

In the absence of a large turnover the range of the types of operations in certificates has been limited. There has been no buying for forward delivery, nor time arbitrage which plays a very important part in the New York market for certificates of deposits. ' Playing the yield curve ' is a much favoured type of operation by dealers in New York wishing to take advantage of discrepancies between yields for long and short maturities and of changes in such discrepancies. As and when the London market will expand such transactions will become a familiar feature, and so will arbitrage transactions with other centres after they too have developed similar markets.

I am convinced that the expansion of the market is only a question of time. For one thing, American depositors are at present prevented by the existing unofficial ban from taking an active hand — though I suspect that some of them at any rate circumvent the ban. Although none of the American bank branches is prepared to issue certificates to American citizens, whether they are resident in the United States or abroad, it is always possible to secure them through the intermediary of some non-American bank. But once the present ban is removed Americans are bound to take a very active interest in the certificates. And once the dollar has ceased to be subject to

185

suspicion, holdings of such certificates are likely to become widely favoured all over the world, in preference to ordinary time deposits or Euro-dollar deposits, or any other kinds of market paper, and even in preference to gold hoarding. Central Banks are likely to acquire a taste for it, as they did for Euro-dollar deposits. Another important permanent source of demand will be created by the banks' desire to spread their liquid assets over a wide variety of easily realisable investments.

Other U.S. banks in addition to those already engaged in issuing certificates are likely to take a hand, if only to avoid losing deposits as a result of the acquisition of certificates of other banks by their depositors. More British banks are likely to follow the example, apart from other reasons, in order to retain their lead in the Euro-dollar market, a lead which might be threatened by a spectacular expansion of the market in certificates issued by American banks. Nor is London likely to remain the only centre in which certificates will be issued or dealt in.

The Bank of England is watching closely the development of this market, not only owing to its possible implications from the point of view of foreign exchange policy, but also in order to discourage any tendency towards over-trading by individual issuing banks. All banks engaged in issuing certificates have to declare the amounts issued in their weekly returns to the Bank. Houses operating in the secondary markets, too, have to make weekly returns on their total turnovers. It was mentioned earlier that the authorities are in favour of the service. The fact that it pays so much attention to the new device in spite of the relatively modest amounts involved at present seems to indicate that authoritative quarters share my belief than an expansion of the issue and turnover of certificates is only a question of time.

Once the advantages of the new device over alternative facilities come to be widely realised its use is bound to be increasingly popular. The extent of its popularity, like that of the Euro-dollars themselves, will have of course its ups and downs. Conceivably certificates in other currencies will also appear and, in given circumstances, they might overshadow the dollar certificates from time to time. Once the knowhow and the mechanism exists and the use of the device is firmly established, it is likely to be used increasingly, subject to temporary declines followed by further expansions, as in the case of the markets in Euro-currencies.

Our next step is to examine the broader implications of the new device, postulating that it has come to stay and that its market will assume considerable dimensions. How is it likely to affect banks within and outside the United States? Is it liable to affect the dollar and other currencies ? Will it contribute towards an increase in the volume of liquid resources, and, if so, to what extent ? Is it a potentially disturbing influence in the foreign exchange markets and in the national economies ? At the present stage any answer to these questions must necessarily be tentative and must rest very largely on sheer conjecture. Nevertheless it is advisable to give some thought to the problems involved, even at this early stage.

Now that certificates amounting to billions of dollars have come to be issued, how is it likely to affect American banks ? The effect on individual banks depends largely on whether they participate in the issue of certificates. If so, the question is whether the amount a bank issues attracts more deposits from other banks than the amount it loses through the issue of certificates by its rivals. This question has been considered in great detail by American banking circles and in American financial literature in connection with the issues of domestic certificates of deposits in the United States. As the amount of London certificates likely to be issued is bound to remain a small fraction of total American bank deposits, or even of domestic certificates of deposits, the problem is one of secondary importance, though not negligible.

Taking the American banking system as a whole, it stands to increase its proportion of time deposits. From this point of view, too, the difference that the issue of London certificates is likely to make is merely one of minor degree.

Although non-American banks are also active in issuing dollar certificates on a large scale, it does not materially affect the American banking system. The basic fact of the situation that is often overlooked is that dollar deposits against which certificates are issued, as Euro-dollar deposits or ordinary foreign-held dollar deposits, are dollars which *must* be held with some American banks in the United States. No matter how many times they change hands as a result of their change of status and change of ownership, they must remain dollars held with American banks in the United States. Changes may result in transfers to other accounts or to other American banks but, unless they lead to withdrawals of deposits in cash and the hoarding of the notes thus withdrawn, they must remain within the American banking system. So the issue of certificates by non-American banks merely results in transfers of dollars from one account to another, or from one American bank to another.

An active turnover in the secondary market for certificates is liable to increase the frequency of transfers of deposits between American banks. Each time the certificates change hands the buyer's bank loses the deposit and the seller's bank gains the deposit. Under the law of averages such gains and losses are liable to cancel each other out in the long run — assuming that all American banks issue certificates and all certificates are equally attractive — but banks have to provide for the possibility of additional withdrawals in the short run.

So long as the issuing of certificates is confined largely to American banks, the operation of the system is likely to reduce the amount of Euro-dollar deposits under the control of non-American holders. For the duration of the deposits obtained by American banks the dollars come under the full control of American banks, in the same way as do Euro-dollars borrowed by American banks in the market. The importance of this point should not be exaggerated, however. After all, as we saw above, dollar deposits in no matter what form, whether owned by residents or non-residents, must necessarily be held in the form of dollars with an American bank. The difference is that so long as the dollars are under the control of a non-American holder there is always the possibility of their withdrawal at any time from the individual bank in question, but if an American bank re-borrows them in the form of Euro-dollars or in the form of deposits against which it issues certificates, it will gain full control of the dollars for the duration of the deposit. It can therefore make use of them without having to envisage their sudden withdrawal. Since, as I pointed out above, the amount involved represents a bare trickle into the vast dollar pool of American banks, the extent of the effect of the issue of London dollar certificates by American banks on their own liquidity provisions is purely marginal. But to that extent it is in a favourable sense as far as the issuing bank is concerned.

The effect of issues of certificates by other American banks tends to be of course in the opposite sense. Even if a bank remains unaffected by the original transaction, there remains the possibility that subsequent transactions in the secondary market might lead to withdrawals of deposits. Or dormant deposits might become active deposits. In other terms, the velocity of circulation of its deposits might increase. But, it must be re-emphasised, any likely change would be purely marginal.

Another question to be examined is the extent to which the dollar is liable to be affected. It depends on whether the issue of certificates means the conversion of a foreign currency into dollars, or merely the conversion of one type of dollar into another. If the certificates are acquired by holders of Euro-dollar deposits the transaction merely changes Euro-dollars into London dollars. If foreign holders of dollars acquire them it increases the amount of foreign-owned dollars re-lent outside the United States. Since, however, the borrowers are mostly American bank branches in London who re-lend most of the dollars to their own head offices, such transactions are not likely to increase the supply of dollars in the foreign exchange market. In fact, since possibly certificates are liable to attract flight-money, their issue might even lead to an increase of demand for dollars. On the whole it seems probable that the overwhelming majority of those who acquire certificates pay for them with dollars they already possess.

Since at the time of writing the Euro-dollar market is many times larger than the market in London dollar certificates of deposits, it is Euro-dollar rates that largely determine interest rates on certificates and the price at which certificates change hands in the secondary market. But this state of affairs may change if and when the volume of such certificates should increase to an extent that it comes to bear comparison with that of Euro-dollar deposits. In given circumstances it is conceivable that the tail might then come to wag the dog from time to time.

How does the new device affect British banking? A number of British banks have embarked on the issue of dollar certificates, adding another profitable line to their existing international banking activities. What is much more important is that British banks have come to be inspired by the example of London dollar certificates to issue sterling certificates of deposits to holders of resident sterling. It has been a logical development, similar to the development of the inter-bank sterling market which was largely inspired by the example of the Euro-dollar market.

There is much to be said in favour of issuing special certificates to holders of external account sterling. It would mop up some of the supplies of Euro-sterling which are now available for speculators against sterling. At times of acute attacks on sterling, speculation is financed largely by borrowing Euro-sterling, mainly over week-ends, and selling the spot exchange. On such occasions short Euro-sterling rates are liable to rise to fantastic figures. Should the by no means unlimited supply of Euro-sterling be reduced as a result of the issue of sterling certificates it would tend to cause an even steeper rise in the cost of short-period speculation, and this would discourage speculation in that form. Admittedly the result would be a widening of the discount on short forward sterling. This has become welcome in British official circles where discouragement of speculation by raising its cost is once more fashionable. But support to forward sterling was always confined to longer maturities so that the authorities never felt strongly against an increase in the cost of short-term speculation.

The most important consequence of the appearance and development of Dollar Certificates of Deposits from a British point of view has been the inspiration it gave for London banks to follow the example by initiating the issue of Sterling Certificates of Deposits. That device has great possibilities.

There remains the question about the effect of the new device on international liquidity. In dealing with this problem briefly we have to differentiate between its effect on official reserves and its effect on credit facilities available for international trade and finance.

As far as official reserves are concerned, the effect depends on whether the new depositors had already possessed the dollars or had to acquire them in the market, and also on whether the change in the form in which foreign-owned dollars are kept affects the likelihood of their use for speculative purposes. We have already observed that, should the certificate become popular, it would tend to increase buying pressure on the dollar. But since it is liable to attract ' hot money ' it would be a blessing of problematic value.

As for the conversion of foreign-held dollars into deposits against which certificates are issued, it is impossible to form any definite opinion whether holders of certificates are less likely to sell their dollars for speculative purposes or through flight from the dollar than holders of Euro-dollars or of ordinary dollars. Nevertheless it seems just possible that, since speculation by them entails first the sale of the certificates and then the sale of their dollars proceeds, there is marginally less likelihood for such use of them, though not less likelihood than for the realisation of, say, U.S. Treasury bills or bank acceptances for the sake of getting out of dollars.

Having regard to the above considerations, it seems possible to conclude tentatively that the new device tends to be moderately beneficial from the point of view of the reserves of the United States. Its effect on the volume of liquid resources available for international trade and finance is likely to be much more important. Since the velocity of circulation of deposits against which certificates are issued is higher than that of ordinary dollar deposits or even that of Euro-dollar deposits of corresponding maturity the same amount of dollars is likely to do more work. A time deposit or a Euro-dollar deposit has to remain idle till maturity, even though the American bank with which it is held is in a position to use the dollars for international financing should it wish to do so. A certificate, on the other hand, can be turned into liquid cash at two days' notice, so that it is more likely to be used actively by the depositor. It means that the same deposit is apt to be used twice — by the American banking system with whom the dollars are held and by the depositor who, having re-lent them to the American bank, has recovered its possession through the sale of the certificate in the secondary market. The original use of the dollars by the American bank does not preclude the use of the same dollars by its depositor who does not have to withdraw them from his American bank in order to be able to recover possession of his money. Even though the buyer of the certificate has to with-draw a deposit from some American bank, the American banking system as a whole will continue to be able to use the dollars in spite of their being used also by the depositor himself. It is only if the buyer of the certificate had intended to make active use of his dollars before deciding to buy certificates that the dual effect would be can-celled out.

This is one of the paradoxes of the modern banking system. All that happens is that the same amount of dollar deposits is doing more work than it would have done if the depositor had tied it down for a definite period in the form of a time deposit. We saw earlier that such an increase in the velocity of circulation of deposits may necessitate larger provision for meeting withdrawals. But the actual extent of such provisions would be infinitesimal unless the volume of London dollar certificates should increase to an amount compar-able to the volume of deposit certificates issued in the United States — which is most unlikely.

London branches of American banks, by issuing certificates, in-crease their resources available for financing foreign trade. If they lend the dollar proceeds of the certificates to their head offices, the latter are enabled to expand credits, including credits for foreign trade. Once the scarcity of credit in the United States comes to an end, a much higher proportion of the dollars borrowed by the Lon-don branches will be re-lent to finance foreign trade.

Beyond doubt, the higher degree of flexibility provided by the new device will tend to place additional resources at the disposal of international trade and finance as a result of the increase in the velocity of circulation of the deposits concerned. Once more, while Treasuries, Central Banks and economists are engaged in endless discussions about the means of increasing international liquidity, practical bankers have found a solution which should go some way towards meeting the growing requirements of international trade and finance. It can achieve that end without increasing the extent to which the international financial system is vulnerable. For there is less likelihood, not more likelihood, for sudden withdrawals of the deposits concerned than there would be if foreign owners of dollars had not acquired certificates.

There is yet another aspect of the new device. Its use should encourage the development of long-term deposits. As it has become possible to extend maturities of certificates of deposits to, say, five years — the same as for Euro-dollars — they provide very useful means for banks to engage in medium-term lending, because they are now able to secure offsetting deposits whose maturities could be made to coincide with those of their medium-term loans. Surely this has been a step in the right direction. For this consideration alone the new device is to be welcomed and its development encouraged.

EURO-DOLLAR RATES IN LONDON

THE following is a list of quotations of Euro-dollar rates in the London market at the end of each month :

1959	CALL	1 MONTH	3 MONTHS	6 MONTHS
March	$3-2\frac{7}{8}$	$3\frac{1}{4}-\frac{1}{8}$	$3\frac{3}{8}-\frac{1}{4}$	$3\frac{1}{2}-\frac{3}{8}$
April	$3-2\frac{7}{8}$	$3\frac{1}{4}-\frac{1}{8}$	$3\frac{3}{8}-\frac{1}{4}$	$3\frac{5}{8}-\frac{3}{8}$
May	$3\frac{3}{16}-\frac{1}{8}$	$3\frac{3}{8}-\frac{1}{4}$	$3\frac{5}{8}-\frac{1}{2}$	$4-3\frac{3}{4}$
June	$3\frac{3}{8}-\frac{1}{4}$	$3\frac{5}{8}-\frac{1}{2}$	$3\frac{3}{4}-\frac{5}{8}$	$3\frac{13}{16}-\frac{11}{16}$
July	$3\frac{3}{8}-\frac{1}{4}$	$3\frac{11}{16}-\frac{9}{16}$	$3\frac{13}{16}-\frac{11}{16}$	$4\frac{1}{4}-4$
August	$3\frac{7}{16}-\frac{3}{8}$	$3\frac{7}{8}-\frac{13}{16}$	$3\frac{15}{16}-\frac{13}{16}$	$4\frac{1}{4}-4$
September	$3\frac{15}{16}-\frac{13}{16}$	$4\frac{3}{8}-4\frac{1}{4}$	$4\frac{1}{2}-\frac{3}{8}$	$4\frac{7}{8}-\frac{5}{8}$
October	$4\frac{3}{16}-\frac{1}{16}$	$4\frac{9}{16}-\frac{7}{16}$	$4\frac{11}{16}-\frac{5}{8}$	$4\frac{13}{16}-\frac{11}{16}$
November	$4\frac{3}{16}-\frac{1}{8}$	$4\frac{1}{2}-\frac{3}{8}$	$4\frac{5}{8}-\frac{1}{2}$	$4\frac{13}{16}-\frac{11}{16}$
December	$4\frac{7}{8}-\frac{1}{8}$	$5-4\frac{3}{4}$	$5-4\frac{3}{4}$	$5\frac{1}{8}-4\frac{7}{8}$
1960				
January	$4\frac{3}{8}-\frac{1}{8}$	$4\frac{5}{8}-\frac{9}{16}$	$4\frac{13}{16}-\frac{11}{16}$	$5-4\frac{7}{8}$
February	$4\frac{1}{4}-\frac{3}{16}$	$4\frac{1}{2}-\frac{3}{8}$	$4\frac{5}{8}-\frac{1}{2}$	$4\frac{3}{4}-\frac{5}{8}$
March	$4\frac{1}{8}-4$	$4\frac{1}{4}-\frac{1}{8}$	$4\frac{7}{16}-\frac{5}{16}$	$4\frac{1}{2}-\frac{3}{8}$
April	$4-3\frac{7}{8}$	$4\frac{3}{16}-\frac{1}{16}$	$4\frac{5}{16}-\frac{3}{16}$	$4\frac{7}{16}-\frac{5}{16}$
May	$4\frac{1}{16}-3\frac{15}{16}$	$4\frac{1}{8}-4$	$4\frac{1}{4}-\frac{1}{8}$	$4\frac{7}{16}-\frac{5}{16}$
June	$4\frac{1}{16}-3\frac{15}{16}$	$4\frac{1}{8}-4$	$4\frac{1}{4}-\frac{1}{8}$	$4\frac{3}{8}-\frac{1}{4}$
July	$3\frac{3}{8}-\frac{1}{8}$	$3\frac{5}{8}-\frac{9}{16}$	$3\frac{7}{8}-\frac{13}{16}$	$4\frac{1}{16}-3\frac{15}{16}$
August	$3\frac{1}{8}-3$	$3\frac{9}{16}-\frac{7}{16}$	$3\frac{11}{16}-\frac{9}{16}$	$4-3\frac{7}{8}$
September	$3\frac{1}{2}-\frac{1}{4}$	$3\frac{13}{16}-\frac{11}{16}$	$4-3\frac{3}{4}$	$4\frac{1}{4}-4$
October	$3-2\frac{1}{2}$	$4-3\frac{7}{8}$	$4\frac{1}{4}-4$	$4\frac{1}{4}-\frac{1}{8}$
November	$3-2\frac{3}{4}$	$4-3\frac{7}{8}$	$4\frac{1}{4}-\frac{1}{8}$	$4\frac{3}{8}-\frac{1}{4}$
December	$4-3\frac{1}{2}$	$4\frac{1}{4}-\frac{1}{16}$	$4\frac{1}{4}-\frac{1}{16}$	$4\frac{5}{16}-\frac{3}{16}$

	CALL	1 MONTH	3 MONTHS	6 MONTHS
1961				
January	$3\frac14$–3	$3\frac{11}{16}$–$\frac{9}{16}$	$3\frac34$–$\frac{11}{16}$	$4\frac{1}{16}$–$3\frac{15}{16}$
February	$3\frac{5}{16}$–$\frac{1}{16}$	$3\frac{9}{16}$–$\frac{7}{16}$	$3\frac38$–$\frac58$	$3\frac{15}{16}$–$\frac{13}{16}$
March	$3\frac12$–$\frac14$	$3\frac58$–$\frac12$	$3\frac{13}{16}$–$\frac{11}{16}$	4–$3\frac78$
April	$3\frac18$–$2\frac78$	$3\frac12$–$\frac38$	$3\frac{11}{16}$–$\frac{9}{16}$	$3\frac{15}{16}$–$\frac{13}{16}$
May	3–$2\frac34$	$3\frac{7}{16}$–$\frac{5}{16}$	$3\frac{11}{16}$–$\frac{9}{16}$	$3\frac78$–$\frac34$
June	$2\frac58$–$\frac38$	$3\frac{5}{16}$–$\frac{3}{16}$	$3\frac{9}{16}$–$\frac{7}{16}$	$3\frac{13}{16}$–$\frac{11}{16}$
July	$2\frac14$–$\frac12$	$3\frac{3}{16}$–$\frac{1}{16}$	$3\frac38$–$\frac14$	$3\frac{11}{16}$–$\frac{5}{16}$
August	$2\frac14$–$\frac12$	$3\frac{3}{16}$–$\frac{1}{16}$	$3\frac38$–$\frac14$	$3\frac{13}{16}$–$\frac{11}{16}$
September	$2\frac78$–$\frac58$	$3\frac{5}{16}$–$\frac{3}{16}$	$3\frac{7}{16}$–$\frac{5}{16}$	$3\frac{15}{16}$–$\frac{13}{16}$
October	$3\frac38$–$2\frac78$	$3\frac{5}{16}$–$\frac{3}{16}$	$3\frac12$–$\frac38$	$3\frac78$–$\frac34$
November	3–$2\frac34$	$3\frac12$–$\frac{7}{16}$	$3\frac{11}{16}$–$\frac{9}{16}$	$3\frac{15}{16}$–$\frac{13}{16}$
December	$3\frac18$–$2\frac78$	4–$3\frac34$	$4\frac18$–$3\frac78$	$4\frac14$–$\frac18$
1962				
January	$2\frac34$–$\frac12$	$3\frac{3}{16}$–$\frac{1}{16}$	$3\frac18$–$\frac{3}{16}$	$3\frac{13}{16}$–$\frac{11}{16}$
February	$2\frac78$–$\frac58$	$3\frac{5}{16}$–$\frac14$	$3\frac{9}{16}$–$\frac{7}{16}$	$3\frac34$–$\frac{11}{16}$
March	$3\frac14$–3	$3\frac{7}{16}$–$\frac38$	$3\frac58$–$\frac{9}{16}$	$3\frac{13}{16}$–$\frac{11}{16}$
April	3–$2\frac34$	$3\frac{5}{16}$–$\frac14$	$3\frac{7}{16}$–$\frac38$	$3\frac{11}{16}$–$\frac{9}{16}$
May	$3\frac18$–3	$3\frac{9}{16}$–$\frac{7}{16}$	$3\frac34$–$\frac58$	$3\frac78$–$\frac34$
June	$3\frac38$–$\frac14$	$3\frac{9}{16}$–$\frac12$	$3\frac34$–$\frac{11}{16}$	4–$3\frac78$
July	$3\frac38$–$\frac18$	$3\frac34$–$\frac{11}{16}$	$3\frac78$–$\frac{13}{16}$	$4\frac14$–4
August	$3\frac18$–$2\frac78$	$3\frac58$–$\frac{9}{16}$	$3\frac{13}{16}$–$\frac14$	$4\frac18$–$\frac18$
September	$3\frac14$–3	$3\frac34$–$\frac{11}{16}$	$3\frac{15}{16}$–$\frac78$	$4\frac{1}{16}$–$\frac{15}{16}$
October	$3\frac12$–$\frac14$	$3\frac{13}{16}$–$\frac{11}{16}$	$4\frac18$–4	$4\frac{5}{16}$–$\frac{3}{16}$
November	$3\frac14$–$\frac14$	$4\frac{1}{16}$–$3\frac{15}{16}$	$4\frac18$–4	$4\frac{3}{16}$–$\frac{1}{16}$
December	5–4	$4\frac{3}{16}$–4	$4\frac{3}{16}$–4	$4\frac{3}{16}$–$\frac{1}{16}$
1963				
January	$3\frac14$–3	$3\frac38$–$\frac14$	$3\frac{9}{16}$–$\frac{7}{16}$	$3\frac34$–$\frac{11}{16}$
February	$3\frac38$–$\frac18$	$3\frac{5}{16}$–$\frac14$	$3\frac12$–$\frac{7}{16}$	$3\frac{13}{16}$–$\frac{11}{16}$
March	$3\frac38$–$\frac14$	$3\frac58$–$\frac12$	$3\frac34$–$\frac58$	$3\frac{13}{16}$–$\frac{11}{16}$
April	$3\frac12$–$\frac38$	$3\frac58$–$\frac{9}{16}$	$3\frac34$–$\frac{11}{16}$	$3\frac{13}{16}$–$\frac34$
May	$3\frac{9}{16}$–$\frac58$	$3\frac34$–$\frac{11}{16}$	$3\frac78$–$\frac{13}{16}$	$3\frac{15}{16}$–$\frac78$
June	$3\frac12$–$\frac38$	$3\frac34$–$\frac{11}{16}$	$3\frac78$–$\frac{13}{16}$	4–$3\frac{15}{16}$
July	$3\frac58$–$\frac12$	$3\frac78$–$\frac{13}{16}$	$4\frac{1}{16}$–4	$4\frac38$–$\frac14$

Euro-Dollar Rates in London

	CALL	1 MONTH	3 MONTHS	6 MONTHS
1963				
August	$3\frac{9}{16}-\frac{7}{16}$	$3\frac{15}{16}-\frac{7}{8}$	$4\frac{1}{16}-4$	$4\frac{3}{8}-\frac{5}{16}$
September	$4\frac{1}{16}-3\frac{15}{16}$	$4\frac{1}{8}-4\frac{1}{16}$	$4\frac{1}{4}-\frac{1}{8}$	$4\frac{1}{2}-\frac{3}{8}$
October	$3\frac{7}{8}-3\frac{3}{4}$	$3\frac{15}{16}-3\frac{7}{8}$	$4\frac{3}{16}-4\frac{1}{8}$	$4\frac{3}{8}-\frac{1}{4}$
November	$3\frac{13}{16}-\frac{11}{16}$	$4\frac{7}{16}-\frac{5}{16}$	$4\frac{5}{16}-\frac{3}{16}$	$4\frac{7}{16}-\frac{5}{16}$
December	$4\frac{3}{4}-\frac{5}{8}$	$4\frac{3}{8}-\frac{1}{8}$	$4\frac{3}{8}-\frac{1}{4}$	$4\frac{7}{16}-\frac{5}{16}$
1964				
January	$3\frac{3}{4}-\frac{5}{8}$	$4-3\frac{7}{8}$	$4\frac{3}{16}-\frac{1}{16}$	$4\frac{3}{8}-\frac{1}{4}$
February	$4\frac{1}{16}-3\frac{15}{16}$	$4\frac{3}{16}-\frac{1}{16}$	$4\frac{1}{4}-\frac{3}{16}$	$4\frac{7}{16}-\frac{5}{16}$
March	$3\frac{15}{16}-\frac{13}{16}$	$4\frac{3}{16}-\frac{1}{8}$	$4\frac{5}{16}-\frac{1}{4}$	$4\frac{1}{2}-\frac{7}{16}$
April	$3\frac{13}{16}-\frac{3}{4}$	$4\frac{1}{8}-\frac{1}{16}$	$4\frac{1}{4}-\frac{3}{16}$	$4\frac{7}{16}-\frac{3}{8}$
May	$4-3\frac{15}{16}$	$4\frac{3}{16}-\frac{1}{8}$	$4\frac{5}{16}-\frac{1}{4}$	$4\frac{1}{2}-\frac{3}{8}$
June	$4-3\frac{15}{16}$	$4\frac{5}{16}-\frac{1}{4}$	$4\frac{7}{16}-\frac{3}{8}$	$4\frac{9}{16}-\frac{1}{2}$
July	$4-3\frac{7}{8}$	$4\frac{3}{16}-\frac{1}{8}$	$4\frac{5}{16}-\frac{1}{4}$	$4\frac{5}{8}-\frac{9}{16}$
August	$4-3\frac{7}{8}$	$4\frac{3}{16}-\frac{1}{8}$	$4\frac{5}{16}-\frac{1}{4}$	$4\frac{1}{2}-\frac{7}{16}$
September	$4-3\frac{7}{8}$	$4\frac{3}{16}-4\frac{1}{16}$	$4\frac{5}{8}-4\frac{9}{16}$	$4\frac{9}{16}-4\frac{1}{2}$
October	$3\frac{15}{16}-3\frac{13}{16}$	$4\frac{1}{4}-4$	$4\frac{9}{16}-4\frac{1}{2}$	$4\frac{5}{8}-4\frac{9}{16}$
November	$3\frac{13}{16}-3\frac{11}{16}$	$5\frac{1}{8}-5$	$5\frac{1}{8}-5$	$5\frac{3}{16}-5\frac{1}{16}$
December	$4\frac{1}{4}-4\frac{1}{8}$	$4\frac{5}{8}-4\frac{9}{16}$	$4\frac{3}{4}-4\frac{5}{8}$	$4\frac{13}{16}-4\frac{3}{4}$
1965				
January	$4\frac{1}{16}$	$4\frac{3}{8}$	$4\frac{1}{2}$	$4\frac{5}{8}$
February	$4\frac{1}{8}$	$4\frac{1}{2}$	$4\frac{11}{16}$	$4\frac{13}{16}$
March	$4\frac{3}{16}$	$4\frac{9}{16}$	$4\frac{13}{16}$	$5\frac{1}{8}$
April	$4\frac{1}{4}$	$4\frac{11}{16}$	$4\frac{7}{8}$	$5\frac{1}{8}$
May	$4\frac{3}{8}$	$4\frac{3}{4}$	$5\frac{5}{16}$	$5\frac{3}{8}$
June	$4\frac{3}{8}$	$4\frac{9}{16}$	5	$5\frac{1}{4}$
July	$4\frac{1}{8}$	$4\frac{3}{8}$	$4\frac{3}{4}$	$5\frac{1}{16}$
August	$4\frac{1}{8}$	$4\frac{3}{8}$	$4\frac{9}{16}$	$4\frac{7}{8}$
September	$4\frac{3}{16}$	$4\frac{1}{2}$	$4\frac{3}{4}$	$5\frac{1}{8}$
October	$4\frac{3}{8}$	$4\frac{9}{16}$	$5\frac{1}{16}$	$5\frac{1}{8}$
November	$4\frac{3}{8}$	$4\frac{5}{8}$	$5\frac{1}{4}$	$5\frac{5}{16}$
December	$4\frac{3}{4}$	$5\frac{3}{8}$	$5\frac{7}{16}$	$5\frac{7}{16}$

The Euro-Dollar System

1966

	Call	1 Month	3 Months	6 Months
January	$4\frac{15}{16}$	$5\frac{3}{16}$	$5\frac{3}{8}$	$5\frac{9}{16}$
February	5	$5\frac{1}{4}$	$5\frac{7}{16}$	$5\frac{9}{16}$
March	$5\frac{3}{8}$	6	$5\frac{13}{16}$	$5\frac{15}{16}$
April	$5\frac{7}{16}$	$5\frac{11}{16}$	$5\frac{13}{16}$	$5\frac{15}{16}$
May	$5\frac{3}{8}$	$5\frac{11}{16}$	$5\frac{13}{16}$	$5\frac{15}{16}$
June	$5\frac{3}{4}$	$6\frac{1}{8}$	$6\frac{1}{8}$	$6\frac{1}{4}$
July	$5\frac{7}{8}$	$6\frac{5}{16}$	$6\frac{7}{16}$	$6\frac{7}{8}$
August	$6\frac{1}{4}$	$6\frac{7}{8}$	$6\frac{7}{8}$	$7\frac{3}{8}$
September	$6\frac{1}{4}$	$6\frac{5}{8}$	$6\frac{5}{8}$	$7\frac{1}{16}$
October	$6\frac{3}{8}$	$6\frac{3}{4}$	$7\frac{1}{16}$	$7\frac{1}{16}$
November	$6\frac{5}{16}$	$6\frac{5}{8}$	$7\frac{3}{16}$	$7\frac{3}{16}$
December	$6\frac{1}{8}$	$6\frac{3}{4}$	$6\frac{11}{16}$	$6\frac{13}{16}$

1967

	Call	1 Month	2 Months	3 Months	6 Months
January	$5\frac{1}{4}$–5	$5\frac{1}{2}$–$\frac{3}{8}$	$5\frac{5}{8}$–$\frac{1}{2}$	$5\frac{11}{16}$–$\frac{9}{16}$	$5\frac{7}{8}$–$\frac{3}{4}$
February	$5\frac{3}{8}$–$\frac{1}{4}$	$5\frac{5}{8}$–$\frac{7}{16}$	$5\frac{5}{8}$–$\frac{1}{2}$	$5\frac{13}{16}$–$\frac{5}{8}$	$5\frac{13}{16}$–$\frac{11}{16}$
March	$5\frac{3}{8}$–$\frac{1}{4}$	$5\frac{5}{8}$–$\frac{1}{2}$	$5\frac{1}{2}$–$\frac{3}{8}$	$5\frac{1}{2}$–$\frac{3}{8}$	$5\frac{9}{16}$–$\frac{7}{16}$
April	$4\frac{1}{2}$–$\frac{3}{8}$	$4\frac{3}{4}$–$\frac{1}{2}$	$4\frac{11}{16}$–$\frac{9}{16}$	$4\frac{7}{8}$–$\frac{5}{8}$	$4\frac{15}{16}$–$\frac{3}{4}$
May	5–$4\frac{3}{4}$	$4\frac{13}{16}$–$\frac{11}{16}$	5–$4\frac{7}{8}$	$5\frac{3}{16}$–5	$5\frac{3}{8}$–$\frac{3}{16}$
June	$5\frac{1}{16}$–$4\frac{15}{16}$	$5\frac{1}{4}$–$\frac{1}{8}$	$5\frac{3}{8}$–$\frac{1}{4}$	$5\frac{1}{2}$–$\frac{3}{8}$	$5\frac{15}{16}$–$\frac{13}{16}$
July	$4\frac{1}{2}$–$\frac{3}{8}$	$4\frac{3}{4}$–$\frac{5}{8}$	$5\frac{1}{16}$–$4\frac{7}{8}$	$5\frac{1}{4}$–$\frac{1}{16}$	$5\frac{13}{16}$–$\frac{5}{8}$
August	$4\frac{1}{2}$–$\frac{3}{8}$	$4\frac{11}{16}$–$\frac{9}{16}$	5–$4\frac{7}{8}$	$5\frac{1}{8}$–5	$5\frac{5}{8}$–$\frac{1}{2}$
September	$5\frac{1}{8}$–5	$5\frac{7}{16}$–$\frac{5}{16}$	$5\frac{5}{8}$–$\frac{3}{8}$	$5\frac{7}{8}$–$\frac{3}{4}$	$5\frac{15}{16}$–$\frac{13}{16}$
October	$4\frac{5}{8}$–$\frac{1}{2}$	$5\frac{1}{8}$–5	$5\frac{11}{16}$–$\frac{9}{16}$	$5\frac{3}{4}$–$\frac{5}{8}$	$5\frac{15}{16}$–$\frac{13}{16}$
November	$4\frac{5}{8}$–$\frac{3}{8}$	$4\frac{7}{8}$–$\frac{3}{4}$	$5\frac{3}{8}$–$\frac{5}{16}$	$5\frac{13}{16}$–$\frac{11}{16}$	$5\frac{15}{16}$–$\frac{13}{16}$
December	5–$5\frac{1}{4}$	$6\frac{1}{4}$–$\frac{1}{8}$	$6\frac{3}{8}$–$\frac{1}{8}$	$6\frac{3}{8}$–$\frac{3}{16}$	$6\frac{9}{16}$–$\frac{3}{8}$

1968

	Call	1 Month	2 Months	3 Months	6 Months
January	$4\frac{3}{4}$–$\frac{1}{2}$	$4\frac{7}{8}$–$\frac{11}{16}$	$5\frac{1}{4}$–$\frac{1}{16}$	$5\frac{9}{16}$–$\frac{7}{16}$	6–$5\frac{7}{8}$
February	$5\frac{1}{8}$–$4\frac{7}{8}$	$5\frac{9}{16}$–$\frac{7}{16}$	$5\frac{11}{16}$–$\frac{9}{16}$	$5\frac{11}{16}$–$\frac{9}{16}$	$6\frac{1}{8}$–6
March	6–$5\frac{3}{4}$	$6\frac{3}{8}$–$\frac{1}{8}$	$6\frac{3}{8}$–$\frac{1}{4}$	$6\frac{1}{2}$–$\frac{3}{8}$	$6\frac{5}{8}$–$\frac{1}{2}$
April	$6\frac{3}{8}$–$\frac{1}{8}$	$6\frac{7}{16}$–$\frac{5}{16}$	$6\frac{5}{8}$–$\frac{7}{16}$	$6\frac{3}{4}$–$\frac{9}{16}$	$6\frac{13}{16}$–$\frac{5}{8}$
May	$6\frac{5}{8}$–$\frac{3}{8}$	$7\frac{3}{8}$–$\frac{3}{16}$	$7\frac{1}{4}$–$\frac{1}{8}$	$7\frac{1}{4}$–$\frac{1}{8}$	$7\frac{1}{16}$–$\frac{5}{16}$
June	$6\frac{3}{4}$–$\frac{1}{2}$	$7\frac{1}{8}$–$6\frac{15}{16}$	$6\frac{7}{8}$–$\frac{11}{16}$	$6\frac{15}{16}$–$\frac{1}{4}$	$7\frac{1}{16}$–$6\frac{7}{8}$
July	$6\frac{1}{2}$–$\frac{1}{4}$	$6\frac{1}{16}$–$5\frac{7}{8}$	$6\frac{1}{4}$–$\frac{1}{8}$	$6\frac{3}{8}$–$\frac{3}{16}$	$6\frac{5}{8}$–$\frac{1}{2}$
August	$6\frac{1}{4}$–6	$6\frac{7}{16}$–$\frac{5}{16}$	$6\frac{3}{16}$–1	$6\frac{1}{4}$–$\frac{1}{8}$	$6\frac{3}{8}$–$\frac{1}{4}$
September	$5\frac{7}{8}$–$\frac{5}{8}$	$5\frac{13}{16}$–$\frac{11}{16}$	$5\frac{7}{8}$–$\frac{3}{4}$	$6\frac{1}{4}$–$\frac{1}{8}$	$6\frac{5}{16}$–$\frac{1}{8}$

Euro-Dollar Rates in London

	CALL	1 MONTH	2 MONTHS	3 MONTHS	6 MONTHS
1968					
October	$6\frac{1}{2}-\frac{1}{4}$	$6\frac{5}{16}-\frac{3}{16}$	$6\frac{11}{16}-\frac{9}{16}$	$6\frac{11}{16}-\frac{9}{16}$	$6\frac{11}{16}-\frac{9}{16}$
November	$6\frac{5}{8}-\frac{1}{2}$	$7\frac{1}{4}-\frac{1}{8}$	$7-6\frac{7}{8}$	$6\frac{15}{16}-\frac{13}{16}$	$7\frac{1}{16}-6\frac{15}{16}$
December	$7\frac{1}{8}-6\frac{7}{8}$	$7\frac{3}{16}-\frac{1}{16}$	$7\frac{1}{8}-7$	$7\frac{3}{16}-7$	$7\frac{1}{4}-\frac{1}{8}$
1969					
January	$7\frac{3}{8}-\frac{1}{8}$	$7\frac{1}{2}-\frac{3}{8}$	$7\frac{5}{8}-\frac{1}{2}$	$7\frac{5}{8}-\frac{1}{2}$	$7\frac{11}{16}-\frac{9}{16}$
February	$8-7\frac{3}{4}$	$8\frac{5}{16}-\frac{1}{8}$	$8\frac{1}{2}-\frac{1}{4}$	$8\frac{1}{2}-\frac{3}{8}$	$8\frac{1}{2}-\frac{1}{4}$
March	$8\frac{1}{2}-\frac{1}{4}$	$8\frac{7}{16}-\frac{5}{16}$	$8\frac{5}{8}-\frac{1}{2}$	$8\frac{9}{16}-\frac{7}{16}$	$8\frac{11}{16}-\frac{7}{16}$
April	$8\frac{3}{8}-\frac{1}{8}$	$8\frac{5}{16}-\frac{3}{16}$	$8\frac{7}{16}-\frac{5}{16}$	$8\frac{11}{16}-\frac{7}{16}$	$8\frac{3}{4}-\frac{1}{2}$
May	$10\frac{3}{8}-\frac{1}{8}$	$11\frac{3}{16}-10\frac{15}{16}$	$10\frac{13}{16}-\frac{9}{16}$	$10\frac{3}{4}-\frac{1}{2}$	$10\frac{9}{16}-\frac{7}{16}$
June	$9\frac{5}{8}-\frac{3}{8}$	$10\frac{3}{8}-\frac{1}{8}$	$10\frac{1}{2}-\frac{3}{8}$	$10\frac{3}{4}-\frac{1}{2}$	$10\frac{3}{4}-\frac{1}{2}$
July	$9-8\frac{3}{4}$	$9\frac{11}{16}-\frac{9}{16}$	$10\frac{1}{2}-\frac{5}{16}$	$10\frac{9}{16}-\frac{3}{8}$	$10\frac{11}{16}-\frac{9}{16}$

APPENDIX III

STATISTICAL PROBLEMS

MANY Central Banks have been endeavouring, during the last year or two, to compile figures relating to the Euro-dollar assets and liabilities of banks in their countries. The Bank for International Settlement has co-ordinated these statistics, at first for the internal use of Central Banks, but later it published them regularly in its Annual Reports.

One of the main difficulties of collecting statistics on Euro-dollars lies in the problem of defining Euro-dollars. According to the definition endorsed, not without some hesitation, by the B.I.S., Euro-dollars are 'dollars acquired by a bank outside the United States and used . . . for lending to a non-bank customer'. This definition is too restrictive, as it excludes a very high proportion of the foreign dollar deposits which have been lent to some non-resident bank but which have not been re-lent to non-banking customers. On the other hand, on the basis of the definition implied by the Bank of England, Euro-dollars are simply synonymous with dollar deposits held by non-residents. The statistical material published by the Bank's *Quarterly Bulletin* simply covers the short-term assets and liabilities of banks in the U.K. in terms of foreign currencies.

This identification of Euro-currencies with foreign currency deposits conveys a misleading picture of the Euro-currency markets. For all foreign currency deposits held by residents outside the countries of the currencies concerned are not necessarily lent in the Euro-currency markets. A resident outside the United States may hold a dollar deposit for various purposes without lending it or intending to lend it to a European bank or to any other borrower. It is, of course, probable that the rise in Euro-dollars in 1968–69 induced most holders to lend their deposits, so that all holdings are a potential source of Euro-dollars. But to include them in the Euro-dollar statistics would be as misleading as was the inclusion of all U.K. holdings of dollar securities into the 'investment dollar pool'. It was because of the failure of the British Treasury to distinguish between investment dollars and potential investment dollars for statistical purposes that the British monetary authorities had overrated the volume of investment dollars and had felt justified in allocating investment dollars for direct investment and for house purchases abroad, thereby causing an unwanted increase of the premium to abnormally high levels.

This mistaken definition found crude expression in the recently published *Everyman's Dictionary of Economics,* according to which Euro-dollars are simply 'private dollar balances held in European commercial banks'. This would mean that even balances on *loro* accounts with U.K. bank are Euro-dollars, and so are balances temporarily retained by exporters for their subsequent requirements, or premium-reserves held in a liquid form by British insurance companies to cover their liabilities on their business in the United States, etc.

The above observations give an idea about the difficulty in compiling statistics on Euro-dollars. It is relatively simple to compile statistics of the banks' short-term assets and liabilities in foreign currencies, though even that task presents some difficult problems. It would be incomparably more difficult to expect banks to discriminate, in their monthly returns to their Central Banks, between those dollars which qualify for being considered Euro-dollars and dollars which do not qualify for inclusion. For one thing, the banks themselves may not be in a position to know whether dollars which they have been lent, or which they hold, are held for the purpose of being lent in the form of Euro-dollars. In the prevailing circumstances the best that they can do is to state their dollar assets and liabilities, and Central Banks have to base their statistics on such inadequate data simply because they are the best that are obtainable.

Fortunately Central Banks are in a position to realise the inadequacy of data compiled on such a basis. They are aware that all short-term assets and liabilities in dollars are not Euro-dollars and can make approximate estimates of the proportion of dollars which serve other purposes. In this respect one of the main difficulties is to form an idea how much of the dollar assets and liabilities represents dollars engaged in interest arbitrage in circumstances in which they have no connection with Euro-dollars.

A major pitfall against which the Bank of England *Quarterly Bulletin* of June 1964 warns is the possibility of double-counting. 'It is possible for funds deposited with a U.K. bank by an overseas resident to be on-lent to a bank abroad and then redeposited with another U.K. bank. In this way the same fund can be counted twice. The extent of such double-counting is not known.' The same deposit, having gone through the hands of several inter-mediaries in various markets, is liable to appear in the figures of several Central Banks based on the monthly returns of the banks in their respective countries.

This possibility has become materially reduced by the co-ordination of the monthly statistics achieved by the B.I.S. as far as the date for which the returns are made is concerned. While originally it was a different day of the month for each country, now the 15th of the month has been adopted by all countries which con-tribute their figures to the B.I.S. But in other essential respects it is difficult to eliminate differences between the methods of the returns in various countries.

The following table, published in the annual report of the Bank for International Settlements for 1968–69, shows the latest amounts of foreign-currency liabilities and assets of the principal countries concerned in Euro-currency transactions :

SHORT-TERM LIABILITIES AND ASSETS OF THE REPORTING
BANKS OF INDIVIDUAL COUNTRIES VIS-À-VIS NON-RESIDENTS

Countries	End of month		Liabilities	Assets	Net position
			(in millions of U.S. dollars)		
Belgium-Luxemburg	1967	December	1,950	1,480	− 470
	1968	March	2,110	1,610	− 500
		June	2,420	1,980	− 440
		September	2,520	2,080	− 440
		December	2,670	2,320	− 350
France	1967	December	2,590	2,850	260
	1968	March	3,390	3,600	210
		June	2,980	3,760	780
		September	3,390	4,190	800
		December	4,640	4,660	20
Germany	1967	December	350	1,170	820
	1968	March	350	1,330	980
		June	400	960	560
		September	510	1,300	790
		December	580	1,640	1,060
Italy	1967	December	2,920	2,940	20
	1968	March	2,980	2,950	− 30
		June	3,080	3,160	80
		September	3,160	3,620	460
		December	3,730	4,470	740

Countries	End of month	Liabilities	Assets	Net position
		(in millions of U.S. dollars)		
Netherlands	1967 December	1,120	1,200	80
	1968 March	1,270	1,310	40
	June	1,350	1,460	110
	September	1,370	1,460	90
	December	1,460	1,560	100
Sweden	1967 December	270	630	360
	1968 March	260	580	320
	June	300	600	300
	September	310	650	340
	December	300	700	400
Switzerland	1967 December	2,800	4,280	1,480
	1968 March	2,870	4,660	1,690
	June	3,050	5,170	2,120
	September	3,390	5,400	2,010
	December	3,350	5,610	2,260
United Kingdom	1967 December	10,520	10,500	− 20
	1968 March	12,150	12,100	− 50
	June	14,660	14,570	− 90
	September	15,690	15,530	− 160
	December	17,130	17,060	− 70
Total	1967 December	22,520	25,050	2,530
	1968 March	25,480	28,140	2,660
	June	28,240	31,660	3,420
	September	30,340	34,230	3,890
	December	33,860	38,020	4,160
Canada	1967 December	2,370	3,500	1,130
	1968 March	2,320	3,420	1,100
	June	2,450	3,660	1,210
	September	2,580	3,970	1,390
	December	2,750	4,240	1,490
Japan	1967 December	3,740	3,700	− 40
	1968 March	3,880	3,670	− 210
	June	3,920	3,890	− 30
	September	3,900	4,070	170
	December	4,210	4,450	240

The following tables, published in the *Bank of England Quarterly Bulletin*, contain figures concerning the Euro-currency deposits lent and borrowed by banks in the U.K. :

Table 1

ANALYSIS BY AREA : ALL CURRENCIES

in millions of pounds

End of period	Total	Overseas sterling countries	United States	Canada	Latin America	Western Europe	Middle East	Japan	Other
U.K. liabilities									
1962	1,038	18	110	162	48	552	94	3	51
1963	1,280	41	152	133	67	652	131	4	100
1964	1,784	82	204	273	90	850	159	7	119
1965	2,108	125	195	170	100	1,165	215	10	128
1966	3,002	200	348	201	135	1,692	234	11	181
1967	4,382	298	588	324	201	2,413	231	16	311
1968	7,131	543	1,119	505	276	3,917	235	26	510
1969 June	10,507	839	1,484	912	426	5,678	333	62	773
U.K. claims									
1962	1,010	2	332	23	27	471	4	106	45
1963	1,268	3	290	37	29	692	17	127	73
1964	1,626	4	435	26	30	840	31	181	79
1965	1,980	24	575	55	76	916	42	209	83
1966	3,020	39	1,244	93	81	1,161	49	249	104
1967	4,374	99	1,709	145	177	1,452	87	451	254
1968	7,109	177	3,058	202	342	2,161	124	695	350
1969 June	10,537	313	5,817	215	436	2,649	118	597	392

Table 2
ANALYSIS BY AREA AND COUNTRY: U.S. DOLLARS

COUNTRIES OUTSIDE EUROPE

End of period	Total	Overseas sterling countries	United States	Canada	Latin America	Middle East	Japan	Other
					in millions of pounds			
U.K. liabilities								
1962	884	18	103	160	45	70	2	37
1963	1,072	37	137	127	62	107	4	78
1964	1,564	76	191	264	77	140	6	94
1965	1,879	116	189	167	90	183	9	106
1966	2,727	189	340	194	127	207	10	156
1967	4,037	278	577	320	178	224	15	282
1968	6,420	503	1,070	489	239	224	25	441
1969 June	9,441	794	1,394	895	380	323	58	696
U.K. claims								
1962	803	2	323	9	25	4	66	38
1963	1,024	3	284	25	27	13	87	66
1964	1,312	4	432	15	29	25	134	73
1965	1,624	23	570	40	71	35	166	78
1966	2,611	38	1,238	67	72	42	223	92
1967	3,836	97	1,694	115	162	82	413	215
1968	6,242	171	3,018	174	277	111	662	288
1969 June	9,332	293	5,743	191	317	98	554	333

WESTERN EUROPE

End of period	Austria	Belgium	France	W. Germany	Italy	Netherlands	Norway	Sweden	Switzerland	Other
					in millions of pounds					
U.K. liabilities										
1962	78	36	40	39	55	21	7	12	129	32
1963	80	25	34	18	52	29	11	7	223	41
1964	79	39	75	25	73	43	22	31	268	61
1965	56	53	112	34	210	37	50	30	371	66
1966	90	88	184	42	260	57	61	31	604	87
1967	149	132	263	189	307	102	100	53	755	113
1968	132	254	389	219	608	168	163	100	1,173	214
1969 June	105	453	548	355	717	363	173	108	1,804	275
U.K. claims										
1962	3	19	50	36	127	21	15	11	19	44
1963	3	69	54	65	173	26	18	28	31	52
1964	8	65	62	100	160	56	24	29	37	59
1965	14	58	72	67	153	51	44	27	69	86
1966	28	78	82	109	184	74	66	32	79	107
1967	52	96	110	74	175	107	79	41	123	202
1968	69	141	218	143	254	108	87	62	210	249
1969 June	56	190	296	205	263	102	81	44	326	240

BIBLIOGRAPHY

ALTHOUGH the number of articles and news paragraphs dealing with Euro-dollars and other foreign currency deposits that appeared in the financial Press since their existence was 'discovered' in 1959 must run into many hundreds, books giving a detailed description and analysing its broader aspects have been very few. There is much material in the annual reports of various Central Banks, the International Monetary Fund, and the Bank for International Settlements, and the monthly or quarterly publications of some Central Banks — especially the Bank of England, the Federal Reserve Bank of New York and the Deutsche Bundesbank — contain also some very useful statistics. An article, ' U.K. Banks' External Liabilities and Claims in Foreign Currencies ', appearing in the *Bank of England Quarterly Bulletin*, June 1964, deserves special attention.

The following is a selection of publications drawn upon by the author for factual material and for comments on the system :

ALTMAN, OSCAR L., 'Foreign Markets for Dollars, Sterling and Other Currencies', *International Monetary Fund Staff Papers*, December 1961

— 'Canadian Markets for U.S. Dollars', *International Monetary Fund Staff Papers*, November 1962

— 'Recent Developments in Foreign Markets for Dollars and Other Currencies', *International Monetary Fund Staff Papers*, March 1963

— 'Euro-Dollars : Some Further Comments ', *International Monetary Fund Staff Papers*, March 1965

BLOCH, ERNEST, *Eurodollars: An Emerging International Money Market*, New York University, 1966

BLOOMFIELD, ARTHUR I., 'Official Intervention in the Forward Market : Some Recent Experiences', *Banca Nazionale del Lavoro Quarterly Review*, March 1964

BOLTON, SIR GEORGE, 'International Money Markets', *Bank of London and South America Quarterly Review*, July 1963

COMMITTEE ON BANKING AND CURRENCY, U.S. HOUSE OF REPRESENTATIVES, Hearings on a Bill to permit Banks to pay higher interest rates on time deposits of foreign Governments

DALLOZ, JEAN-PIERRE, *Euro-dollars et Euro-devises*, memorandum presented to the Association des Instituts européens in April 1964

EINZIG, PAUL, 'Statics and Dynamics of the Euro-dollar Market', *Economic Journal*, September 1961
— 'Some Recent Developments in Official Forward Exchange Operations', *Economic Journal*, June 1963
— 'Dollar Deposits in London', *Banker*, January 1960
— 'Towards an International Money Market', *Statist*, November 17, 1961
— *A Dynamic Theory of Forward Exchange*, 2nd ed., 1962
— 'Has the Euro-Dollar a Future?', *Statist*, October 11, 1963
— 'The Euro-Dollar Market has Achieved Permanency', *Commercial and Financial Chronicle*, March 14, 1963
— 'Euro-Dollars Receive Official Blessing Abroad', *Commercial and Financial Chronicle*, June 18, 1964
— 'Some Recent Changes in the Euro-Dollar System', *Journal of Finance*, September 1964
— 'Character and Significance of the Euro-Dollar Market', *Commercial and Financial Chronicle*, September 24, 1964
— *The Euro-Bond Market*, London 1969
— *A Textbook on Foreign Exchange*, 2nd ed., 1969
HOLMES, ALLEN R., and KLOPSTOCK, FRED. H., 'The Market for Dollar Deposits in Europe', *Federal Reserve Bank of New York Market Review*, November 1960
INTERNATIONAL REPORTS INC., *The Euro-Dollar Market — Methods and Meaning*, New York 1963
JOHNSON, MORRIS O., *Eurodollars in the New International Money Market*, First National City Bank, New York 1964
KLOPSTOCK, FRED. H., 'The International Money Market: Structure, Scope and Instruments', *Journal of Finance*, March 1965
— *The Euro-Dollar Market*, Princeton 1968
KVASNICKA, J. G., ' Euro-Dollars — An Important Source of Funds for American Banks ', *Business Conditions*, June 1969, Federal Reserve Bank of Chicago
MARTENSON, G. CARROLL, *The Euro-Dollar Market*, New York 1964
MORGAN GUARANTY TRUST COMPANY, 'Dollars that go Abroad — But Not Really', *Morgan Guaranty Survey*, December 1961
STEVENSON, R. B., 'The Euro-Currency Market', *Journal of the Institute of Bankers*, August 1964
SWOBODA, A. K., *The Euro-Dollar Market*, Princeton 1968
TUROT, PAUL, 'Le marché des capitaux à court terme en Europe et l'Euro-Dollar', *Banque*, Paris, April 1961

INDEX

Altman, O. L., 195
'Amero-Currencies', 59-60
Arbitrage :
  Hedging —, 46, 50
  Interest —, 28, 38, 42-6, 48, 50, 96, 116, 139
  Space —, 12, 38, 46-7
  Time —, 12, 16, 38, 46, 48-9, 146
  Trader —, 46, 49-50
  Triangular —, 101

Banca Nazionale del Lavoro Quarterly Review, vii, 204
Bank for International Settlements, 17, 27, 69, 132, 146, 149, 158-9, 175-6, 198-200, 213
Bank of England, 17, 29, 67, 108, 114, 172, 176, 180, 184, 186, 204
Bank of England Quarterly Bulletin, 176, 198-9, 204
Bank of France, 120-1, 131, 148
Bank of Italy, 114
Bank of Japan, 114, 122
Bank of London and South America Quarterly Review, 204
Bank Rate, 6-7, 82, 100, 115, 118, 126
Banker, The, 204
Banque, 8, 204
Banque Commerciale de l'Europe du Nord, 30
Basle Agreement, 174
Belgium, 9, 36, 119
Berlin, 3-4
Bloomfield, A. I., 204
Bolton, Sir George, 17, 204
Borrowing of Euro-Dollars :
  American Bank branches, 7, 19, 40-1, 52-60, 104-5, 149, 152-9
  Banque Commerciale de l'Europe du Nord, 30
  Belgian Treasury, 36
  Bullion hoarders, 6, 46, 49, 116
  Canadian Banks, 41
  Central Banks, 30, 35-6, 56, 103-4, 106, 118, 166

Borrowing of Euro-Dollars—*contd.*
  Communist Banks, 30-1, 36, 51, 72-3, 84, 140, 150, 170, 186
  For Financing European Dollar Bonds, 135-7
  For Financing Foreign Trade, 5, 8-9, 35, 38-40, 49-50, 53-4, 60, 90, 93, 105, 110, 116
  For Financing Home Trade, 5, 17, 38, 40, 99
  France, 31
  Germany, 24, 41
  International Brokers, 20
  Italy, 3, 7, 39, 41, 45, 67, 99, 111, 121, 168
  Japan, 1, 7, 38-40, 54, 67, 99, 111, 122, 175
  Latin American, 54, 99, 141
  Middle East, 11
  Moscow Narodny Bank, 30
  Speculators, 97-8, 116-17, 166

Central Banks, 5, 7, 25, 27, 32, 35-6, 56-7, 66, 82-3, 86, 103-4, 106, 108-9, 112-22, 126, 138, 151, 174
Clearing Banks, Commercial Banks, 19, 27-8, 107-8, 125
Commercial Paper, 26, 42
Congress of the U.S.A., 27, 52, 54, 107
Crassus, Marcus Licinius, 3
Creditanstalt, Austrian, 66
Current Account Balances, 28-9

de Gaulle, General Charles, 155
Deposit Certificates, 25, 34, 155, 177-192
Deutsche Bundesbank, 51, 117, 120-121
Diversifying Investments, 32
Dollar Bonds, European, 134-7, 157

Economic Journal, The, 204
Einzig, Paul, *The History of Foreign*

206

Index